SOCIALIST PERSPECTIVES

edited by
Phyllis Jacobson
and Julius Jacobson

with contributions by
Pyotr Adovin-Egides, Harry Brill, Lynn
Chancer, Melvyn Dubofsky, Julius Jacobson,
Richard Lichtman, Manning Marable, Jiri Pelikan,
Daniel Singer, Dan Smith, Alan Wald, Alan Wolfe

KARZ-COHL PUBLISHING, INC.
Princeton • New York

C ^{,,}

Burgess

HX
542
.S56
1983
copy 1

Library of Congress Cataloging in Publication Data
Main entry under title:

Socialist perspectives.

    Bibliography: p.
    1. Communism and society—Addresses, essays, lectures.
I. Jacobson, Phyllis, 1922-   . II. Jacobson, Julius.
III. Adovin-Ediges, Pyotr.
HX542.S56   1983   335.43   83-4356
ISBN 0-943828-51-1
ISBN 0-943828-52-X (pbk.)

Published in the United States by
KARZ-COHL PUBLISHING, INC.
320 West 105th Street, New York, N.Y. 10025

Introduction

W HO WOULD HAVE THOUGHT, in 1970, just two years after a sitting president had been forced into early retirement by the political and moral force of the anti-war movement, that just ten years later, a Reagan, catering to the most primitive and base prejudices, would win election, sweeping almost every state in the Union?

How could a movement of such power and dynamism have disappeared leaving so few traces? Etched on our memories are the dramatic demonstrations, the hundreds of thousands protesting in the streets, the dignity of non-violent resistance. A movement of the rebellious young, determined to end an unjust, immoral war, reached every city, town, and village in the country, making converts not only of the young but of their parents—in Idaho as well as San Francisco, in West Virginia as well as New York. And, finally, it was successful; it helped topple a president and end the war.

There are many reasons for the demise of the movement—its composition, its refusal to go beyond the immediate issue of the war itself, its isolation from other social movements. But its disregard for theory and ideology best explains its failure to leave a political legacy. Theory was needlessly sacrificed for the sake of action and, while the movement was responsible for profound social and cultural changes in the US, it provided no continuity between the radicalism of earlier decades and the present.

Yet, after a period of reactionary backlash and two years of Reaganism, there is once again interest in left wing thought and history—greater interest than has been manifested in many years. Even before Reagan's election, there were signs of radical renewal in the growing anti-nuclear, feminist and ecology movements. Today, the signs of revitalization are unmistakable. Rooted in the revolt against Reaganism with its callous war against the people, its intoxication with B-1 bombers, MX and cruise missiles, and its cynical alliances with repressive regimes from El Salvador to South Africa, and inspired by the heroic working class uprising in Poland, there is awakened interest in socialism, its history and basic definition.

SOCIALIST PERSPECTIVES is a response to that awakened interest. To those who may question the need for yet another socialist publication, we would like to point out that in a country with a population of approximately 250 million, we are not exactly inundated with socialist journals. Even if there were a larger number, we would not hesitate to publish SOCIALIST PERSPECTIVES which differs from the others because it clearly reflects opposition to the systems and politics of *both* power blocs. It is uncompromisingly anti-capitalist and anti-Stalinist, which is not to suggest a narrow "line" publication. On the contrary, this general perspective accommodates a wide diversity of views, conflicting analyses, and debate. There is room for multiformity: differences about the interpretation of socialist history and theory, about the nature of the superpowers' societies, the outlook for capitalism, for Stalinism, the future of the labor movement, the road to equality for women and blacks, and countless other areas that lend themselves to socialist analysis and interpretation.

IN THIS VOLUME, there are clear-cut and important differences on a question of theoretical and political significance—the strategy for social change in Eastern Europe. Daniel Singer and Jiri Pelikan—both socialists—express distinctly different views. And to appreciate the palpable life force that emerges in the analysis of Soviet society by Adovin-Egides, a man who spent 11 years in Russian prison and psychiatric cells, is not necessarily to endorse his conception of the social character of the Russian state.

Harry Brill's theory on the origins of the current crisis in capitalism differs sharply with the views of a number of radical political economists whose opinions would be no less welcome in these pages. Nor do we have a "line" about the relationship between race and class/blacks and socialism discussed in depth by Manning Marable. There are other positions equally appropriate for publication in SOCIALIST PERSPECTIVES. The same is true for Lynn Chancer's analysis of the feminist movement. There might well be lively debate on her perceptions of radical and socialist feminism, as well as the course of action she proposes.

In his insightful article, Alan Wolfe concludes that the left is of two minds about modernity; one tendency strongly pro, the other ready to call a halt to growth. He feels that the left should face the difficult task of deciding what kind of modernization it wants, what kind should be resisted; a subject certain to produce controversy.

In these volumes, there is no room for support of or rationalizations for the nuclear ambitions—limited or otherwise—of either superpower. But within an anti-nuclear context, there can be genuine differences on the strategy to be pursued against the madness of both power blocs. We do not suggest that Dan Smith's view of the anti-nuclear struggle, for example, is the only one possible.

The labor movement, its history and development, has always been a central socialist concern. Melvyn Dubofsky's essay discussing the problems faced by the trade unions today, in a period of economic decline, and his evaluation of the union leadership's response is but one of a number of possible approaches.

Alan Wald's voyage back to the thirties and forties to trace the political roots of the New York intellectuals raises a number of controversial questions, as does Richard Lichtman's thoughtful essay on socialist freedom, a crucial question for socialists.

A special point must be made about articles by the editors. We too have a right to express a view without the assumption being made that an editor's opinion represents an editorial declaration, closing out other analyses. In this volume, Julius Jacobson's point of view in his discussion of fascism and Communism is by no means the last word on this subject. On this question, as on others, SOCIALIST PERSPECTIVES does not seek ideological conformity.

We are interested in essays on all aspects of socialist thought and history, on concrete political as well as theoretical questions. We hope to carry articles that are serious and thoughtful, unafflicted by the academicism and portentousness of so much that has appeared in left wing publications taxing the reader's endurance and assuring a limited life span for such journals. Good scholarship and political clarity do not necessarily require the absence of polemical fervor.

A project like this has at least one built-in limitation: not all important issues can be covered in a particular volume. We are, for example, well aware of the absence in this first volume of articles on Latin America, the Middle East, aspects of socialist theory, etc. We can only attempt to make up for this lack in future volumes.

As we mentioned earlier, a sign of the current revitalization of radicalism is the search for socialist roots, socialist ancestry. There has been a hiatus between the radical upsurge of the thirties—generally of the pre-WW II period—and the present. That lack of continuity of the socialist movement in this country has had a devastating effect on several generations of radicals. Not only has it made orphans of them, but for each new generation the search for a meaningful socialist past has been more difficult, leading further back in time.

The editors of SOCIALIST PERSPECTIVES represent a connection with the socialist past. We grew up in the socialist movement of the late thirties and have remained committed socialists to this moment. Hopefully, in the pages of this publication we can help forge a link between that past and the present.

We want to go beyond the reservoir of known and previously published authors, to reach younger writers who are part of the radical renewal. We know you are out there but since we have no way of locating you, we urge you to contact us with ideas and articles. Please send correspondence and manuscripts to: SOCIALIST PERSPECTIVES, 234 Fifth Avenue, New York, N.Y. 10001.

Julius Jacobson
Phyllis Jacobson

March 1, 1983

Contents

Page

INTRODUCTION   v

1. The Politics of European
Nuclear Disarmament
   DAN SMITH   3
2. Which Side Are You On?
   MELVYN DUBOFSKY   21
3. The Unreformable
Economy: Origins of the
Current Economic Crisis
   HARRY BRILL   41
4. Why Black Americans
Are Not Socialists
   MANNING MARABLE   63
5. The Current State of
the Feminist Movement
   LYNN CHANCER   97
6. Reflections on Fascism
and Communism
   JULIUS JACOBSON   119
7. The New York Intellectuals
in Retreat
   ALAN WALD   155
8. Is America Modern?
   ALAN WOLFE   185
9. Socialist Freedom
   RICHARD LICHTMAN   201
10. Poland in Perspective
   DANIEL SINGER   229

CONTENTS

11. Can "Real Socialism"
Be Reformed?
   JIRI PELIKAN   253
12. Currents within
Soviet Dissidence
   PYOTR ADOVIN-EGIDES   269

INDEX   289

SOCIALIST PERSPECTIVES

The Politics of European Nuclear Disarmament

DAN SMITH

> *We are entering the most dangerous decade in human history. A third world war is not merely possible, but increasingly likely. Economic and social difficulties in advanced industrial countries, crisis, militarism and war in the third world compound the political tensions that fuel a demented arms race.*

THESE ARE THE OPENING SENTENCES of the appeal for European Nuclear Disarmament, issued on 28 April 1980.[1] The background against which the appeal was issued included the evident breakdown of superpower detente, the growing crisis in both blocs, the qualitative and quantitative developments of the nuclear arsenals of the superpowers, and the development of strategic concepts of "limited" nuclear war and "usable" nuclear weapons. With "the most dangerous decade" now well under way, more and more people are coming to agree with the judgments contained in those sentences as the evidence for them, not least in 1982, becomes impossible to ignore.

The appeal, however, did not only seek to draw attention to the perils of our time and call for a massive effort to counter them. It also sought, from its opening sentences, to direct attention to the politics which underlie and produce these perils. It did this, not for the fun of it, but because for the authors

DAN SMITH, *freelance researcher and writer, is the Chairperson of European Nuclear Disarmament, a member of the National Council of the Campaign for Nuclear Disarmament and its former General Secretary. He is the co-editor with E.P. Thompson of* Protest and Survive *(Monthly Review Press, N.Y.)*

of the appeal there was no way that the situation could be changed if it were not first understood. We now stand at a point, especially in Europe, when every last ounce of effort must be invested in practical action to change the situation, and yet when it has never been more important to understand it.

The Mass Movements

IN THE FIRST YEARS OF THE 1980s, developments in the field of nuclear strategy and weapons have all been bad, extending the depressing and dangerous tendencies of developments in the 1970s. But these years have also seen the emergence of massive public movements against nuclear weapons. Their first stirrings in Europe pre-date by some months (and, in some cases, much longer) the appeal for European Nuclear Disarmament. Their most immediate focus has been resistance to the planned deployment of new nuclear missiles to Western Europe. Their most spectacular manifestation to date has been the series of demonstrations in the last quarter of 1981, involving well over two million people in most of the Western European countries. But those rallies were in all cases built on the foundations of a growing tide of popular consciousness, expressed in a network of small, local groups publicizing the problem of nuclear weapons and the need for nuclear disarmament in their own communities.

For some time it appeared that, with help from Japan and Australia, the Western European disarmament movements were shouldering the responsibility for introducing some elements of sanity into the high counsels of the two blocs and the superpowers. But in 1982 we saw also the emergence of an American Disarmament movement, focusing on the limited but important demand for a "nuclear freeze" and on the general appeal of the broad disarmament slogans of the June 12, 1982 rally in New York. And at the same time, in the most difficult of conditions, independent movements or committees for peace have appeared in East Germany, Hungary and the USSR.

These movements face a severe test. According to the NATO plan, 1983 is the year when the first cruise missiles will be deployed to Greenham Common in Britain and Comiso in Sic-

ily. The implementation or cancellation (or tactical postpone-
ment) of the plan will mark a potentially decisive moment in
Atlantic politics. The movements which have grown so extra-
ordinarily in the past two years must now be sustained and
developed into permanent features of European politics, able to
take in their stride reverses, small successes and the mere passage of time—and all three pose different but equally sharp
problems. We face a range of powerful pressures. In the USSR,
members of an independent peace committee were arrested in
the Summer of 1982 to prevent them from meeting the Scandinavian Women's Peace March. In East Germany, peace activists face insidious but increasing harassment from the authorities. In Sicily, the anti-cruise movement is faced by the Mafia
which has been speculating in land around the Comiso base
area, ready, presumably, to build night clubs and brothels for
when the American boys arrive. Elsewhere in Europe, smears
in the press about disarmament movements or leading individuals are common currency—and in Britain a film, whose pre-
miere was graced by a member of the royal family, tells how a
terrorist group operating in the Campaign for Nuclear Disarmament, kidnaps the US Ambassador and British Foreign
Secretary, only to be foiled by the SAS. Beyond this, we cannot
afford to be complacent about the possibilities of infiltration,
sabotage, and *agents provocateurs*.

At this point, however, these external pressures are less
important in determining the movements' development than
the decisions which the movements themselves make about
priorities and strategies. There is clearly little point in relying
on US-Soviet negotiations in Geneva as a way of turning back
the missiles. The American negotiating position—Reagan's
"zero option"—offered to trade all existing Soviet theatre
nuclear missiles against non-existent but planned American
weapons. I would like to see the USSR accept the trade, but few
serious people can expect it to do so. Within the rules of the arms
control game the Reagan proposal was blatantly one-sided and
out of order. So if we are to resist cruise missile deployment
successfully, it will be because of the efforts of the mass movements in their unconditional opposition to NATO's plans.

Within Europe, the political struggle around cruise missiles
has come, for both sides of the argument, to carry a political

symbolism which makes the struggle harder and will make success more important. Should we win the campaign against cruise, thousands of nuclear warheads will still remain in Western Europe. The task of disarmament will not even have been started; we shall merely have succeeded in preventing one measure of rearmament. That, however, will also be a massive political defeat inflicted on NATO strategy and its reliance on nuclear weapons. Success in the anti-cruise campaign will mean the withdrawal of popular consent to NATO strategy.

IF THE POLITICAL MEANING OF SUCH A SUCCESS is properly understood, two things become clear. First, the concentration on resisting cruise and Pershing II missiles reflects a sophisticated judgment about campaigning against important but vulnerable targets. Second, the US disarmament movement ought rightly to share that judgment and devote a considerable part of its own effort to stopping cruise and Pershing II.

There are many on the left, both in North America and in Western Europe, who deride the disarmament movements as nonpolitical. They are not only to be found in small sectarian grouplets. They object to the narrowness of the movements' goals—focusing on the symptom, not the underlying sickness, dealing with the weapons of war, not with the causes. Though they may be emotionally moved by campaign literature graphically depicting the pornography of ultimate destruction and the tragic waste of resources involved in the arms race, they argue that an appeal to humanitarian instincts cannot prepare the way to overcome the real political obstacles which block disarmament. They seek to inject politics into the disarmament movements. Their arguments carry a great deal of intellectual weight, but all suffer from one major flaw: they concentrate too much on how the issue of nuclear weapons and disarmament is presented, neglecting to assess the issue itself.

This is certainly an easily understood error. For it is undeniably true that, both at the center of many of the movements and on their fringes, there are other groups that want to avoid politics altogether. For them, it is precisely the humanitarian appeal which is the only successful way of campaigning, the only way of engaging a broad range of political forces in the campaigns. They want to have the support of constituencies with real political clout, and they do not want to put them off with what they consider to be spurious political rhetoric.

The arguments of these two very different groups are equally familiar and take similar forms on both sides of the Atlantic. But I think it is probably the case that in Western Europe the disarmament movements have been more successful in steering a path between the pitfalls which both groups dig. The main pitfall provided by those who would "inject" politics is the danger of becoming locked into a political ghetto without real leverage. The main pitfall provided by those who seek to "avoid" politics is the dissipation of the movement's energies into supporting demands which are either so general that nobody really thinks they can be achieved, or so minimal that achieving them will not change anything. My main criticism of both groups stems from blank incomprehension at the argument that a movement for nuclear disarmament can be nonpolitical. Politics is about power: if nuclear weapons are not about power, then nothing is. It is therefore pointless to try to avoid politics. The politics are present and will make their presence felt whatever you do. Equally, the point is not to inject politics into the issue, but to bring them out into the open where they belong. To do otherwise, to suppress the politics of disarmament, would be dishonest, and while dishonesty has proven to be a successful political strategy for politicians backed by corporate dollars and media barons, it is unwise and short-sighted, as well as immoral, for a popular movement which does not have and will not get that kind of backing.

Millions of people are quite rightly alarmed by the prospect of nuclear war and believe that nuclear disarmament is required to remove that threat. This alarm is based on an increasing awareness of how awful nuclear weapons are, and on a growing understanding that the strategies of both superpowers include the willingness to use nuclear weapons in a future war. Neither the awfulness of nuclear weapons nor readiness to use them is new. What is new is the extent of awareness. The result is that it is now possible for those millions of people to seek to explore the reasons why the nuclear threat exists. And this provides the opportunity for the disarmament movements to develop understanding of the relationship between the threat to our survival posed by nuclear weapons and the power structures which produce and require nuclear weapons. For what we must then go on to argue is that it is only if those power structures are challenged, that we shall have a chance of winning nuclear disarmament.

Survival and Politics

THE PROBLEM OF NUCLEAR WEAPONS is primarily a problem of survival. A limited nuclear war would kill very large numbers of people. Thanks to radioactivity, nuclear weapons kill across space and time in a way which makes them qualitatively different from conventional and chemical weapons. Unlimited nuclear war risks omnicide. Once the literature on the effects of nuclear weapons has been read and absorbed, these are the fundamental facts which must dominate and shape discussion.

While such sentiments would be accepted by all participants in disarmament movements, whatever their other political views, they are not thereby nonpolitical. For the proponents of the new nuclear weaponry of the 1980s, the basic problem is not survival but confrontation with the USSR and the cohesiveness of the Western alliance (or, from the other side, confrontation with the US and the cohesiveness of the Soviet alliance). The orthodox framework for debating these issues has, for over three decades, begun with the perspective of the Soviet threat (initially political, now military) and proceeded from there to argue for nuclear weapons as one of the required countermeasures. When people come together as a movement for nuclear disarmament, they begin by displacing the orthodox framework and substituting another more compelling one.

But if we make this political action of substituting one framework for another (and most campaigning work for nuclear disarmament begins with that act), we must nevertheless understand the truth which is contained within the orthodox framework. Nuclear weapons are not an aberration. They are not a mistake made by thoughtless people in positions of power who would have done differently if they had known better. They are integral to the international political order, the binding constituent in the cement which holds the American-led Western alliance together. What they have done is to prevent relaxation of the Cold War and to insure the division of Europe, a division created by the Cold War. Whatever the fluctuations of East-West relations, the fact is that each side can blow the other up with monstrously powerful weapons. It is utterly banal to point out how that single fact cannot but create deep suspicions of the other side throughout the population, but it is perhaps necessary.

It is clear to everybody that in human terms the nuclear issue is enormous, affecting the very conditions and possibility of human existence. In political terms, the nuclear issue is of comparable dimensions. In these terms, the nuclear issue is essentially about division and, after that, of leadership. It is about the division of most of the industrialized countries into two blocs, and about each superpower's leadership of its bloc.

This is also, of course, the essence of the Cold War—both the original one starting in the 1940s and the current one starting from the late 1970s into the 1980s. It is a fundamental mistake to view the Cold War as being primarily about either the aggressive designs of one superpower against the other or, in the "revisionist" version, the designs of US capital against the Third World. The Cold War is primarily about order and stability. In the West, this means the order and stability which are necessary for the successful functioning of an international capitalist economy. It would appear that these conditions can be provided only when a single state can by itself regulate the world order—Britain in its imperial heyday, the US since 1945. The crisis of the 1920s and 1930s and the current crisis can in part both be traced to the weakness of international regulation and the decline of a leading world power.

But the US-led order since 1945 shows three marked dissimilarities with the British-dominated order of the 19th century. First, it includes many more states; second, it has bound many of those states into explicit military alliances which have strengthened political and economic ties; third, it specifically excludes certain states. It has ordered the affairs of those states within the system and it has bound them together against those states which are outside it.

The economic rise of Western Europe and Japan and the costs of the international policing role assumed by the US have led to the weakening of this international order. In the

1940s and through the 1950s, the US was economically, politically and militarily dominant among capitalist states. Now, it remains the largest single economic power but its margin of superiority has been drastically cut; its political credibility and leadership is fast failing; its military dominance remains, yet the utility of its military strength in far-flung corners of the globe has declined. What remains, unchallenged among capitalist states, is its nuclear dominance—it still provides the nuclear "umbrella" upon which Western European and Japanese military planning is predicated.

My argument has, evidently, cut a long story short in order to arrive at this point. In Western Europe, the real power of the US is represented by its troops in Europe, by NATO's reliance on its war-planning, on trans-Atlantic reinforcements and by American nuclear weapons—the ones deployed in and around Europe and the strategic forces.

Consequently, if in Western Europe we begin by seeking a solution to the very human problem of the threat of nuclear destruction, we are immediately confronted with the political problem of the relationship between Western Europe and the US. To seek a nuclear-free Europe is inevitably to seek a changed relationship with the US.

THE POSITION IN EASTERN EUROPE, however, is not symmetrical. The USSR's dominance over its European allies is less a function of its nuclear forces and has more to do with its military occupation of four of the six countries. Yet the international position of the USSR as the alternative pole to the US is heavily underscored by its formidable nuclear arsenal. The Cuban government could well be forgiven for believing that the only thing restraining American anti-communism from a direct assault is the possibility of a Soviet nuclear response. The Vietnamese government might be forgiven for having similar thoughts in relation to China. In fact, I would doubt if the deterrent effects of Soviet nuclear forces really figure in US or Chinese calculations about Cuba or Vietnam; I doubt that the Soviet leadership would sacrifice Kiev for the sake of Havana or Hanoi. But the ideological effect of nuclear protection by a superpower does not have to be related directly to a detailed assessment of the odds. The fact is that, as a global superpower, the USSR is comparable to the US only in military strength, and the appearance of military weakness would be as troubling to the Soviet leadership as to the US.

Thus, despite the importance of the nuclear element in the USSR's global policy, a nuclear-free Europe does not imply such a decisive change in relations between Eastern Europe and the USSR as between Western Europe and the US. Soviet military occupation would remain the determining factor. Even so, the scaling down of military confrontation in Europe, focal site of confrontation, would ease the pressure on Eastern Europe and erode the ideological rationalization for continued repression. If this process were accompanied by a decisive shift in Western European military planning toward a truly and obviously defensive posture—as is widely argued in Western Europe now, and not only in the disarmament movements—the pressure would be still further eased, the ideological basis for repression further eroded.

It is here that the decisive link is to be found between nuclear disarmament and political liberties. But the link is not an automatic mechanism. We cannot credibly argue that European nuclear disarmament would necessarily create greater liberties in Eastern Europe. But we can argue that it could create the room in which some progress in that direction might be made with less immediate offense to Soviet paranoia. This would be no small achievement.

Nuclear Strategy and Politics

THE MAIN LINES OF DEVELOPMENT of nuclear strategy in the current period can best be grasped through two key concepts: "limited nuclear war"—i.e., one which does not result in mutual annihilation of the superpowers—and, relatedly, "nuclear utility"—i.e., nuclear forces which can be used without inevitably ushering in mutual annihilation. It is far more satisfactory to use these concepts rather than the concept of deterrence which has so many meanings. It is, for example, quite legitimate to argue that willingness to start a nuclear war, which is part of NATO's strategic posture, can be intended to deter, but this is not what most people understand by nuclear deterrence.

However, using these concepts does not mean that the nuclear strategy of either the US or the USSR will then make sense. Having taught courses about nuclear strategy, I am familiar with the constant complaint that "I don't understand this; it doesn't make sense." The complaint confuses two things—whether you understand it is different from whether it makes sense.

Many people do assume that if the US has a strategy of protracted but limited nuclear warfare, then the strategy must make sense, that it must conform to a rational pursuit of rational interests. Depending upon their political standpoint, such people either assume that the strategy really is good for the defense of the populations of the US and its allies, or they conclude that the strategy really reveals a current US intention to start a nuclear war. In both cases, they are wrong. The true situation is simply that the strategy does not make sense.

The fundamental problem of nuclear strategy is how to use nuclear weapons without running the risk of national suicide. The best evidence and the most serious analyses reveal that in most conceivable circumstances, initiating a nuclear attack must run the risk of uncontrollable nuclear war. The reasons for this are many and varied, and include technical problems in the weapons themselves and in associated communications systems, as well as political and human problems in the command system. The exceptions appear to be circumstances in which attack and initial retaliation involve only a handful of weapons, in which case the risk exists but is reduced, or in which the attack is made against a state with no nuclear weapons and with no superpower protection. Accordingly, since each superpower can wipe out the other, together with all its allies several times over, the sensible thing is not to deploy weapons and develop strategies suitable for limited nuclear war, because if the other side comes to think you are planning such a war, that may be the motivation for launching its own pre-emptive nuclear attack.

All of these arguments are, of course, highly speculative. In discussing nuclear strategy, we must remember that nobody really knows how a nuclear war would proceed. But it does seem to be clear that strategies of limited nuclear war and nuclear utility make impossibly stringent demands on technical capabilities, human performance and on the other side's acceptance of the rules of the game. As a result, they fail to solve the problems to which they are addressed and actually increase the danger of nuclear war occurring in a time of political crisis. These risks have been pointed out over the past two decades with increasing frequency, vigor and cogency. Many of the critics have been people who have held positions of power in the American military establishment.[2] It is therefore important to ask why these strategies have been developed.

One track to follow in seeking the answer is to start from the response of many people to the whole business—that it is quite insane. It would be possible to consider the social psychology of nuclear strategists and politicians, the cultural roots of their obsession with power and strength. This approach is certainly capable of producing important insights, but they would need to be fitted into a framework which includes the international political role of nuclear weapons. It might be possible to show that nuclear strategy reveals a psychological condition which is socially abnormal, possibly deriving from the way in which particular institutions, such as the military, take to extremes certain elements of American culture—for example, its emphasis on achievement, competition, being "number one," white male values. But it would also be necessary to show how this abnormality (if such it is) can be socially and politically acceptable and even valued.

For this, we should look not simply at the strategies themselves, but at their political underpining. How can the idea of limited nuclear war and nuclear utility be fitted in to our understanding of the international political order, even if the idea does not make sense?

I HAVE ALREADY COMMENTED THAT the fundamental problem of nuclear strategy is how to use nuclear weapons without risking national suicide. This can be understood as a political problem, a problem of power, of how to translate military strength into political power. Billions of dollars have been spent on an awesomely destructive nuclear arsenal, and billions of rubles on another. The result is a nuclear face-off in which the nuclear arsenal of one superpower neutralizes the nuclear arsenal of the other. But nuclear weapons are not only about relations with the other bloc; they are also about relations within the bloc. Yet if the US's nuclear arsenal is effectively neutralized by the USSR's, the US nuclear guarantee to Western Europe becomes devalued. Always in discussion of NATO strategy there is the nagging question: to save Bonn from Soviet conquest, would an American president unleash a nuclear war which would eventually destroy Washington? To those who both doubt the credibility of an American threat to gamble in this way and want to strengthen the nuclear guarantee, the answer has appeared to be the development of limited nuclear warfighting capabilities. If an American president could use nuclear weapons in a way which would not lead to the destruction of the US, the credibility of the guarantee would be increased. This has led to the paradox of preparing Europe as the nuclear battleground of the future, to which the nuclear war would be limited, while declaring this willingness to sacrifice Western Europe makes it more secure. By and large, Western European governments have accepted this paradox, France being the major exception. At the same time, readiness for limited nuclear war could strengthen the US's hand in political and economic conflicts involving the less developed countries.

The particular importance of this since the early 1970s has been two-fold. Following the war in Indochina, the political costs of fighting conventional wars, even if they are economically less punitive to the US, have been very obvious and extremely inhibiting. Limited nuclear war has seemed a way of avoiding the need to commit American troops in large numbers. At the same time, Western Europe and Japan have followed economic and political trajectories which have taken them away from their former dependence on the US. It should not be forgotten that the US established the political order and conditions for economic growth of both these centers of economic rivalry. Yet it is very easy to forget that in the quarrels and conflicts of interest which pervade current relations between the US and its former proteges. Strategies of limited nuclear war have thus seemed a way of reasserting American leadership where it is challenged, of binding the allies back into a unity led by the US. Today, as throughout the nuclear age, nuclear strategy is a political instrument in the effort to maintain the order of an international economic system. Over the past decade it has become an attempted counterweight to the relative economic and political decline of the US.

It is here that one can understand the particular significance of the planned deployment of cruise and Pershing missiles to Western Europe. These weapons are intended both as visible reminders of the importance of the US to Western European defense and security, and as ways of making the nuclear guarantee to Western Europe credible. Their actual operational utility in a war with the USSR is rather secondary in this perspective. That much has been virtually admitted by proponents of the new missiles, whose most important arguments are couched in terms of the need to maintain NATO's unity. From the beginning of the controversy, they have represented opposition to cruise and Pershing as opposition to US leadership of Western Europe. For clarifying the issue in this way they deserve our thanks.

Thus, while the strategy of limited nuclear war does not make sense, the motivation which lies behind it does. Remove the strategy, and remove the weaponry and military infrastructure associated with it, and a decisive change will have been effected in trans-Atlantic relations. In a certain sense, the strategy of limited nuclear war is the strategy politically appropriate to the condition in which the American-led alliance now finds itself. It is also an extremely dangerous strategy that could easily explode in the faces of all of us, including those who promote and seek to benefit by it. For the sake of survival, we have no choice but to force the removal of the strategy. Accordingly, we have no choice but to be political.

Europe

THESE ISSUES TAKE ON A PARTICULAR DIMENSION and sharpness in Europe. This results first from Europe's role as the potential battleground for a limited nuclear war, in which the definition of "limited" is strictly geographical—what might seem limited from an American perspective will seem total from ours. It does not seem likely that a future European war will be European in its proximate cause, merely in its location. Accordingly, the dismantling of nuclear confrontation in Eu-

rope, the creation of a European nuclear-free zone, while it will
not render us immune from nuclear attack, will contribute to
our chances of survival. And even if, as seems likely, this development does not end confrontation between the US and the
USSR, it would end its currently most embedded and immediate form. It would therefore create a breathing space in which
other steps to de-escalate confrontation might be taken.

Europe's role as potential nuclear battleground is part of
what holds the Cold War division of the continent in place. As I
have already argued, diminishing and abolishing that role
could create the room for reforming tendencies to make some
ground. Much greater changes are required, over a very long
period, before genuine liberty flourishes in Eastern Europe, but
weakening the hold of Soviet militarism by easing the pressure
from Western militarism would be a step in the right direction.
Certainly, entrenched confrontation and a renewed Cold War
are the worst possible conditions for reform. *Solidarność* was
sacrificed on this altar.

THE WESTERN EUROPEAN POLITICAL AND ECONOMIC trajectory
has been away from dependence on the US. Continuing military and strategic dependence on the US is out of "sync" with
that trajectory. Conversely, the nuclear disarmament movements in Europe are in tune not only with our desire to live as
long as possible, but also with the emerging political mainstream of Western Europe. Within Europe, this represents a
major crisis and challenge for the generation of politicians
reared as Atlanticists—pro-American, in the sense of accepting
American leadership as the very context of European politics.
If the nuclear disarmament movements ever appear to be anti-
American, it is because they are inescapably anti-Atlanticist.
Atlanticism has become the ever shallower apologia for con-
signing our fate into the hands of American decisions, for
accepting the strategy of limited nuclear war, for agreeing to be
disposable. And the same politicians who in Europe preach
Atlanticism in military affairs, are at war with the present US
administration over interest rates, steel, the Middle East.

The result is that the European disarmament movements can
affect both our chances for survival and our political possibili-

ties in Europe. Improving our chances of survival is directly related to reducing superpower domination of our affairs.

One consequence of this is that we cannot conceivably accept confinement to bilateral or multilateral negotiations as the approach to reducing confrontation. To do that would be again to surrender our fate and our politics into the hands of the superpowers, conducting their business in diplomatic forums which are intrinsically beyond our reach. The way in which these negotiations have been conducted—in the endlessly deadlocked talks on conventional force reductions in Vienna, in the negotiations on the eventually unratified SALT II treaty which would still have let each superpower increase its strategic warheads by about 50 percent, in the Reagan "zero option"—gives us no cause for confidence that the multilateral path to disarmament can be effective. The essential case for nuclear disarmament for Western Europe is that these weapons cannot be used for our defense, if the word "defense" is to have any meaning. The urgency of the case is that the use of these weapons for our destruction is increasingly likely with current developments in both technology and strategy. The wider relevance of the case is that reducing confrontation in Europe, even if only on one side, will diminish the likelihood of global destruction and might begin to give some impetus to arms reductions by the superpowers and efforts to prevent nuclear proliferation. Unilateral nuclear disarmament therefore represents an effective strategy for the Western European peoples to reassert some degree of control over our fate and contribute to world peace.

There are no apologies or half-heartedness about our espousal of unilateralism. If it were not for a belief that unilateral nuclear disarmament can improve our chances of having a future, the Western European disarmament movements would not exist. And if it were not for those movements, nuclear disarmament would not be on the world's political agenda in even the most marginal form.

It may, however, be worth adding that the choice of unilateralism is not lightly made. We do not and cannot ignore the USSR's nuclear arsenal, including that portion of it which is specifically directed against Western Europe—most notoriously, but not exclusively, about two-thirds of its SS-20 missiles. Nor can we ignore the size of the USSR's conventional forces and the density of armored forces within them. Nor can we ignore the grinding continuation of the USSR's military industrial effort. What we cannot accept is that the best way of living next to this giant is to further increase NATO's own nuclear forces and develop strategies for fighting and winning a nuclear war. What we recognize is that Europe is a well-prepared site for nuclear war, but an unlikely cause of that war. And what we take on ourselves is our responsibility to diminish the current confrontation between the superpowers—even without their permission.

Most of the advocates of multilateralism as the only approach to nuclear disarmament turn out on closer inspection not to be advocates of disarmament at all. They are, rather, advocates of various ways of diverting disarmament movements up blind alleys. If I am right in my argument that ridding Europe of nuclear weapons would effect a decisive change in relations between Western Europe and the US, then in principle it does not matter whether that goal is achieved unilaterally or multilaterally. Nuclear weapons are an integral part of the world order. Their removal would change that order. It is here that the basic politics of nuclear disarmament lie and here that the bedrock of resistance is to be found.

I must add that these remarks are *not* to be taken as comments upon the demand for a bilateral nuclear "freeze." I regard this as a valuable initiative of great political significance, and crystal clear in its even-handedness to anybody who is aware that both the US and USSR can blow each other up many times over. Were it to be accepted, it would halt the nuclear colossi in their tracks. Like a nuclear-free Europe, it could provide a breathing space in which something more could be accomplished. But these remarks *are* comments upon those in the US, as well as in Western Europe, who urge us to await the outcome of negotiations about cruise and Pershing II missles. That we cannot do, for reasons I hope I have made clear.

ONE OF THE MOST COMMON CRITICISMS I have heard of unilateralism in Western Europe, even in its relatively limited form of unconditional opposition to cruise and Pershing II missiles, is that its consequence will be a US withdrawal into isolationism and "fortress America." Frankly, I do not believe the US would ever give up the game so easily. It does not ring true to the US's responses to reverses in other parts of the world, responses which are generally remarkable for their flexibility and versatility. But the truth contained within this criticism is that, should Western Europe follow the path sought by the disarmament movements, the change in relations with the US will necessitate a rethinking of those relations within the US itself. This need is urgent and is accompanied by a need for rethinking the US's global relations. It exists regardless of the Western European disarmament movements. To the extent that the Reagan Administration has a strategy for foreign affairs, it is a matter of reestablishing US primacy. So far, all the signs are that it will not work. If it does not work, the result will be a series of failures in foreign policy likely to lead to increasing panic and desperation. The more that military strength is used in an attempt to counterbalance other failings, the more dangerous the process will be. In the end, it does not matter what anybody except the US administration thinks about limited nuclear war. The evidence of the past decade, despite recent efforts to be a little more tactful, is that the US is all too tempted by nuclear warfighting strategies. If it believes, now or in the future, that it can fight, contain and win a limited nuclear war, it is possible it will try to do it. Unless the political mainstream in the US becomes convinced that it cannot regard Western Europe as its possession or the rest of the world as its stomping ground, nuclear war may be the logical destination.

This, finally, returns us to the campaign against cruise and Pershing II missiles, and to the need for the American disarmament movement to put a major effort into that campaign. For the battle over the cruise and Pershing II has become a battle about limited nuclear war. While we cannot hope in a short time to achieve a nuclear-free Europe, let alone global nuclear disarmament, we can and must hope and work to inflict a decisive setback on the strategy and politics of limited nuclear war.

The issue of the moment which encapsulates that strategy is the plan to deploy cruise and Pershing missiles to Europe starting in 1983. Americans and Europeans have an equal stake in preventing that plan from being implemented.

Footnotes

1. The full text of the appeal is in E.P. Thompson & D. Smith, eds, *Protest and Survive* (New York: Monthly Review Press, 1981).
2. Not least among them was Harold Brown, Defense Secretary under Carter who, in the Defense Deparment Annual Report for the Fiscal Year 1982 (released January 19, 1981), stated his view that nuclear war could probably not be limited, although he was not thereby deterred from developing strategic concepts for limited use of nuclear weapons—i.e., for limited nuclear war.

Which Side Are You On?

MELVYN DUBOFSKY

EVER SINCE THE LATE 1970s it has been commonplace to refer to the crisis of the American labor movement. Some commentators have indeed gone so far as to suggest that no American labor *movement* exists. In the words of one observer, "organized labor has kept the forms of a social movement while jettisoning most of the content." In 1978, Nicholas Von Hoffman wrote in *Harper's* about "The Last Days of the Labor Movement," and A.H. Raskin described for *Fortune's* corporate readership the rut in which "big labor" found itself immobilized.

The crisis of American labor to be sure is part of a much larger, more general historical conjuncture. For 25 years after WWII, the world's industrial nations experienced a cycle of economic expansion and prosperity unparalleled in the history of capitalism. This boom enabled the United States to build an "affluent society" and American trade unions to provide their members with steadily rising real wages, widened fringe benefits, and a level of job security heretofore unimaginable. Economic growth, moreover, provided the resources with which every national administration from Truman through Nixon expanded welfare benefits and transferred some of the surplus accumulated by the successful to the poor and unfortunate. Global capitalist expansion provided a setting in which Ameri-

---

MELVYN DUBOFSKY *is Professor of History and Sociology at the State University of New York-Binghamton. He is the author of* We Shall Be All, *a history of the IWW, co-author of a biography of John L. Lewis and has written numerous other books and essays on US labor and general history.*

can trade unions flourished as never before and the United States erected a partial welfare state for its citizens.

But in the 1970s a global economic contraction began. Throughout the industrial world, Japan excepted, productivity and employment levels declined. Inflation and capital disaccumulation occurred simultaneously, the combination of high prices and reduced investment causing mass unemployment reminiscent of the Great Depression of the 1930s. By the start of the 1980s even the most highly unionized of American workers found their real wages and living standards threatened. The global economic contraction forced American workers and their labor movement to face a crisis of unexpected dimensions.

The crisis consisted of both institutional and structural factors, the former linked directly to changes in the size and influence of trade unions, the latter flowing from a transformation of the American social and economic structure. In the remainder of this essay I want first to delineate and analyze the primary characteristics of the current crisis as it affects labor. Next I will explain why the crisis is *not* an unprecedented historical phenomenon, and how a fuller comprehension of American labor's past can render its present and future possibilities more discernible. Finally, I will move from description and analysis to prescription, suggesting tactics and strategy through which trade unions might turn the contemporary crisis to their advantage.

THE MOST OBVIOUS SIGN OF LABOR'S INSTITUTIONAL decay is in the relative decline of trade unionism. Although more workers belonged to unions at the end of the 1970s than at the start, the number of full-time workers had grown even more rapidly. By 1978, only 26.6 percent of nonagricultural workers belonged to unions compared to 34.7 percent in 1954, and 35.5 percent (the peak) in 1944. In only a quarter of a century then, the proportion of the unionized labor force fell almost 25 percent. Unions suffered their worst damage in the primary manufacturing sector, the stronghold of the labor movement since the upheaval of the 1930s. Between 1974 and 1978 alone, unions in manufacturing lost more than a million members (9,144,000 to 8,119,000), or over 11 percent of total membership. And in 1981 and 1982 as auto and steel experienced steep declines in demand for their products, mass layoffs spread. In February 1982, the UAW averaged 300,000 fewer members than in 1979 (1,255,000 to 1,530,870). In 1981, even after the reaffiliation of the UAW, the AFL-CIO had fewer members than at its founding in 1955. More threatening still to the labor movement was its inability to keep pace with the growth of the labor force in the non-manufacturing sector. While employment in that sector rose 37 percent between 1968 and 1978, union membership increased only 13 percent, resulting in a decline in organized labor's share of non-manufacturing workers from 24.6 to 20.0 percent.

The relative decline in union strength was also evidenced in the results of NLRB employee representation elections. Ever since the 1940s, an NLRB-conducted election rather than a strike had been trade unionism's primary instrument to organize the unorganized. Yet the rate of union success in NLRB representation elections declined steadily, from a peak of 80 percent in 1946, to a low of 47 percent in 1977. As *Business Week* noted in December 1978: "American business has by and large never really accepted unionism." This reality and the evidence on all sides of a renewed corporate campaign to create a "union-free environment" led an eminent reporter to describe the nation's top labor leaders as enveloped by "a sense of insecurity."

A SERIES OF FEDERAL JUDICIAL RULINGS, reaching back to the 1940s, but increasing in number and impact by the 1970s, also intensified trade union insecurity. Although many legal decisions strengthened unions as institutions and secured labor leaders against rank-and-file rebels, the same rulings stripped unions of vital weapons. Federal judges reinterpreted the Norris-LaGuardia Anti-Injunction Law and Wagner Act to sanction anti-strike injunctions, even in the absence of union-management agreements containing no-strike provisions. The Supreme Court ruled that workers could not strike when their grievances were subject to arbitration. As Karl Klare has noted in an enlightening recent article on "Labor Law as Ideology": Judicial decisions have paved the way for collective bargaining to function as "a system for inducing workers to participate in their own domination by managers and those whom managers serve."

Just as court decisions over the last decade have curtailed workers' right to strike, they have also circumscribed rank-and-file initiatives. No matter how unresponsive a union leadership may be to the interests of its members, judicial precedents require dissidents to observe union rules and contractual obligations that maintain the power of incumbents. And in a Supreme Court decision in June 1982, a 5 to 4 majority ruled that unions may ban outside contributions to candidates for union office. In effect, this ruling stripped away one of the assets insurgents might use in their campaigns to unseat officials who control the union international staff, the union journal, and the union treasury.

In their eagerness to stabilize, routinize, and harmonize both labor-management relations and internal union affairs, judges have built a firm doctrinal wall against worker shop-floor initiatives and direct forms of labor action. Where initial New Deal legal reforms liberated workers and their unions from judicial oppression, their more recent interpretation and implementation have sought to recork the genie of labor militancy.

Judicial decisions, of course, are not rendered in a political vacuum. For four decades after the Roosevelt "revolution" of the 1930s, the American labor movement relied on its influence within the Democratic Party to protect labor's interests and advance welfare legislation. A few exceptions to the general rule of union political behavior notwithstanding, organized labor had been fully incorporated into the national Democratic Party. For most of the WW II and postwar years this political strategy, on balance, produced positive results. By the late 1970s, however, labor's political influence was in a shambles. After pouring its resources and manpower into the campaign for the election of Jimmy Carter and a Democratic Congress in 1976, the labor movement found itself at a political loss. Congress refused to enact labor's most desired bills. As the *AFL-CIO News* announced after the adjournment of the 95th Congress in 1978, what it left behind was "not a monument to forward-looking legislation but a tombstone."

Not only did the AFL-CIO lose its battle to reform federal labor law; Carter's Democratic Administration fought inflation through a tight-money policy that raised unemployment to levels not experienced since the 1930s. This was doubly galling because Carter, as a candidate, had promised to reward his union supporters. As President, he betrayed them. First, Carter conscripted workers as cannon fodder in the war against inflation. Second, he failed to use presidential muscle to build a congressional majority for labor law reform. All the AFL-CIO had sought were minimal changes in the National Labor Relations Act that would have accelerated hearings on unfair labor practice cases and representation elections; increased penalties for employer violations of the law; withheld federal contracts from willful violators; and given organizers an equal opportunity to address employees in representation elections. As the dean of the Michigan Law School said about the reform proposals, they would not alter "the balance of collective bargaining power as between unions and organized employers."

Still employers united nearly as one in fighting labor law reform. From the reactionary National Right-to-Work Committee to the mainstream US Chamber of Commerce to the "corporate liberal" Labor-Management Group, businessmen fought labor. George Meany aptly characterized the emerging anti-labor alliance as "a heavily financed, well orchestrated coalition between big business and right-wing extremists."

ITS SUCCESS IN CONGRESS and the equally evident paralysis of labor's political muscle encouraged business to attack unions more aggressively. The NAM strengthened its Committee on a Union Free Environment, labor-management consulting firms peddled their sophisticated anti-union services widely, and even General Motors, for a time in 1978-79, imperiled the "civilized relationship" it had built after 1948 with the UAW. When General Motors abetted anti-union elements among workers in new assembly plants being opened in Oklahoma and Mississippi, UAW president Douglas Fraser warned: "GM has given us a Southern strategy designed to set up a non-union network that threatens the hard-fought gains won by the UAW. We have given stability and been rewarded with hostility."

It was the same union president, Fraser, who, in resigning in July 1978 from the prestigious Labor-Management Group, presciently characterized organized labor's dire new predicament in an open letter. Accusing corporate leaders of breaking the fragile compact, which had bound management and labor together since the end of World War II, Fraser charged that the "leaders of the business community, with few exceptions, have chosen to wage a one-sided class war." He resigned from the Labor-Management Group because he could scarcely sit with employers "while they try to destroy us and ruin the lives of the people I represent." Fraser was equally scathing in his denunciation of the Republican and Democratic parties as ". . . weak and ineffective . . . with no visible clear-cut ideological difference between them, because of business domination."

Where then did that leave organized labor politically? In the event, nowhere! In the 1980 election the union hierarchs, as usual, campaigned for Carter and the Democrats. In their view, anything and anyone was preferable to Ronald Reagan. Not that they were wrong. Yet labor leaders had so lost touch with their followers that almost half of all union members and their families voted for Reagan. Now not only had labor leaders lost political clout in Washington; they also had been deserted politically by masses of their own troops.

Reagan and his Republicans did not disappoint their union enemies. For the first time since the creation of the Department of Labor in 1913, a president chose a secretary without friends in either the labor movement or the liberal-left reform community. Reagan's "supply-side" economic program, which simultaneously cut general welfare expenditures while reducing taxes for the wealthy, in the words of the new ALF-CIO president Lane Kirkland "fails every test of justice and equity."

The Summer 1981 air controllers' strike disclosed graphically the anti-labor animus of the Reagan Administration and the paralysis in the will of American unions. However ill-advised and ill-planned the strike may have been, however excessive several of the controllers' demands seemed, however "criminal" the walkout may have been in strictly legal terms, the strikers were motivated by substantial, legitimate grievances that Reagan's negotiators refused to address. Instead of bargaining constructively with the air controllers, federal officials declared the walkout illegal, sought injunctions against the strikers, and arrested, chained, and jailed several local PATCO officials. Not since the 1922 national railway shopmen's strike had the national government so directly and brutally suppressed a union action. And Reagan made the air controllers pay an even heavier price than the defeated railroad strikers of 1922 (or for that matter Debs' American Railway Union members after the 1894 Pullman Boycott). The President summarily fired all the strikers, proclaimed that they would never be rehired for their former positions or pardoned, and had their union decertified as a legitimate bargaining agent.

For organized labor the most ominous aspect of the air controllers' strike was that Americans overwhelmingly endorsed the President's action. Moreover, private sector union members failed to support public employees, whose salaries were paid from taxes. No other unions struck in sympathy with their PATCO brothers and sisters, and many union members freely crossed picket lines. In 1981, as so often before, solidarity among American workers proved a chimera.

Labor's paralysis enabled the Reagan Administration to put its economic policy into practice. The result was disastrous for workers. By the end of 1982, unemployment was pushing 11 percent nationally, and had reached depression-era levels in such states as Michigan, Ohio, Indiana, Oregon and Alabama, such industries as auto, steel, and construction, and among such workers as nonwhites and teenagers (black teenage unemployment exceeds 50 percent). Once again, workers and poor people paid the price for a political war against inflation.

BUT THE CURRENT CRISIS OF AMERICAN LABOR is only partly a result of the changing institutional milieu in which unions function. It is also much more basically a consequence of fundamental changes in the American economic and social structure.

In July 1982, for the first time in United States history, employment in the consumer, financial, and service sectors surpassed the job total in primary production—manufacturing, mining, and construction. In three decades total employment in the white collar service sector tripled to account for more than 27 percent of the nation's nonfarm payroll jobs, while over the same time period primary production employment fell from 41 percent to under 27 percent.

This trend has spelled trouble for the American labor movement for two reasons. Traditionally, union strength has been concentrated among adult male blue collar workers in the skilled crafts (construction, transportation, and mining before 1937) and the mass-production durable goods sector after 1937. True, from the mid-1960s through the mid-1970s, unions made their greatest strides among white collar employees concentrated in state and local government jobs. The American Federation of Teachers and the American Federation of State, County, and Municipal Employees (AFSCME) became two of the fastest growing unions, the latter becoming one of the five largest in the AFL-CIO. But by the late 1970s, state and municipal employment stopped expanding and in many regions actually declined.

Meantime, the areas in which white collar jobs continued to grow were precisely those that trade unions failed to penetrate. As Emma Rothschild pointed out in a 1981 article in the *New York Review of Books*, such fast-food franchises as McDonald's and Burger King now employed more workers than the auto or steel industry. These workers, typically teenagers earning minimum wages, tended to enter and leave the job market rapidly. They were also scattered among so many small, isolated locations that the expense of organizing them appeared to exceed the potential benefits to a union. A similar pattern evidenced itself among supermarket employees organized by one of the more successful service employee unions, the United Food and Commercial Workers (UFCW). That union's Portland, Oregon local, the largest in the state, experienced an annual membership turnover exceeding 75 percent, mostly among newly-hired high school graduate checkout clerks.

Not all or most white collar jobs were filled by young adults earning minimum wages. An even larger number included well-educated men and women hired by financial, insurance, and high-technology firms as accountants, bookkeepers, engineers, and technicians. These workers, too, proved largely resistant to trade unionism. The firms that employed them practiced a system of labor relations pioneered and perfected by IBM. They sought to guarantee job security for employees, who also received a plethora of fringe benefits, from healthcare insurance and attractive retirement packages to membership in company country clubs. Typically, workers in such firms held jobs with status-laden titles that led them to identify themselves as part of a professional or management team.

Linked to the shift from primary to secondary and tertiary sector employment was a change in the sexual composition of the labor force. The bulk of blue collar production jobs are still held by men. But the growth in service sector employment has drawn more and more women into the workplace. Today, the largest single occupational category, clerical workers, remains, as always, a female bastion. Sixty-six percent of all women workers as contrasted to 43 percent of men are concentrated in the white collar sector, most heavily among secretarial-clerical jobs. With women now composing over 40 percent of the total labor force and with more than 50 percent of all women seeking full-time waged work, that reality holds promise and peril for the labor movement.

Another factor reminiscent of the American past has recomposed the labor force over the past decade: the streams of legal and illegal immigration. Both streams have been composed overwhelmingly of non-white workers, the legal immigrants numbering hundreds of thousands of Asians and the illegals, millions of Hispanics from Mexico, Central America, and the Caribbean. As in the past, the presence today of millions of new immigrant workers acts as a divisive factor within the American labor movement. Immigrants compete with American-born nonwhites for marginal low-wage jobs, while the millions of illegals offer employers an ideal reserve labor army, one as disposable as it is employable, to avert union organizing drives.

Yet as the composition of the work force steadily changes, the labor movement remains a white male-led institution. As in the past, this causes the union leadership to neglect nonunion areas employing mostly female and nonwhite workers while in unionized firms with growing numbers of women and minority workers the gap between leaders and members widens.

The structural changes in the kinds of people working and the sorts of work they do are also steadily being transformed by the imperative at the heart of capitalism: the absolute need to accumulate capital through the profit mechanism. As capital competes on an ever widening global scale, the search for profits and the drive for accumulation affects American workers in two ways. First, capital relentlessly seeks the cheapest labor markets, whether in Mexico, Korea, Taiwan, or Singapore. Capital internationalizes, workers remain prisoners of national borders. Hence American clothing, textile, shoe, electrical appliance, and now auto and steel workers impotently watch their jobs shift overseas. Second, in order to compete in a global market and still produce at home, American capital strives to reduce the price of domestic labor. It does so in two ways. One reduces material standards and the other eliminates jobs. The former method requires workers to accept wage increases less than the rate of price increases or even to "give back" to employers benefits long taken for granted. The latter, more threatening and insidious, simply substitutes capital for labor, using robots in place of human hands. "Robots," noted a *New York Times* labor reporter, "bring to their work several special qualities. For one thing, they are perfect—they never make a mistake. For another, they never get bored." Yet another attraction of robots is their cost. It has been estimated that a programmable robot costs only one-third to one-quarter of the wages of a UAW member. That reality has led automotive industry engineers to estimate that by 1995 at least 50 percent of the direct assembly of cars would be done by automated machines. It has also been suggested that the new technology of micro processors and smaller, less costly central computers will inevitably reduce employment in the primary growth sector of the labor market, the white collar secretarial and clerical trades.

In the best of times such a technological transformation in work processes would prove painful for employees. Although debate has raged for more than two centuries, ever since the first industrial revolution, about whether technological change creates more jobs than it destroys, one thing is clear. Those who lose their jobs to technology, especially if they are older, more established workers, rarely get the new jobs. Instead they become the human refuse deposited on the scrap heap of capitalist progress. In the worst of times, such as the present, it is not even clear that technological change creates as many jobs as it eliminates. As unemployment throughout the industrial world runs in the 9 to 13 percent range and high interest rates prevail, it seems quite unlikely that those workers displaced by robots and microprocessors will find other jobs. More depressing still, new entrants to the labor force, secondary school graduates especially, today find limited opportunities. Everywhere in the Western world the ranks of the unemployed have been swelled by masses of older teenagers and young adults. The United States, of course, has been no exception to this trend. Just as during the Great Depression of the 1930s economists addressed the issue of structural stagnation (what some called "the maturation of capitalism"), economists and policy makers in the 1980s must again deal with an apparent secular stagnation in the capitalist system.

There was also a rise in protectionist sentiment among many trade unionists in 1982 as a result of the economic crisis. Ever since their emergence as stable institutions in the late 1930s, most large mass production unions have supported liberal international trade policies. The leaders of the auto, steel and electrical industry unions, unlike their brothers and sisters in the more labor intensive, competitive clothing trades, believed that their members benefitted materially from liberal trade policies. But as foreign cars and steel eroded the domestic American market in the 1970s, sentiment among mass production workers shifted. By the end of the 1970s, the United Steel Workers and especially the United Auto Workers were in the vanguard of a movement to establish more protectionist trade policies. Indeed, in its 1983 session, Congress will consider a bill sponsored by the UAW which mandates that foreign car companies with large shares of the American market must manufacture a substantial portion of component parts in the US. So far has such protectionist sentiment penetrated that Michael Harrington, leader of Democratic Socialists of America, has publicly endorsed the UAW demand for "domestic content" legislation. Whether protectionism will bring workers more benefits than free trade internationalism remains debatable.

THE CURRENT ECONOMIC CRISIS HAS ALSO reexposed and magnified a dilemma in American trade unions that has existed ever since their stabilization and maturation at the end of the nineteenth and start of the twentieth centuries: the gap between leaders and led. As high union office became a career not a calling, as union officials gained tenure in office and substantial salaries, and as they socialized with employers and government officials, union leaders came to inhabit a universe vastly different from that of their followers. The officers had steady jobs and annual salaries; their followers were paid by the hour and lacked job security. Union members lived in working class neighborhoods, frequented local taverns, belonged to ethnic-fraternal societies, and enjoyed only brief paid vacations. Their leaders lived in private homes in exclusive neighborhoods, banqueted with corporate and government leaders, golfed at country clubs, and holidayed in Florida and even Europe. Over time, as unions grew in size, as their treasuries flourished, and orderly collective bargaining became the norm in industrial relations, the distance between union leaders and followers widened. As John Kenneth Galbraith pointed out in *The New Industrial State* (1967) and William Serrin elaborated in his history of the UAW and General Motors, *The Company and the Union* (1970), union leaders and corporate executives built a mutually symbiotic relationship. Both made concessions to each other that were intended to stabilize their respective institutions, the company and the union. Put bluntly, if simplistically, the union enabled the company to control its workers more completely and effectively while the company enabled labor leaders to administer their union more efficiently and securely.

Stagflation and the dire predicament of many large American corporations have magnified the historical split between union leaders and led. Aware of the economic weaknesses of auto, steel, and rubber firms, among others, international union officers evince as much interest in protecting the firms' stability as in advancing the claims of *all* their members. Rather than see a major corporation fail, union leaders prefer to temper their wage claims and even to "give-back" current benefits. Many union members, especially the younger ones among them, experience a different reality. They, too, must exist with economic stringency. For them, reduced real wages and "give-backs" mean less opportunity to achieve an "American standard of living" and its most notable feature, private home ownership. More disquieting to younger workers are the longer term aspects of "give-back bargaining." Wherever such bargaining has occurred, the tendency has been for union leaders to concede wage, fringe benefit, and work rule features of the contract in return for corporate promises to preserve an agreed minimum of current jobs. The effect of such agreements has been to protect employment for older workers with seniority or to enhance the pensions of those about to retire at the expense of newer employees, particularly females and nonwhites. Another insidious feature of union concessions flows from corporate plans for future investment of the savings from reduced wage costs. Many major firms plan to invest more heavily in robots and numerically controlled tools, which will certainly reduce total job opportunites for young workers.

In a sense, then, American labor leaders are caught between Scylla and Charybdis. If they refuse to offer concessions to economically imperiled corporations, capital faces bankruptcy or threatens to run away to nonunion territory at home or abroad. In either event, union membership declines and the trade union as an institution shrivels. If union officials defer to corporate demands for concessions, they save their institutions and many jobs in the short run—but only at the expense of future institutional crisis and the jobs of younger workers. Whatever choice union leaders make, they are damned. In the economic conjuncture of the 1980s they simply cannot serve their members best by focusing on what has become the conventional American means of advancing the workers' welfare —voluntary, private collective bargaining.

HAVING PAINTED SUCH A BLEAK LANDSCAPE for the present and future of the American labor movement, can one also splash some brighter colors on the canvas? Perhaps! One must bear in mind that the history of the American labor movement has not been one of steady, linear progress. Rather it has been a story of cycles, of sudden rapid advances punctuated by equally rapid retreats. Historically, the bulk of union membership growth has been concentrated in four periods: 1897-1903, 1916-1919, 1936-1937, and 1940-1944. It should be noted that three of the four periods were times of rapid economic expansion and/or war. Except for the most recent period, the eras of union growth were followed by absolute as well as relative declines in union membership, the steepness of such drops varying considerably.

As might be expected, the union retreats were closely associated with economic contractions and corporate counterattacks. Thus the plight of the American labor movement in the 1980s is not an historical anomaly.

Indeed the situation of labor today calls to mind the plight of trade unions in the decade 1923-1933. A labor movement, which between 1917 and 1920 became larger, more successful and more militant than ever, found itself reduced almost to impotence in just a few years. Between 1919 and 1922 a concentrated corporate attack on unions buttressed by state and local governments, as well as the judiciary, eliminated labor's wartime gains. Capital proved especially successful in rooting unions out of the basic mass-production industries. After 1923, only the conventional, conservative, narrowly-based construction trades unions and the teamsters concentrated in noncompetitive local cartage were spared the ravages of declining memberships and falling treasuries. In the mines, on the railroads among nonoperating employees, in the metal trades, and in the clothing industry, unions reeled from one defeat to another. In the basic steel, auto, and electrical goods industries, labor made no headway after 1919. A combination of welfare capitalism (the carrot) and the American Plan (the stick) paralyzed unionism. Impotent economically, the labor movement proved equally deficient politically. It opposed unemployment insurance, national health care, old-age retirement plans, and all the other features of the emerging modern welfare state that conflicted with the hoary AFL tradition of "voluntarism."

Union leaders also showed little interest in organizing the legions of semi-skilled operatives in the mass-production industries, those workers Dan Tobin of the Teamsters was to dismiss as late as 1935 as the "rubbish at labor's door." Rather than advance new ideas or develop new plans to unionize the unorganized, most union leaders seemed content to defend their own institutional realms, however much the labor movement's overall size and influence shriveled. Careerists, not missionaries or reformers, the typical union officials of the 1920s shunned risk and innovation.

The Great Depression made such labor leaders even less daring. By 1932-33, as the depression reached its nadir, critics and commentators on American trade unionism saw no prospect for the movement to renovate and revitalize itself. Almost without exception, they dismissed trade unions as a factor in transforming the society, economics, and politics of Depression America. In 1932, American trade unions as a group neither repudiated Herbert Hoover and the Republicans nor endorsed either Franklin D. Roosevelt or a leftist political alternative. Thus what happened among workers and unions ephemerally in 1933-34 and more durably in 1935-37 came as a surprise, if not total shock, to most students of labor. Few who were familiar with the character of American trade unions in 1932 could have imagined that within eight years the labor movement would be larger than ever before in American history and for the first time securely based in the mass-production industries.

Such a brief survey of the past should give pause to those who today dismiss the future prospects of American trade unions and consider labor dead as a social movement. 1982 is not 1932. Nor is the current economic crisis yet comparable to the Great Depression. And Ronald Reagan is certainly not Franklin Roosevelt! But American labor in 1982 is clearly in a stronger position to advance the interests of workers and to act as a force for general socio-economic transformation than it was only half a century ago. Fifty years ago trade unions numbered less than 3 million members, had scarcely any presence in the basic industries, and exercised almost no national political influence. Today, by contrast, unions claim more than 23 million members, function effectively in almost all sectors of the economy, and carry real political weight nationally as well as locally. If the future was not foreclosed for unions in 1932, it is even more open today. The options for change and success exist; it is incumbent on American workers and their leaders to seize the opportunities.

It is also worth considering that in the history of American labor and trade unions the impulse for basic change has rarely originated from within the institutions of labor. As one of the most astute labor historians, David Brody, has observed, the trigger for trade union expansion was rarely in the labor movement, but in the larger environment. In his view, the decisive factors governing worker militancy have arisen from fundamental shifts in the national economic and political situations. Just as the crisis of the 1930s precipitated a structu-

ral transformation and expansion of American trade unionism, it is conceivable that the crisis of the 1980s will do the
same.

For those who believe that the labor movement and trade
unionism have not outlived their usefulness, that wage and
salary workers, broadly defined, maintain the ability and will
to reshape their environment in a more progressive humanitarian direction, several questions remain to be answered. First,
who and where are the people and influences within the trade
unions with the will to turn the current crisis to labor's advantage? Second, what sort of tactics and strategies should unions
develop to turn the crisis to their benefit? Because the two
questions are inseparable, it is best to discuss them together.

One should not expect too much from the hierarchs of the
AFL-CIO or from the aging leaderships of most national and
international unions. During the 1930s their predecessors resisted most of the fundamental changes that revitalized the
labor movement. But the established union leadership does
include a small number of more daring and innovative officials,
such people as Tony Mazzochi of the Oil, Atomic, and Chemical
Workers, "Wimpy" Winpisinger of the Machinists, and many
top leaders of such white-collar and service unions as the
Service Employees' International Union, the UFCW, and
AFSCME. Such union leaders must be willing to challenge
openly more conventional labor officials and even to go their
own ways if the hierarchy resists innovation.

More important for the future, trade unions have a vast reservoir of second-line officers, largely at the local, state, and
regional levels, unencumbered by paralyzing traditions and
not captive to antiquated union precedents. These people,
many of whom matured and became politically conscious in the
protest movements of the 1960s, are much more sensitive to the
concerns of younger workers and the character of the contemporary labor force. Not reflexively hostile to leftist politics and
receptive to a larger universe of ideas, these younger union
officials, given the opportunity, could provide the labor movement with precisely the spark it lacks.

And that is just the point. To grow rather than atrophy,
American trade unions must open themselves to influences
from below. Unions must practice internal democracy as well

as preach it. Instead of repressing insurgent movements and discouraging rank-and-file initiatives, union leaders must listen more sympathetically to voices from the ranks. Rank-and-file militancy must be encouraged not restrained. Unions have enjoyed their greatest periods of growth not when labor-management cooperation was the norm, but rather when workers and their organizations fought vigorously for labor's rights. If older union leaders would act more tolerantly and open their institutions to democratic and popular tendencies, they would discover that American unions include numerous younger officers and members eager and willing to behave militantly to advance labor's interests.

In the summers of 1980 and 1981 I directed National Endowment for the Humanities seminars for labor leaders in which I came into close contact with more than two dozen younger labor leaders from all parts of the country and all sectors of the economy. As a group, they were receptive to the play of ideas, to leftist politics, and to more militant forms of union action. Unlike the New Left of the 1960s, in which some of them participated, these 1980s-style labor leaders see trade unionism as a positive, vital force in American society and politics. No longer do even the most radical among them dismiss workers as Marcusian "one-dimensional" people, or unions as the disciplinary agents for corporate capital. Rather, they view unions as the major bulwark defending workers against corporate subjugation and they seek to enhance, rather than dilute, the strength of existing unions.

Just as younger leaders must be given more opportunity in the labor movement, unions must encourage greater participation from women, nonwhite, and high-technology workers. It is not enough simply to recruit women and nonwhites who work for unionized firms. They must obtain leadership positions more in accord with their enlarged role in the labor force. The AFL-CIO executive council should have more than one token female member and two nonwhites from marginal unions. Moreover, such international unions with large nonwhite memberships as those in steel, auto, rubber, and clothing must develop a leadership that represents the labor force of the 1980s, not the 1950s, 1940s, or 1930s. Just as the union rebels of the 1930s found the will and the way to organize the semiskilled mass-production workers who had long been neglected by the dominant craft unions, union insurgents in the 1980s must find a strategy to unionize workers in high technology firms. As long as IBM, Texas Instruments, Hewlett-Packard, and others remain resistant to trade unionism, the American labor movement cannot rest secure.

WHILE OPENING ITSELF TO INFLUENCES from below, transforming itself from a homogeneous white male movement to a more heterogeneous one, and organizing the unorganized, the labor movement must simultaneously turn "give-back" bargaining to its own advantage. In return for discussing deferrals of wage increases and COL adjustments as well as reductions in holidays and fringe benefits, unions must compel capital to negotiate about technological innovation, plant closings and capital investment decisions. It can be done! In 1945-46 General Motors endured a strike of more than 100 days in order to defend its managerial prerogatives, especially to deny the union the right to bargain about the relationship among prices, wages, and profits. Twenty-five years later in 1981, a less economically secure and profitable General Motors negotiated with the UAW over precisely the issues it had defined in 1946 as solely managerial prerogatives. Simply put, if troubled firms seek union cooperation, they must concede labor a greater role in corporate policy-making. Corporations must be compelled to bargain about prices and profits as well as wages and fringes, capital investment and plant location as well as coffee breaks and vending machines. Unions must demand no less. Even less so than in the 1940s, in the 1980s no sharp line can be drawn between the prerogatives of capital and the rights of labor.

Even while unions democratize internally and bargain with capital on a broader range of issues, they must also innovate politically. Throughout American history and increasingly so after the Great Depression and New Deal, government has played a vital, sometimes determining, role in the relationship between labor and capital. Unless unions succeed in ousting Reaganite Republicans, their conservative Democratic allies, and their judicial hatchetmen from power, any institutional changes labor attempts will be for naught. Corporate capital will make few, if any, concessions to labor so long as it can rely on the national government to defend its vital interests against unions. Thus unions must become more active and independent politically. They must join with women's groups, nonwhites, activist citizens' bodies, and democratic socialists to create a real alternative to the antiquarian romanticism of the Reagan Republicans and the stale New Deal reforms of the conventional Democrats. Solidarity Day, 1981, hinted at the form such a new labor politics might take. As that massive demonstration in the nation's capital united young and old, white and non-white, male and female, private and public employees, old-style blue collar workers and new-style technical and scientific workers, so must the new labor politics. Unions must assume the lead in building a new political coalition to replace the partly discredited and partly debilitated New Deal one first put together in the 1930s. Only such a new coalition, whether it is built within the Democratic Party or takes shape as an independent left-wing alternative, will politicize the masses of poorer citizens divorced from electoral politics. If unions can mobilize their own members politically, build working coalitions with nonunion women's and citizens' groups, and activate the mass of poor nonvoters, the labor movement can alter the national political agenda and transform the structure of party politics.

In seeking to accomplish the goals suggested above, unions must act from strength not weakness. They must recognize that they represent the largest single organized group in the United States. No other institution can claim 23 million members. Union voters and their families are numerous enough, if united, to determine electoral results at all governmental levels. Capital, moreover, simply can no longer function effectively without the cooperation of labor. As *Forbes* magazine oberved in February 1978: "Organized labor is ... so interwoven into the fabric of the US economy, especially in basic industries, that any sudden and serious loss of its authority would probably distress management more than please it."

CAN LABOR SURVIVE THE CRISIS OF THE 1980s and perhaps gain new strength and direction from it? Right now the portents do not look promising. Most observers inside and outside the unions see the labor movement as having less and less impact on society and behaving as a largely spent force in the national life. But the same reality was truer in 1932. If the labor movement's future was not predetermined then, neither is it now. The future history of labor remains to be made by its subjects: male and female, white and nonwhite, young and old, union and nonunion.

The Unreformable Economy: Origins of the Current Economic Crisis

HARRY BRILL

To EXPLAIN THE CAUSES of the current economic crisis, the left has produced a number of propositions to be used as points of departure; among them, "capital flight and plant closings," "conglomerate concentration," and "inflation." Although these are compelling issues which provide us with clues for unraveling thorny contemporary problems, they do not serve to further our understanding of recurring economic crises in the United States for the past 60 years. For example, they are not particularly relevant to understanding the causes of the Great Depression, a phenomenon that must be examined if we want to understand the modern history of economic crises. A review of the period prior to WW II should help us determine the roots of the current crisis and to identify those factors that acted as deterrents to recession and depression. Particular attention will be directed to dispelling a view, with many adherents among the left, that serious downturns are brought about by working class advances.

A fairly sophisticated version of this view, which has several variants, is presented in *What's Wrong With the U.S. Economy,* published by the New York City-based Institute for Labor Education and Research (ILER). Its principal author is David M. Gordon, a prominent member of the Union of Radical Political Economics (URPE) which, as its name indicates, is devoted to radical economic analysis. The position in brief is that the

HARRY BRILL *is an Associate Professor in the Sociology Department of the University of Massachusetts, Boston. He has been writing on economic matters, particularly unemployment, for over 20 years in articles that have appeared in* The Nation, Social Policy, In These Times, Commonweal *and* The Progressive.

workers' rebellion of the mid-sixties, encouraged by an economy close to full employment, improved their bargaining position and that the gains they won, as a result, exceeded productivity advances. "From 1965 to 1973," they say, "corporate power began to erode. US workers and government clients fought back, reclaiming 'many of their earlier losses." So workers' share of corporate income increased at the expense of profits, which discouraged investment and triggered a high rate of inflation. Corporate earnings and real wages then declined, setting off a downturn in the economy.

An alternative view, which will be developed here, is that although workers have made real gains, these improvements have inadequately reflected their expanded capacity to produce. This pattern remained essentially unchanged for most of the early post-World War I years. The state, primarily an ally of capital, promoted investment by favoring capital over labor, thereby assuring the corporations a larger, not smaller, share of profits. It also made large-scale public investments on behalf of corporate America, the costs of which have been borne disproportionately by working people. Rather than taxes impinging heavily upon corporate profits, as ILER also suggests, tax policies have guaranteed that working people would carry the burden of subsidizing the corporations. These policies have been reducing workers' spending power, thereby creating an enormous potential for economic crisis.

Although capital with the aid of the state has prevailed in the long run, it has not, of course, been omnipotent. Working people, as both wage earners and public citizens, have been able to make important gains, which have increased their standards of living. Also, their struggles have resulted in the creation of jobs, an achievement that has played an important role in postponing and ameliorating economic downturns.

However, enormous advances in productivity have given capital a most important edge. Improvements in worker output per hour have more than offset increases in earnings. So even real advances in wages are accompanied by a decline in workers' share of profits, and conversely, an increase in the rate and magnitude of corporate profits. As a result, there is a growing gap between the ability of workers to purchase goods and services and what is actually produced, eventually erupting into a crisis for capital as well as labor.

The permanent war economy has been a major response to economic uncertainty. Military oriented expenditures have provided the corporations with an alternative source of income in varying degrees and have resulted in the creation of jobs in various sectors of the economy. But, contrary to the widely held view that military spending is good for the economy, its net long range impact has been to erode aggregate employment.

* * *

THERE WERE NO SUBSTANTIAL MILITARY expenditures from 1921-1929 and still employment grew by almost 25 percent. (It took almost 18 years after the end of WW II—a period of relatively heavy defense spending—to match this growth.) Although most people were poor during the twenties, the standard of living increased, along with illusions of prosperity. For the first time, such appliances as the radio, refrigerator, and the automobile became available to working people, often through installment buying which squeezed meager incomes.

Responding to broad-based business pressure, federal and state governments played an indispensable role in stimulating the economy through road building programs. As the Keynesian economist Alvin Hansen observed, the road building activities were "comparable in magnitude with the gigantic task in an earlier period of covering the entire country with a network of railroads." Without the extremely expensive public subsidy —around $28,000 per mile—it is difficult to imagine how the enormous expansion of the 1920s would have occurred.

By 1929, there were almost 23 million cars registered, climbing from 11 percent to about 25 percent of the population. The automobile and its satellite industries employed nearly 4 million workers, almost 10 percent of the work force, not including the jobs generated as a result of the additional spending power. There were several million trucks on the road, sparking a major shift in the movement of goods. The construction industry was also stimulated by the automobile which produced changes in residential and shopping patterns.

Since business wanted to avoid a resurgence of the militancy that characterized the period immediately after WW I when 4 million workers went on strike, it made some concessions during the 1920s, including some improvement in wages. But the increases never approached the level of productivity advances. Manufacturing wages rose about 10 percent from 1923-1929 but, according to the Department of Labor, productivity increased by over 30 percent, so production soared well beyond the ability of working people to consume what was being produced. Government spending of about 8 percent of the Gross National Product (GNP) provided a stimulant to the economy, but apparently not enough to offset the Depression. The state, in favoring capital, which in the short run encouraged investment, also created the conditions that produced the nightmare of the 1930s.

There are several important lessons to be learned from the experience of the Great Depression. It provided testimony to the potential of a peacetime economic revival, the effectiveness of working class militancy even during hard times, and the enormous capacity of capital to resist and even retaliate against working class advances. Unemployment and underemployment remained high until WW II. However, it would be a serious mistake to neglect the gains achieved from 1933-37. GNP grew by over 9 percent annually, and the volume of industrial production finally surpassed the pre-Depression level. The number of workers employed climbed almost to the 1929 average. For those fortunate enough to be working, real annual earnings exceeded those of 1929.

Significantly, real hourly wages in manufacturing rose during this period by over 25 percent, appreciably exceeding the 10 percent gain made in productivity. It was a period characterized by militant labor activity. In 1937, 400,000 workers were involved in plant sitdowns. There were 4,700 strikes that year, twice the number that occurred only two years earlier. Strike activity would have exceeded the unprecedented 1919 level except for the dispiriting impact of another severe downturn.

The economy collapsed again in 1937, causing industrial production to drop 2½ times as swiftly as it had in 1929. Joblessness climbed by over 2½ million, which increased the unemployment rate by more than a third within one year. The significance of this dismal event is that it represented the nation's first economic downturn engineered by business and executed by the federal government.The government had been responding to mass protests by injecting billions of dollars into the economy. But the slow pace of business investment limited growth and put a cap on the ability of the economy to recover more fully.

Although from a business perspective, caution seemed understandable, growing public expenditures justified higher levels of investment. As the business journal, *Fortune*, explained, "businesses may profit from government spending but they are afraid to expand; they believe that sooner or later this spending must stop, when the props will be pulled out." *Fortune* might have added that it was the corporations which had been doing their best to pull the props out, or at least to assure against any further expansion of the welfare state.

The New Deal had increased corporate taxes, passed labor-oriented legislation, and allocated substantial funds for programs benefitting the poor and the unemployed. A segment of the business community had supported the New Deal programs, but only to the extent that they might keep protests under control. Corporate America, as a whole, would not support such growing public expenditures as the basis for capital accumulation. Instead, capital went on strike.

In direct reaction to widespread and growing labor unrest, big business circles provoked the 1937 depression. Responding to business anxieties, the Federal Reserve adopted a restrictive monetary policy by substantially reducing bank reserves from the middle of 1936 to early 1937. This seriously depressed the growth rate of bank loans and investments to only 14 percent of the previous year's figure, and it induced an increase in the cost of capital which discouraged investments.

The policy had been urged by the Federal Reserve Bank of New York president, who frankly told his colleagues that it would cause a contraction, of which he approved. The Federal Reserve Bank's chief economist concurred, claiming that the business situation "was going beyond the normal state," implying that the labor situation was out of control. When the Federal Reserve increased its reserve requirements, it was applauded by big business. The major corporations could still readily raise capital, including use of its own savings, but the rest of the business community was more vulnerable to shifts in monetary policy.

Also, the federal government drastically reduced the number of workers on WPA payrolls, cutting back from 2.9 million workers in the peak level of March 1936 to 1.5 million in September 1937. Other cuts were made reflecting a complete turnabout by the federal government. The 1930s provided a grim lesson. The big corporations, taking a long view, precipitated a severe depression. It was not what they wanted ideally, but since the economy was beginning to revive on terms unacceptable to them, they were quite willing to bring about again what they had inadvertently brought on in the first place.

WORLD WAR II SOLVED THE PROFIT CRISIS for business, but its impact on working people has been greatly misunderstood. National income increased tremendously and both unemployment and underemployment virtually disappeared. But why? The most important factor was the siphoning of up to 12 million men into the armed services. The war created fewer jobs than one might have expected from the extraordinary levels of government spending. Employment increased by only 7 million from 1940 to its peak in 1943. With considerably less pump priming, more jobs were created during the upturn in the depression from 1933 to 1937. Had 10 million workers magically disappeared from the civilian work force in 1937, a labor shortage would have resulted at that time, too.

The war severely depressed the civilian sector of business. According to Dunn and Bradstreet, the number of businesses declined by over a quarter of a million from 1940 to 1944. Domestic oriented production either ceased or was severely reduced. Automobiles and houses were not built, nor were major appliances and other goods produced since many peacetime facilities were converted to war production, and raw materials were in extremely short supply, if available at all, for the civilian market. Also, due in part to huge productivity gains in the armament industry, employment declined by about 10 percent in Summer 1944, from its peak in 1943. The increase in the size of the armed forces that year prevented an unemployment problem.

As for workers' income, average real hourly earnings in manufacturing increased during the war by under 4 percent a year as a result of wage controls. Much of that small increase reflected additional overtime work. The unions had signed a no-strike pledge and, with few exceptions, they interpreted their role as policing their members. However, the rank-and-file was not to be manipulated. There were over 14,000 strikes during the war, exceeding the number during any period of comparable length in US history. A large number of the strikes was over productivity issues, resistance to employer attempts to institute and enforce harsh working conditions. These were radical struggles, challenging a fundamental prerogative of capital: the unrestricted right to manage.

As in the post WW I period, capital's supremacy over labor after WW II had to be reestablished as a basis for capital accumulation. Again, the state assisted the corporations. The removal of price controls raised the cost of living by a third in three years. Strikes broke out in almost every major industry, signaling an attempt by workers to restore their standard of living and establish some control over the workplace.

Although the war was over, the government used its war powers to seize industries and compel strikers to return to work. Union leaders, rather than capitalizing on rank-and-file militancy, obediently cooperated. The government also became formally involved in mediating disputes between employers and labor. Labor was expected to compromise on wage demands, but capital was not required to compromise on price increases. In 1947, Taft-Hartley was enacted, weakening the ability of unions to organize and make significant gains.

On the right to manage issue, union leaders cooperated with capital and, as a result, areas of negotiation were narrowed. Major gains achieved by employers included the abolition of the right to strike during the life of the contract, and the development of unwieldy, bureaucratic grievance procedures which removed control from the shop floor. Rank-and-file rebellion and wildcat strikes continued over working conditions and speed-ups but the union leadership systematically discouraged grass roots militancy, replacing issues of control with wage and hour concerns.

During the mid-fifties, for example, fear of automation, along with the specter of unemployment rekindled interest in workplace democracy. The response of the union leadership was to redirect these concerns to negotiating for supplementary unemployment benefits and away from challenges to managerial prerogatives. In the 1959 steel strike, the companies exchanged wage increases for the expansion of management control over work rules.

Productivity bargaining also came into vogue. Initiated by General Motors, it was adopted by other corporations and industries as well. This tied wage increases to gains in productivity in ways which guaranteed that capital would be the main beneficiary of speed-ups and technological advances. Of course, workers were in a much better position to improve their standard of living during that period. Pressure from the rank-and-file compelled labor leaders to deliver better contracts. Nevertheless, like the 1920s, a basis for capital accumulation was established but the rules of the game intensified the American economy's vulnerability to crisis.

* * *

As ALREADY MENTIONED, many left economists have an entirely different interpretation of the current crisis. In a highly publicized *Monthly Review* article, R. Boddy and J. Crotly attributed economic downturns to the squeeze on profits due to higher labor costs, a reflection of wage increases advancing faster than productivity gains. In J. Campen's discussion of the economic crisis in a recent issue of *Radical America*, we are told that capitalists have been doing worse than working people. He claims that not only have the 1970s been "at least equally grim for *corporations and capitalists who own and control them,"* (sic) but, Campen insists, "Our separate looks at how the 1970s affected the economic fortunes of working people and of capitalists suggests that while both groups were hit hard, compared to how they did in the 1960s, capitalists were hit harder." In *The Nation*, S. Bowles, D. Gordon and T. Weisskopf offer data to prove that "the productivity slowdown lies at the heart of the U.S. economic crisis." All these left scholars, incidentally, are prominent members of URPE. Through its journals, conferences, and the publications of its individual members, URPE has been most influential in shaping a left critique of American capitalism.

Their analysis fails to give sufficient weight to the considerable power and flexibility of capital to establish a context that favors its interests. Working people have, of course, made great advances, often over what appeared to be insurmountable obstacles. However, the burden to prove their thesis is certainly upon those who believe, as these economists apparently do, that within the framework of monopoly capitalism, the working class, in the long run, can appreciably reduce corporate profits to a point which precipitates severe economic crises.

The difference between their analysis and the one presented here is reflected in the dissimilar data sources used, a matter of more than a little significance. These economists do not consider that government data may be seriously biased and, as a result, they make no attempt to ascertain the direction of these biases.

The federal government collects and assembles a vast amount of extremely useful information. But to accept as accurate such politically and economically sensitive material as profit and productivity data, risks slanting the analysis unjustifiably in a direction congenial to establishment interpretation.

The annual productivity rate reported by the Department of Labor for the private business sector is as follows: 1948-66: 3.17(%); 1966-73: 2.34; 1973-79: 0.80. These figures show a huge decline in hourly worker output from one period to the other. However, they present numerous problems. The most serious among them is the innaccuracy of the construction component of the index, which accounts for almost 60 percent of the drop in the third period. According to the data for construction, worker output per hour declined in absolute terms by over 16 percent from the prior period. A study by the Department of Commerce found these figures without basis and, moreover, the Department of Labor has made other estimates showing an increase in construction worker productivity. However, they have not yet been integrated into the productivity series.

It is important to distinguish between reduced productivity due to the short run impact of economic decline, and a long term, chronic slowdown in productivity-oriented technological advances, reflecting changes in investment patterns. During downturns, production frequently drops more swiftly than lay-offs, resulting in declining productivity rates. In fact, during the steep 1974-5 recession, productivity in the private non-farm sector dropped as sharply in absolute terms as it did in the 1945 recession and in the depression years between 1929-33. This adversely affected the productivity rates for the entire 1973-79 period.

The issue of productivity is of more than academic interest since Labor Department statistics are often used to justify lower wage increases. Its failure to adjust this data by screening out factors that are artifacts of the business cycle, so as to produce statistics which really reflect hourly worker output is grievously one sided. The Labor Department adjusts other statistical series as, for example, seasonal adjustments to unemployment data, which give the economy the appearance of greater stability. More serious, however, is that the productivity figures are grossly inaccurate.

It would be more useful to consider the statistics for manufacturing because there is an alternative procedure for estimating productivity. According to the Labor Department's figures—1948-66: 2.9 (%); 1966-73: 3.3; 1973-79: 1.5—annual productivity improved in the second period, but dropped drastically, by over half, between 1973-79. Until 1973, the capital-labor ratio, that is, the amount of physical capital each worker uses, was increasing. Moreover, a growing share of domestic investments were made to purchase machinery and equipment, which generally improves productivity, while new plants, oriented toward expansion, were being built in countries offering cheaper labor. We should suspect, then, that America's productivity achievements are far more impressive than Labor Department statistics suggest.

Productivity rates can also be determined by integrating the industrial production data of the Federal Reserve Bank and the aggregate hours worked by production workers reported in the Census Survey of Manufactures. From the early post WW II period until 1973, productivity growth averaged 4 percent annually. It dropped during 1973-79 to 2.7 percent, which, although lower, is still high, and 80 percent higher than the Labor Department's figures. Moreover, the long term productivity improvement for this period was even larger. Capital's profit-making strategy has been to reduce labor's share of corporate income rather than to increase domestic capacity and production.

The results are evident from the US Census of Manufactures. For industrial corporations, the corporate share of value added, which is the net selling price less non-labor costs, has consistently increased during the post WW II period. For production workers, wages as a percent of value added declined between 1949-1973 from 40 to 29 percent. From 1973 to 1977 (the latest year available) the ratio dropped further to under 27 percent. Working people have been losing because the corporations have been gaining.

The claim by various URPE and establishment economists of a long term decline in profits is based on reports from the Department of Commerce which obtains its data from the IRS. However, corporate earnings reported for tax purposes are much lower than actual profits, which appear in annual reports. Numerous changes in the tax laws, particularly, but not only with regard to depreciation, have, over the years, appreciably reduced the percentage of income declared as profits. Two economists at IBM have calculated that the gap between profits reported to IRS and book profits has been growing substantially. For the period they reviewed, from the midfifties to 1974, the ratio of tax to book profits shrank from 77 to 60 percent. Using the IRS based figures for comparative purposes, then, is misleading.

The Department of Commerce also makes adjustments that misinterpret the significance of inflation in promoting profit. Business sells goods at a mark-up based upon current costs although a certain percentage of its sales comes from inventory purchased at lower prices. The Department of Commerce discounts these gains as idiosyncratic, and so deducts them from aggregate profits. However, they are not at all unusual; to one extent or another, the economy has exhibited an inflationary bias for the entire post WW II period. The level of inventory profits can be substantial: for example, $45 billion in 1980.

In addition, since inflation increases the price tag on fixed investments, the Department adjusts corporate profits to take account of replacement costs. It contends that to acknowledge only what business paid for its plant and equipment during periods of inflation exaggerates profits. The Commerce Department's rationale is unjustified because net business income is based upon past investment costs. The higher costs of new plant and equipment will be reflected in future earnings, and, undoubtedly, in highter prices as well. In 1980, the adjustments reduced reported profits by an additional $17 billion. Along with the deductions for inventory profits, 25 percent of corporate profits were discounted.

Commerce Department adjustments are also one sided. Business accumulates enormous liabilities, which, during periods of inflation, are retired with cheaper dollars. Yet there are no adjustments to reported earnings reflecting the gains made as a result of borrowing during inflationary periods. The Department of Commerce's interest is in understating profits, and like establishment professionals generally, it provides technical justifications for politically motivated juggling.

The profit figures relied on here come from the Federal Trade Commission reports on industrial corporations. Although the FTC in recent years has excluded billions of dollars of corporate earnings from certain foreign sources, it remains the best historical public record available to determine profits. Here is the record from 1950-1979. Pre-tax earnings are presented so as to exclude the favorable impact of revised tax laws on profits in recent years.

Profits of Manufacturing Corporations, 1950-79
Billions in 1972 dollars

1975-79	77.8
1970-74	65.8
1965-69	64.7
1960-64	44.3
1955-59	40.5
1950-54	40.2

Taking profit averages for five year periods, it is clear that real profits have continually improved. The last half of the seventies, far from being stagnant, as has been claimed, witnessed the highest reported profits for the postwar period.

Compared to the period a decade earlier, during the Vietnam War, corporate earnings were 20 percent higher. The decade of the seventies was much better for business than either of the previous two.

Return on investment, in addition to aggregate profits, is the most important measure of corporate profitability. The rate of profit on investment (stockholders' equity) for the late seventies averaged 23 percent, higher than it was for the previous five years and the comparable period a decade earlier. In fact, it was even comparable to the rate during the highly profitable Korean War period. In any case, a 23 percent yield on investment produced the largest aggregate profits in the post WW II period, which certainly does not suggest that corporate earnings were either a source or even a symptom of the crisis.

Moreover, the actual magnitude of corporate profits, and the extent to which they have improved from one period to another, has been understated here. Briefly, converting current to constant dollars is based upon Department of Commerce annual estimates of the inflation rates for industrial companies. But in the concentrated manufacturing industry, many corporations are highly integrated, owning or controlling everything from the sources for raw materials to finished products. One subsidiary or division purchases from another in the same company, setting artificially high prices. In reality, these concentrated corporations experience nowhere near the extent of inflation claimed.

A CONSEQUENCE OF GROWING BUSINESS CONCENTRATION has been to exacerbate the risk of crises. A third of all workers now earn their salaries or wages from firms with 5,000 or more employees. About two-thirds of all workers employed in manufacturing are on the payroll of the 500 largest industrial corporations. These large enterprises are in the best position to invest in machines and equipment that greatly advance productivity, and also to relocate, often abroad, thereby undermining the ability of workers to make even the inequitable gains they achieved in the past. Also, through subcontracting, big business controls the fate of a substantial number of small businesses and their work forces. They can and do shift production elsewhere when strikes occur or unacceptable wage increases are won.

Just as in 1936-37, big business has turned to the government to help discipline workers by inducing recessions. Federal fiscal and monetary policies played a major role in promoting the severe 1974-75 recession. Prices climbed tremendously in 1974, precipitating increased strike activity to make up for losses in real wages. By 1975, the severity of the recession reduced the percentage of the work force on strike to its lowest level in over ten years. From the perspective of big business, whose savings provide it with considerable leeway, a short run decline in business is preferable to long term concessions to labor.

So the trend continues: the productivity of workers increases but wages lag. The situation appears to be approaching the breaking point, with not much left for the corporations to squeeze. One signal is that finally corporate profits are feeling the sting.

It is not surprising that a major part of corporate strategy in the post WW II period has been to obtain the federal government as a permanent customer. A substantial number of the nation's largest corporations, and many small businesses as well, have diversified significantly, entering into the defense sector. Corporations in the durable goods industries are especially sensitive to the ups and downs of the business cycle. So even if a relatively small share of their business is derived from military sources, it provides these firms a degree of stability. The current Administration's commitment to an expanding military budget at a time when business orders are falling precipitously is not coincidental.

But military expenditures are costly to the American people. As a result of a shift from labor to capital intensive industries, with its inflationary implications, real income and buying power are reduced, thereby unfavorably affecting employment. More important is that defense spending often results in capital flight which has lost the American economy millions of jobs. A major function of defense expenditures is to create a favorable climate for foreign investments and to protect these investments when necessary. (An important consideration for the government's economic and military support of dictatorial governments.) The protection of business interests, particularly in times of economic instability, requires nurturing military power.

* * *

THE ELEMENTS FOR A SERIOUS DEPRESSION have long been present in the economy. Unlike the 1920s, however, large scale spending by all levels of the government has postponed and reduced the risk of another economic holocaust. According to the Department of Labor, public sector spending accounts for 26 percent of all employment through both direct hiring and local and federal government contracts awarded to private enterprise. If we add what is not included in its estimate—jobs generated as a result of increased spending power—we find that roughly one-third of all jobs are the result of public sector spending.

The ability of the private sector to create jobs without public sector stimulus is much weaker than generally realized. From 1948 to 1966, a period of relatively rapid growth, public expenditures created about 7 out of every 10 new jobs. Within the public sector, neither the defense budget nor even the entire federal budget has been the major source of employment. The state and local sectors account for two-thirds of all employment resulting from government spending.

Although the extent to which the public sector generates employment may seem surprising, these estimates are based upon data provided by the Department of Labor which tends to underestimate the impact of public spending on creating jobs. The Institute for Labor Education and Research claims an even higher figure, but due to some ambiguities in the data, it is more appropriate to make a conservative estimate. In any case, the public sector has been crucial for sustaining high levels of employment.

As the economy deteriorates, greater public sector spending is required. But in 1975, public spending began leveling off. So although real per capita government expenditures had reached their historically highest level, they could not sustain an ailing economy. What is more, the steeper the economic decline, the greater the fiscal stimulus required. Although per capita government expenditures have grown in the last decade, unemployment has, nevertheless, climbed significantly. The many years of accumulated stress are finally weighing the economy down.

While additional dosages of public spending will no longer readily restore the economy, the policies of the current Administration are hastening the nation's economic decline. Reaganomics is depressing the standard of living by redistributing income to big business and the wealthy. Huge cuts in domestic programs are reducing the social wage, thereby depriving working people of numerous public amenities and compelling them to dig more deeply into their earnings.

Domestic program budgets are being diverted in part to finance the huge increase in military expenditures. Whatever the foreign policy rationale for defense spending, the major beneficiary is big business, which receives the lion's share of military contracts. The cuts are also financing the Administration's tax reductions which disproportionately benefit the upper class. As in the past, the small short run gains made by working people will be offset by the impact of inflation, moving people into higher tax brackets without increasing their real income. Statistics from the Federal Advisory Commission on Intergovernmental Relations show that since the early fifties, despite tax reductions, the average family pays a much larger percentage of its earnings for taxes. The extraordinary increase in defense spending along with the tax cuts for business and the rich assure that, one way or another, the tax burden will continue to be borne by working people.

No less certain as a result of Reagan's policies is an inordinate increase in deficit spending. The interest payments on these debts reap huge profits for the financial institutions and rich investors. In 1981, interest on the public debt exceeded $95 billion, and even Reagan has acknowledged that it will climb considerably.

The rather extreme economic policies of the Reagan Administration have understandably, but mistakenly, been blamed for the current depression. Actually, the Administration inherited a stagnant, ailing economy, characterized by high rates of unemployment and inflation, although Reaganomics is exacerbating the crisis. Unlike periods of rapid economic expansion, inequitable public policies are directly experienced as a reduction in the standard of living.

Nor, as many believe, does Reaganomics represent a sharp

break with the past. The Administration's specific objectives, regressive tax measures, larger defense outlays, the curtailment of domestic programs are not recent innovations. In 1963, John F. Kennedy, a Democratic president, proposed what was then the largest tax cut in American history. The legislation finally enacted reduced the maximum corporate tax rate from 52 percent to 48 percent and individual taxes from a maximum of 91 percent to 70 percent. Kennedy's own tax message to Congress recommended even more favorable tax treatment for business and the wealthy.

His successor, Lyndon Johnson, increased the military budget considerably as a result of manipulating the nation into the Vietnam War. Since he did not enact substantial tax increases to finance the war, the deficit and, accordingly, Treasury borrowing appreciably increased. Business profited greatly during this period, but successfully escaped its responsibility for paying an appropriate share of the costs.

The Carter Administration adopted practices even more conservative than those of his Democratic predecessors. He increased the military budget and, in 1978, initiated inequitable tax reductions. Voicing strong commitment to a fiscally responsible budget, Carter also constrained the growth of domestic spending. On behalf of business, the regulatory functions of numerous agencies were limited. Certainly not least of all, this presumably fiscally responsible president accumulated more than $180 billion in public debt in his four years of office. Reagonomics, rather than inaugurating a new economic policy, is Carternomics plus.

Many liberals who consistently supported deficit spending are now among its most ardent opponents. They are especially troubled by public borrowing that is not intended to finance human services. The liberal faith in deficit spending as a stimulant to the economy no longer seems justified.

Deficit spending to provide human services and other progressive programs has traditionally served to overcome business resistance, a costly approach, saddling future generations of working people with extortionate payments primarily to the financial institutions and wealthy investors. It has always been an alternative to higher taxes for business and the rich. In a most revealing article in *The Nation*, John McDermott shows that reduced taxes for the corporations from 1960 to 1980 deflected almost $640 billion from the US Treasury, accounting for the entire rise in the federal debt during those decades. This extraordinary transfer of income to the corporations and the banks, accomplished by prior administrations, has contributed appreciably to class inequality, and set the stage for high unemployment and economic crisis.

Despite protestations, then, the persistence of annual federal deficits has been advantageous to big business. Its public stance against deficits in favor of fiscal responsibility, properly translated, really reflects its opposition to social spending. Deficits certainly did not trouble the business community this time around. In fact, even the *Wall Street Journal,* a stalwart of fiscal conservatism, became Keynesian for a while, assuring its readers not to worry about deficits. "Reign of Panic" was the caption of one of its editorials criticizing opponents of deficit financing.

And although the influential banking industry carefully avoids publicizing its enthusiastic support for deficit financing, it is certainly partisan on this issue. Chase Econometrics, the economic forecasting subsidiary of the nation's third largest bank, warned its clients that the "solution to large deficits are not deficits that are too small.... Thus, any program which reduces the expected deficits below the $75-$90 billion range (based on realistic assumptions) would not provide the sufficient stimulus to fuel an economic recovery."

Pro-business public policies are almost invariably justified as serving the public interest. In William Greider's *Atlantic Monthly* interview with Budget Director David Stockman, the latter is quoted as saying, "Whenever there are great strains or changes in the economic system, it tends to generate crackpot theories, which find their way into legislative channels." The "crackpot theory" that has justified Reaganism has been supply side economics. Its major tenet is that the stagnant and now declining economy reflects, not insufficient demand, but inadequate levels of business investment. Therefore, to spur investment, tax reductions should primarily benefit business and upper income households whose savings add to the pool of investment capital.

The fatal flaw, indeed the absurdity, of supply side economics is that it is advanced in a period when plants are closing and idle capacity increasing as a result of declining aggregate demand. Under these circumstances, tax incentives, no matter how lavish, would not persuade business to reverse its course in favor of expanding its facilities. Nor would the Reagan Administration dream of proposing a tax bill compelling business to invest as a condition for reducing the tax rate.

Supply side economics serves not as a guide but as a justification for Reagan's economic policies. We learn from the interview with the Budget Director that the theory is not taken seriously by the Administration. Moreover, he confesses that the three year income tax cut was a ploy to reduce taxes for the wealthy, which supply side theory attempted to legitimate.

The widely held belief that the Reagan Administration has been seriously attempting to restore the economy but is misguided in its approach is a measure of the success of ruling class ideology. Actually, Reaganomics is accomplishing just what the Administration's policy makers intended. And that certainly does not include revitalizing the economy in the interests of working people.

THE REASONS FOR THE RECURRENCE OF ECONOMIC CRISES go far beyond a critique of Reagonomics, or even of the economic policies of previous administrations. The central and underlying tendency of the American economy is to expand production while limiting, and even throttling, consumption. Even when real wages improve, leading to an increase in buying power, productivity and productive capacity show an even greater advance. Sooner or later, this state of affairs sets off an economic crisis.

There have been occasions when workers successfully increased their share of corporate earnings by achieving gains that exceeded the additional income produced as a result of productivity advances. But the bitter economic and political resistance of capital rendered these gains short-lived. When the economy declines, reform measures can soften the impact of a downturn. But as long as capitalism survives, it will be marked by economic crises.

Selected Bibliography

Books

Blair, John M., *Economic Concentration* (New York: Harcourt Brace Jovanovich, 1972).

Brecher, Jeremy, *Strike!* (San Francisco: Straight Arrow Books, 1972).

Brody, David, *Workers In Industrial America* (New York: Oxford University Press, 1980).

Chase, Stuart, *Prosperity and Myth* (New York: Charles Boni, Jr., 1929).

Friedman, Milton, and, Schwartz, Anna *Monetary History of the United States* (Princeton: Princeton University Press, 1963).

Ginzberg, Eli, et al., *The Pluralistic Economy* (New York: McGraw-Hill Book Co., 1965).

Hansen, Alvin H., *Full Recovery or Stagnation?* (New York: W.W. Norton & Co., 1938).

Hayes, Douglas A., *A Case Study of the Recession of 1937* (Ann Arbor: University of Michigan Press, 1951).

Institute for Labor Education and Research, *What's Wrong With the U.S. Economy?* (Boston: South End Press, 1982).

Keyserling, Leon H., *"Liberal" and "Conservative" National Economic Policies and Their Consequences, 1919-1979* (Conference on Economic Progress, September 1979).

Melman, Seymour, *The Permanent War Economy* (New York: Simon & Schuster, 1974).

Roose, Kenneth D., *The Economics of Recession and Revival* (New Haven: Yale University Press, 1954).

Zinn, Howard, *A People's History of the United States* (New York: Harper & Row, 1980).

Articles

Bennett, Paul, "American Productivity Growth: Perspectives on the Slowdown," *Federal Reserve Bank of New York Quarterly Review,* Autumn 1979, pp. 25-31.

Boddy, R. and Crotly, J., "Class Conflict, Keynesian Policies, and the Business Cycle," *Monthly Review,* October 1974, pp. 1-17.

Bowles, S., Gorden, D.M., Weisskopf, "Falling Productivity Debate," *The Nation,* 10-17 July 1982, p. 43 ff.

Brown, E. Cary, "Fiscal Policy in the 30's," *American Economic Review,* December 1956, pp. 868-69.

Campen, Jim, "Economic Crisis and Conservative Economic Policies," *Radical America,* Spring 1981, pp.33-54.

Greider, William, "The Education of David Stockman," *Atlantic Monthly,* December 1981.

Loomis, Carol J., "Profitability Goes through a Ceiling," *Fortune,* 4 May 1981, pp. 114-120.

McDermott, John, "The Secret History of the Deficit," *The Nation,* 21-28 August 1982.

Nathanson, Charles E., "The Militarization of the American Economy," in

Corporations and the Cold War, ed. Horowitz, David (New York: Monthly Review Press, 1969).

Tannenwald, Robert, "Federal Tax Policy and the Declining Share of Structures in Business Fixed Investment," *New England Economic Review*, July/August 1981.

Tucker, John T., "Government Employment: An Era of Slow Growth," *Monthly Labor Review*, October 1981, pp. 19-25.

Wassily, Leontiff, "Is Technological Employment In?" *Challenge*, March/April 1982, pp. 22-30.

"The Effects of Government Spending on Private Enterprise," *Fortune Magazine*, March 1939, p. 59 ff.

"Roads," *Hearings Before the Committee on Roads*, H. & R., 17th Congress, First Session, January 23-February 15, 1928.

"Sources of War Time Labor Supply in the U.S.," *Monthly Labor Review*, August 1944, pp. 264-278.

"Steel Jacks Up Production," *Business Week*, 12 October 1981, p. 84 ff.

Official Statistical Sources

Census of Manufacturers, U.S. Department of Commerce, Bureau of the Census, 1977.

Economic Report of the President, February 1982.

Employment and Training Report of the President, 1981.

Handbook of Labor Statistics, Bulletin 2070, U.S. Department of Labor, Bureau of Labor Statistics, December 1980.

Historical Statistics of the U.S.: Colonial Times to 1970, Parts 1 & 2, U.S. Department of Commerce, Bureau of the Census, 1975.

Productivity and the Economy: A Chartbook, U.S. Department of Labor, Bureau of Labor Statistics, October 1981, Bulletin 2084.

Quarterly Financial Reports, Federal Trade Commission.

The State of Small Business: A Report of the President, March 1982.

Statistical Abstract of the United States, 1981, U.S. Department of Commerce, Bureau of the Census.

Reports

Advisory Commission on Intergovernmental Relations, *Significant Features of Fiscal Federalism: 1980-81 Edition*, December 1981, U.S. Government Printing Office, Washington, D.C.

Chase Econometrics Associates, "U.S. Macroeconomic Forecasts and Analysis," 25 February 1982.

Why Black Americans Are Not Socialists

MANNING MARABLE

> *The chief hope [for socialism] lies in the gradual
> but inevitable spread of the knowledge that the
> denial of democracy in Asia and Africa hinders its
> complete realization in Europe. It is this that
> makes the Color Problem and the Labor Problem
> to so great an extent two sides of the same human
> tangle. How far does white labor see this? Not far,
> as yet.*
>
> W.E.B. DuBois, *The Negro Mind Reaches Out,*
> 1925.

MARXISTS HAVE ALWAYS BEEN CONSCIOUS of the symbiotic
relationship between racism and capitalism. Marx himself
made the point succinctly in *Capital:* "labor with a white skin
cannot emancipate itself where labor with a black skin is
branded." A half century later, W.E.B. DuBois, radical black
scholar and founder of the NAACP, observed that "more and
more the problem of the modern workingman is merging with
the problem of the color line." For DuBois, socialism was an
impossible goal unless anti-racist politics dominated labor
organizations. "So long as black laborers are slaves," he concluded, "white laborers cannot be free."[1] Thus, the relationship
between race and class, and the political link between racial
equality and the emancipation of the working class was clearly
stated a long time ago.

MANNING MARABLE *is Professor of History and Economics and
Director of the Race Relations Institute at Fisk University. He is the
author of a number of books, the most recent,* How Capitalism
Underdeveloped Black America, *and one of the most widely read
black political theorists in the country. His syndicated column,
"From the Grassroots," appears in over 135 newspapers in the United States and the United Kingdom.*

Although objectively, as the most oppressed section of the working class, blacks should be in the forefront of a class conscious movement for a socialist America, actually relatively few black workers, activists or intellectuals have joined socialist organizations.

The first part of this essay explores some of the reasons for the failure of socialism within black America, taking up the legacy of racism on the left, examining the political development of black socialists and the path they took to Marxism as differentiated from the one followed by white leftists, and noting some of the sociological factors which have retarded the development of a broad based socialist consciousness in the black community from 1865 to the present. In the second section, there is a discussion of the current black struggle and the continued gap between major black organizations and the American left.

The Racist Legacy

THE HISTORY OF THE RELATIONSHIP between blacks and American white radicals is filled with broken promises, ethnocentrism, and outright contempt. Racism has blunted the critical faculties of white progressives from the colonial period to the present. Any proper understanding of black historic reluctance to support calls for socialism by radical intellectuals and white workers must begin with this twisted heritage of racism.*

---

*Part of the rationale for some black nationalists' fears that Marxism is a form of "left-wing racism" must be attributed to the writings of Marx himself. Marx's vicious statements about German socialist leader Ferdinand Lassalle were both racist and anti-Semitic: "It is now quite clear to me that, as shown by the shape of [Lassalle's] head and . . . hair, that he is descended from the negroes who joined the flight of Moses from Egypt (unless his mother or grandmother . . . were crossed with a nigger). This union of Jew and German on a negro foundation was bound to produce something out of the ordinary. The importunity of the fellow is also negroid." David McLellan, *Karl Marx: His Life and Thought* (New York: Harper and Row, 1973), p. 322.

In Marx's letter to Friederich Engels, dated June 14, 1853, he argued, in a comparison between black Jamaicans and slaves in the US, that the former "always consisted of newly imported barbarians," whereas Afro-Americans are "becoming a native product, more or less Yankeefied, English speaking,

   Blacks have seen an endless series of prominent white liberal and progressive allies betray their trust and embrace the politics of white supremacy. Populist Tom Watson, the Georgia lawyer in the early 1890s, became the fiercest proponent of lynching and racist hatred the South had ever known.* Elizabeth Cady Stanton's call for women's right to vote at Seneca Falls, New York in 1848, was seconded by black abolitionist Frederick Douglass. As Angela Davis notes, "Douglass was responsible for officially introducing the issue of women's rights to the Black Liberation movement, where it was enthusiastically welcomed."[2] Stanton repaid black supporters with this racist diatribe:

> As long as [the Negro] was lowest in the scale of being, we [white women] were willing to press his claims; but now, as the celes-

---

etc., and therefore *fit for emancipation.*" See Marx-Engels correspondence reprinted in Shlomo Avineri, ed., *Karl Marx on Colonialism and Modernization* (Garden City: Anchor Books, 1969), p. 454.

At one point, Marx described Mexicans as *"les derniers des hommes."* Engels was even worse. In one work he asserted that "the Germans were a highly gifted Aryan branch" of humanity, an "energetic stock" who have the "physical and intellectual power to subdue, absorb, and assimilate its ancient eastern neighbors." Obviously, it may be unfair to judge the founders of historical materialism by the standards of the late twentieth century. But these and many other blatantly racist statements by the early proponents of socialism must give pause to many contemporary would-be black leftists. See M.M. Bober, *Karl Marx's Interpretation of History* (New York: W.W. Norton, 1965), pp. 69-70.

* In the election of 1892, Watson drafted the Populist Party's platform on a united front between black and white farmers. "You are kept apart that you may be separately fleeced of your earnings. You are made to hate each other," Watson declared, "because upon that hatred is rested the keystone of the arch of financial despotism which enslaves you both." Biographer C. Vann Woodward declares that "Watson was perhaps the first native white Southern leader of importance to treat the Negro's aspirations with the seriousness that human strivings deserve." With the collapse of Populism, Watson turned to racism and anti-Semitism with gusto. By 1904 he favored the abandonment of the Fifteenth Amendment. In 1910 he bragged that he would no more hesitate to lynch a "nigger" than to shoot a mad dog. Even Booker T. Washington, the model of Negro accommodation, was too radical for Watson. He closed a racist diatribe against the black educator with the statement: "What does Civilization owe the negro? Nothing! Nothing!! NOTHING!!!" See C. Vann Woodward, *Tom Watson: Agrarian Rebel* (New York: Oxford University Press, 1970), pp. 220-221, 374, 380, 432-433.

tial gate to civil rights is slowly moving on its hinges, it becomes a serious question whether we had better stand aside and see "Sambo" walk into the kingdom first... Are we sure that he, once entrenched in all his inalienable rights, may not be an added power to hold us at bay? Why should the African prove more just and generous than his Saxon peers? ... It is better to be the slave of an educated white man, than of a degraded, ignorant black one.[3]

Birth control advocate Margaret Sanger championed black and white workers' rights, and for a time maintained close ties to the Socialist Party. By 1919, however, Sanger defended birth control as "more children from the fit, less from the unfit." In a letter to one associate, Sanger confided, "We do not want word to get out that we want to exterminate the Negro population."[4] Such was the profound racism that has underscored American politics, right to left.

An early socialist whose career parallels Watson's, Stanton's and others, was Orestes A. Brownson. Two decades before the 1848 revolutions and the publication of the *Communist Manifesto,* Brownson pursued a radical labor organizing career. A Universalist minister, Brownson was a supporter of the Robert Owen-Frances Wright faction of the Workingmen's Party. In the 1830s, he was a strong advocate of black emancipation. "We can legitimate our own right to freedom," Brownson wrote in 1838, "only by arguments which prove also the negro's right to be free." After 1840, Brownson had begun to believe that laborers "are neither numerous nor strong enough to get or to wield the political power of the State." With his renunciation of radicalism, Brownson also abandoned any support for black liberation. By 1844, he supported South Carolina Senator and slaveholder, John C. Calhoun, for the Democratic Party's presidential nomination. After the Civil War, he protested black suffrage, warning that black voters "will always vote with the wealthy landowning class, and aid them in resisting socialistic tendencies." He applauded Jim Crow laws, taunting his abolitionist opponents, "you will never make the mass of the white people look upon the blacks as their equals."[5]

Marxists have always insisted that the flow of social history is determined by the relationship between the subjective and objective factors—the superstructure or ideological, cultural and political apparatuses and the base, or forces of production. But what most American socialists and Marxists adhered to was a philosophy not of Marxism—which also suggests that the relations between superstructure and base are reciprocal, one affecting the other—but of economic determinism, not unlike that of American historian Charles Beard.[6] The left economic determinists held that the base, the means of production, strictly determines the character of all other human institutions and thought. Racism was, therefore, only part of the larger class question. The rights of Negroes, *per se*, were no different in any decisive respect than those of Polish-American factory workers in Chicago or white miners and lumberjacks in the Great Northwest. This is not to suggest that all white socialists who held this view were racists or insensitive to racism. Eugene V. Debs made it a point of principle never to address any racially segregated audience. The Socialist Party would "deny its philosophy and repudiate its own teachings," Debs said, "if, on account of race consideration, it sought to exclude any human being from political and economic freedom." Socialist historian Albert Fried applauds Debs' enlightened views, but adds that Debs "and probably most socialists" during the early 1900s "reduced the Negro problem to a class problem. They assumed that equality would prevail in America the moment capitalism ceased to exist. Until that day they preferred to keep the race issue as far out of sight and hearing as possible."[7]

This theoretical rigidity produced two political by-products. First, militant socialists like Curaçao-born Daniel De Leon who were sympathetic to black demands for civil rights nevertheless "regarded the plight of the Negro as essentially a class issue," according to historian David Herreshoff. De Leon did not take seriously the loss of black voting rights in the 1890s, because in his own words, "the tanglefoot Suffrage legislation while aimed at the Negro ostensibly as a Negro, in fact aims at him as a wage slave." De Leon personally opposed racist legislation, but he believed "it was a waste of time for socialists to explore the differences between whites and blacks" as to their relative degrees of race/class exploitation.[8] The second and more devastating result was that white American socialists *never* made the issue of racism a basic point of struggle either internally or propagandistically. Thus, socialist John Sandgren was not censured for expressing the view in the Party's newspaper that blacks, women and migrant workers "can in no manner be directly interested in politics." No one pressed for the expulsions of centrist leader Morris Hillquit and newspaper editor Hermann Schlueter for championing the exclusion of immigration of "workingmen of inferior races— Chinese, Negroes, etc."[9]

White social democrats repeatedly disappointed black leftists in their tolerance, and sometimes outright approval, of racism. In a 1911 speech before the New York City Socialist Party, DuBois publicly attacked white leftists for refusing to combat racism.[10] In 1913, he urged the American Socialist Party to redouble its efforts to recruit blacks. "There is a group of ten million persons in the United States toward whom Socialists would better turn serious attention," he declared.[11] DuBois' campaign to force white leftists into the struggle for racial justice was effective, in certain respects. Moderate socialist/social worker Jane Addams supported DuBois' research activities at Atlanta University. Addams and more militant intellectuals in the Socialist Party, like Mary White Ovington, William English Walling, and Charles Edward Russell, were founding members of the NAACP.[12] However, other white socialists either ignored DuBois' call or simply restated the popular racist bigotry of the age. A typical example was Victor Berger, powerful leader of the Milwaukee socialists and head of the Wisconsin AFL, who said that "the negroes and mulattoes constitute a lower race," and were a menace to white labor. The "free contact with the whites has led to the further degradation of the negroes."[13] The Socialist Party in the South was for "whites only," and some party theoreticians expounded the view that "socialism would bring complete segregation: blacks and whites should not live in the same areas or even work in the same factories."[14]

Even some of the most "progressive" white socialists who were actively involved in anti-racist work could harbor a private hatred for blacks. For example, in December 1928, Molders Union leader John P. Frey was the AFL speaker at a large interracial meeting in Washington D.C. Publicly, Frey supported black civil rights; privately, he was "a notorious racist."

Despite the AFL's long record of racist exclusion Frey claimed that the Federation "not only organized the negro, but brought him into the white man's unions." He added that racial prejudice against Afro-Americans in unions was no greater than that experienced by Italians, Jews or Poles. DuBois and NAACP assistant secretary Walter White denounced Frey's speech. Seeking to resolve the dispute, William English Walling counselled White to halt public attacks on Frey. As a leading Socialist Party theoretician and a member of the NAACP executive board, Walling openly fought the "color line" but privately condemned his black co-workers. In a letter to Frey, Walling described DuBois and other black NAACP critics of the AFL as "nasty reds. Labor's attitude on the color question is 100 percent o.k. and it has nothing to be ashamed of." Frey's response to Walling charged that blacks themselves were to blame for their "low" representation in all-white unions![15]

FROM ITS ORIGINS, THE COMMUNIST PARTY always maintained better relations with the black movement than the Socialists. Initial black recruitment efforts were unsuccessful. During the 1920s only 200 black Americans joined the Party, but among them were some of the most gifted writers and organizers of the "Harlem Renaissance," like Cyril Briggs, founder of the revolutionary black nationalist organization, the African Blood Brotherhood. The Party's real growth did not occur until the Great Depression. Communists established integrated Unemployment Councils and led "hunger marches" in dozens of state capitols and in Washington D.C. Two black Communists organized a sharecroppers' union at Camp Hill, Alabama in 1931, that quickly mushroomed into a mass movement among black rural farmers in the state. The Party launched the National Miners' Union which promptly elected a black Indiana miner, William Boyce, as its national vice president. Thousands of blacks supported NMU strikes and organizing activities because, in Boyce's words, "it fights discrimination, segregation, Jim Crowism and disenfranchisement." Black Party leader James W. Ford, secretary of the Harlem Section, was instrumental in organizing tenant and worker protests reaching tens of thousands of poor blacks.[16] During those years of astronomically high unemployment, vast numbers of poor blacks acquired a deep respect for the Communist Party, the first socialist organization in their experience to emphasize racial egalitarianism in theory and practice.

But subsequent Communist activity lost the Party black support. When black social democrat A. Philip Randolph organized the Negro March on Washington Movement in 1941, to pressure the Roosevelt Administration to desegregate defense plants, Communists opposed the mobilization. After Nazi Germany's attack on the Soviet Union, the Party "frowned upon any struggles that might interfere with the war effort," writes historian Philip S. Foner. Thus, black Communist spokesperson Ben Davis urged blacks to put aside "all questions of discrimination" and to "sacrifice" for the war effort. The Party's newspaper, the *Daily Worker,* told blacks to sign "no-strike pledges," and charged that black protesters involved in the August 1943 Harlem riot were "fifth columnists and pro-fascists." The Party was silent about the immoral internment of thousands of Japanese-Americans in West Coast camps, and applauded the use of the atomic bomb on Hiroshima. "It was to be exceedingly difficult for the Communists to overcome the resentment among blacks created by the Party's wartime policies," Foner observes. "The Communists never completely erased the feeling in sections of the black community that they had placed the Soviet Union's survival above the battle for black equality."[17]

Since 1945, American Marxists have generally supported the struggle for equal rights, but their contributions to the black movement have not been decisive. White social democrats provided financial support for Martin Luther King's Montgomery bus boycott in 1955-56. Many "red diaper babies," of the New Left generation, joined the Student Nonviolent Coordinating Committee (SNCC) in the early 1960s. Most white social democrats, however, were bewildered when the civil rights cause turned into a struggle for "Black Power." They thought that Malcolm X was a racist or a madman; they could not comprehend Stokely Carmichael or H. Rap Brown. Conversely, some of the younger white radicals applauded any angry black spokesperson—Eldridge Cleaver is a sorry example—without any serious analysis of the dynamics of race and class in American society. Small wonder, then, that by the 1980s, no socialist or communist organization, Old Left or New, had won over any significant number of black activists, intellectuals or workers.

At the core of the left's legacy, therefore, is the ongoing burden of racism. In the 1920s, DuBois characterized American social democracy and the white working class as "autocratic and at heart capitalistic, believing in profit-making industry and wishing only to secure a larger share of profits for particular guilds." After WWI and the successful revolution in Russia, however, there existed the faint possibility for a democratic movement for socialism which was anti-racist. For DuBois, the logical question was: "Will the new labor parties welcome the darker race to this industrial democracy?" Reflecting critically on the United States, DuBois had to admit that the long term prospects were decidedly bleak:

> White laborers can read and write, but beyond this their education and experience are limited and they live in a world of color prejudice. The propaganda, the terrible, ceaseless propaganda that buttresses [white racism] . . . has built a wall which for many centuries will not break down. Born into such a spiritual world, the average white worker is absolutely at the mercy of its beliefs and prejudices. Color hate easily assumes the form of a religion and the laborer becomes the blind executive of the decrees of the "punitive" expeditions; he sends his sons as soldiers and sailors; he composes the Negro-hating mob, demands Japanese exclusion and lynches untried prisoners. What hope is there that such a mass of dimly thinking and misled men will ever demand universal democracy for all men?[18]

The overwhelming majority of white American socialists have yet to confront this question seriously.

The Black Path to Socialism

A FEW BLACK WORKERS AND INTELLECTUALS were attracted to socialist ideas as early as the 1870s. One of the nation's most prominent black trade unionists, New York engineer John Ferrell, was a socialist and a leader of the Knights of Labor. Peter

H. Clark, the principal of the Colored High School of Cincinnati, Ohio was "probably the first American Negro Socialist," according to Foner. During the 1877 railroad strike, Clark publicly hailed black-white unity and "called for socialism as the solution for labor's grievances." Probably the most effective black leftist before 1900 was the militant editor of the *New York Age,* Timothy Thomas Fortune. In a series of newspaper and periodical articles, Fortune demanded that "Southern capitalists give their wage workers a fair percentage of the results of their labor. If there is any power on earth which can make the white Southern employers of labor face the music," he wrote, "it is organized white and black labor."[19] Fortune called for a class struggle to liberate black Americans. "What are millionaires, anyway, but the most dangerous enemies of society?" he asked his readers. Fortune was convinced that black people had to adopt a socialist analysis to comprehend the economic forces that exploited them. "The revolution is upon us, and since we are largely of the laboring population, it is very natural that we should take sides with the labor forces in their fight for a juster distribution of the results of labor."[20]

Lucy Parsons was one of a number of black women socialists who have been buried in the pages of history. Born in 1853, Parsons joined the Socialist Labor Party in her mid-twenties. She married a radical Southerner, Albert R. Parsons, who had served briefly in the Confederate Army. Even before her husband was indicted for complicity in the deaths of seven policemen during the Haymarket Square riot of May 4, 1886, and executed in November 1887, Lucy Parsons traveled the country in support of anarchism. Most socialist historians have ignored her writings and activities against sexism and lynching. A few have even questioned her racial identity.[21] Her contemporaries knew her as a militant supporter of the Industrial Workers of the World, and a defender of the Scottsboro Nine in 1931. Parsons joined the Communist Party in 1939, and died three years later.[22]

Some black leaders advanced socialist ideas after 1900, but relatively few joined the Socialist Party. J. Milton Waldron, a Jacksonville, Florida Baptist minister, was a supporter of cooperatives and black-white labor unity. In 1901, he organized the Afro-American Industrial Insurance Society, and four

years later joined DuBois' Niagra Movement, the black political opposition to accommodationist educator Booker T. Washington. Politically, however, Waldron aligned himself with the
Democratic Party through an all-black organization, the National Independent Political League. J. Max Barber, assistant
editor of the *Voice of the Negro*, was another Niagra Movement
activist who sympathized with socialist reforms.[23] In Harlem,
street propagandist and black nationalist organizer Hubert
Harrison had, by 1914, begun to combine the issues of race and
class into a unique political program. Younger Harlem black
radicals involved in union organizing, A. Philip Randolph and
Chandler Owen, joined the Socialist Party. Randolph's subsequent career as the leader of the Brotherhood of Sleeping Car
Porters and founder of the National Negro Congress in 1935 is,
of course, well known. But for our purposes, it has relatively
little relationship to Marxism. By 1920, Randolph had broken
with militant socialism, and by the end of his life had become
an apologist for crude anti-Communism and white racism
inside the AFL-CIO.[24]

Among the thousands of blacks who joined the Communist
Party during the Great Depression, Angelo Herndon is, perhaps, the best known. Born in 1913, Herndon was a construction laborer and worked in the Kentucky coal mines. In 1930, he
joined the Party-led Unemployment Council of Birmingham.
Two years later, he was arrested and jailed for possession of
Marxist literature, provoking labor violence and trying "to
establish a group and combination of persons, colored and
white." The case of Angelo Herndon became a national cause
for the left and many white liberals. Randolph drafted a resolution to free Herndon which was presented to the 1936 AFL
Convention. NAACP attorney Thurgood Marshall supported
the Herndon defense. In 1937, the Supreme Court narrowly
reversed Herndon's conviction in a five-to-four vote. Of interest
here is not Herndon's subsequent career—he broke with the
Party after World War II—but the political evolution that led
him to socialism. In his youthful autobiography, *Let Me Live*,
Herndon explained that his "conversion" to Communism was
virtually a religious awakening:

The Negro leaders tell us that the poor white workers are responsible for our sufferings. But who controls the powerful weapons with which to spread anti-Negro propaganda. . . ? Decidedly, it could not be the poor white workers who had all they could to keep themselves alive. Therefore, it could only be the rich white people who were our oppressors, for they controlled the churches and the schools and the newspapers and the radio. . . [To] secure their profits from human sweat and brawn they fall back upon these wicked methods of "divide and rule," divide the white workers from their Negro brothers.[25]

For Herndon and other unemployed black workers, Marxism manifested itself first in *racial* terms as a theory of human equality and social justice.

THE MOST SIGNIFICANT NATIONAL BLACK LEADER won to socialism during the first half of the twentieth century and who remained a militant leftist throughout his public career was W.E.B. DuBois. As a radical journalist, he stood above De Leon, Fortune and Randolph; as a pioneering social scientist, his voluminous writings, from *The Soul of Black Folks* (1903) to *Black Reconstruction* (1935), influenced scholars worldwide. For decades his name was the personification of the black freedom struggle in the US, the West Indies and Africa. For these reasons his evolution as a Marxist merits considerable attention.

DuBois viewed himself as a socialist by 1904. In his early journal, *Horizon*, and later in the NAACP publication, *Crisis*, he "advised the socialists that their movement could not succeed unless it included Negro workers, and wrote that it was simply a matter of time before white and black workers would see their common economic cause against the exploiting capitalists."[26] Like Parsons, Randolph and Herndon, DuBois was impressed with the nonracist personal behavior of many white socialists, and probably gravitated to leftist politics because they seemed to share his burning commitment to racial equality. As early as 1908, DuBois made this point quite clearly: "the only party today which treats Negroes as men, North and South, are the Socialists."[27] Thus, he vigorously applauded Los Angeles socialists for nominating a black man for city council in 1911.[28] Afro-Americans view society through the prism of race, and when they come to radicalism it is as a response to and rejection of racism and the inherent irrationality of capitalism. In August 1927, for example, DuBois noted in *Crisis* that several blacks in Louisville, Mississippi had been "burned alive" because of the "widespread indignation at the refusal of Negroes traveling in slow, second-hand Fords to give the road to faster cars." Small wonder, DuBois exclaimed, that some black Americans were turning to "bolshevism." Given the level of racist atrocities, he thought larger numbers of blacks would turn to Marxism.[29]

However, DuBois' conversion to Marxism did not begin until well after the Bolshevik Revolution. Although, in September 1916 he predicted that the war would create "the greater emancipation of European women, the downfall of monarchies . . . and the advance of true Socialism,"[30] when the autocracy fell in St. Petersburg six months later, DuBois worried "whether the German menace is to be followed by a Russian menace."[31] In the summer of 1921, the black editor was criticized by novelist Claude McKay for neglecting to mention the accomplishments of the Soviet Union. DuBois tartly rejected the slogan, "dictatorship of the proletariat," and informed McKay, "[I am] not prepared to dogmatize with Marx and Lenin." He urged blacks not to join a revolution "which we do not at present understand."[32] DuBois' leap toward the left only began in earnest with a two month visit to the Soviet Union in 1926. He was not surprised to see so many poor people, food lines and "orphan children, ragged and dirty, [crawling] in and out of sewers." What impressed DuBois was the Soviet government's commitment to "the abolition of poverty. . . . Schools were multiplying; workers were being protected with a living wage, nurseries for children, night schools, trade unions and wide discussion." Ever the puritan, DuBois noted that "there were no signs of prostitution or unusual crime . . . some drunkenness, but little gambling."[33] Summarizing his experience in *Crisis*, DuBois declared with enthusiasm:

> I stand in astonishment and wonder at the revelation of Russia that has come to me. I may be partially deceived and half-informed. But if what I have seen with my eyes and heard with my ears in Russia is Bolshevism, I am a Bolshevik.[34]

Even earlier, DuBois believed that the essence of the socialist revolution and the most important product of Bolshevism "is the vision of great dreamers that only those who work shall vote and rule."[35]By1931, he urged *Crisis* readers to study *Capital.*[36]

During the Depression, DuBois' affection for the Soviet model of socialism grew. Visiting Russia again in late 1936, he was pleased with what he felt to be the nation's progress: "There were no unemployed, all children were in schools, factories, shops and libraries had multiplied, and there was evidence of law and order everywhere. The peasant was in close cooperation with, and not in revolt against, the factory worker."[37]

In retrospect, though, DuBois' silence on the massive Soviet political upheavals during those years is more than curious. The "liberals" in the Politburo, particularly Leningrad chief Sergei Kirov, Vice Premier Rudzutak, Kalinin and Voroshilov, were being displaced (or in Kirov's case assassinated on Stalin's orders). The "trial of the sixteen," which included former Comintern leader Grigori Zinoviev, occurred in August 1936. Former Soviet leaders Piatakov, Radek and fifteen others were "tried" for committing crimes against the state in January 1937. One of Marxism's greatest theoreticians, Nikolai Bukharin, would be executed on false charges the following year.[38] By 1939, one quarter of the entire Soviet officer's corps was imprisoned; one million party members were expelled. "The Great Purge destroyed a generation not simply of Old Bolshevik veterans of the anti-tsarist struggle but of very many of their juniors who had joined the movement after 1917 and served as active implementers of Stalinism in its first phase," political scientist Robert Tucker writes. "It virtually transformed the composition of the Soviet regime and the managerial elite in all fields."[39] To all this terror, DuBois remained blind and mute.

His support for Communism increased with the beginning of the Cold War. Persecuted by the federal government, his passport revoked and his books banned from public libraries and universities, DuBois concluded that Russia was the only hope for liberating the oppressed peoples of color across the world. He later acknowledged the crimes of Stalinism but argued that the Soviet state deserved praise for what he believed to be its positive influence on the national liberation movements in Africa, Asia and the Americas.[40]

Since his death in 1963, no single Afro-American leader has emerged to articulate the socialist vision with anything approaching DuBois' skill and power. Congressperson Ronald V. Dellums and Georgia State Senator Julian Bond are members of the Democratic Socialists of America but neither is known particularly as a socialist among blacks. Angela Davis, the Communist Party's Vice Presidential candidate in 1980, known for her work in black and feminist history, is a prominent activist in struggles which involve poor and working class blacks but it is certainly questionable whether her activities are helped by her identification with the Party. Since 1968, a number of black scholar/activists, including Adolph Reed, Robert L. Allen, Damu Imara Smith, William W. Sales, William Strickland, James Foreman and Earl Ofari have become socialists of various ideological hues, but none has the means that were available to DuBois to reach millions of black workers.[41]

From Timothy Thomas Fortune to W.E.B. DuBois and those mentioned above, blacks have become radicals, socialists and Marxists as a result of their *commitment to black liberation*, which usually involved protest activities and organizing in the black community. White socialists could express solidarity with the black struggle, but precious few actually incorporated militantly anti-racist politics into the core of their own writings and activities; for them, the race question has always been secondary to the class question. On the other hand, for black socialists race and class have been an interdependent dynamic. They discovered Marx on the road to black liberation.

Historical Impediments to Black Socialist Consciousness

THE BASIC THEME OF BLACK US HISTORY is the schism between protest and accommodation, struggle and compromise, radicalism and conservatism. Most leftists accept as given the proud heritage of black resistance—Nat Turner, Frederick Douglass,

W.E.B. DuBois, Sojourner Truth, Fannie Lou Hamer, Malcolm X, Martin Luther King, Jr., Paul Robeson. Yet, for each of these gifted women and men, there were many Afro-American leaders who did *not* openly fight racism, Jim Crow laws and economic exploitation. Most Black Reconstruction politicians were cautious and pragmatic, ready to campaign for voting rights and civil liberties, but unwilling to call for armed self-defense of the black community and a radical divestment of the white planters' property. From 1865 until the eve of the Great Depression, over 80 percent of all black people were Southern farmers and sharecroppers. Today, we fail to appreciate the fact that, historically, blacks' sense of nationality, racial pride and culture are essentially rural in origin. Rural attitudes toward life and labor tended to be fairly orthodox and were reinforced by the rigid code of racial segregation. Any strict caste system retards the internal social/cultural/economic dynamics of the oppressed group. New ideological and cultural currents expressed by a subgroup are repressed; the race/class interests of those in authority are often infused into the world view or "common sense" of the oppressed. Protest in any racist, totalitarian order like the US South between 1877-1960 was difficult even under the best of conditions. It should not surprise us, therefore, that the majority of black leaders emerging from such a racist society would not propose a socialist program.

Historically, the central political demand of any oppressed peasant class is the redistribution of the land. In this country, that was translated into the call for "forty acres and a mule." Those black leaders closest to the agricultural production process called for small proprietary holdings which would free blacks from the yoke of tenancy. With the migration of blacks to the Northern cities in the 1930s this demand found its Northern echo in programs with the slogan: "Don't buy where you can't work." Such policies, which it was hoped would lead to greater black employment, were supported by both the Garveyites and the NAACP, but they did not attack the root of black joblessness—capitalism. Those who migrated to the cities took their rural ideological limitations with them in the form of "Black Capitalist" programs for the Afro-American ghetto.

The role of religion in the black community provided yet

another barrier to socialism. The language of black politics has always been conditioned by the idiom of the church. Opposition to Marxism and socialism often comes from black preachers and those most heavily influenced by them. Atheism could never be popular among a peasant and working class people whose nationality and identity were forged in part through faith in their churches and in a just God. For example, on Herndon's admission into the Party's Unemployment Councils, he "bubbled over with enthusiasm" and talked to his relatives and friends "about Negroes and whites fighting together against their bosses so they might live like human beings." Without exception, his friends were aghast and warned Herndon "that I had better stay away from those Reds who were wicked people blaspheming against God." Older religious blacks lamented that the young man had fallen into the atheist movement.[42]

Hosea Hudson's experiences with the black church were even more bitter. Born in 1898, in rural Wilkes County, Georgia, Hudson had attended church since childhood. For years, his ambition was to become a minister, like his brother. When he joined the Communist Party in September 1931, he says, "I lost sight of that preaching, I lost sight of the Bible." Church-going blacks had little interest in Hudson's concern about the Scottsboro Nine case. Black ministers urged black Communists to "quit talking about" Scottsboro, and demanded that Hudson "keep that devilment out of the church." Devout friends denounced him as "a terrible something, an infidel." In his later years, Hudson wrote, "We turned a lot of people away . . . that's the way they looked upon Reds, Reds didn't believe in no God. They's dangerous." He blamed the capitalist ruling class for "whipping up the minds of people" to oppose socialism on religious grounds. But even after a half century in the Communist Party, Hudson did not escape his social and cultural origins. "I never did finally stop believing in God," he admits. "I haven't stopped believing yet today. I don't argue about it. I don't discuss it, because it's something I can't explain."[43]

ANOTHER FACTOR RESPONSIBLE for the black community's indifference, even hostility to socialism was the negative influence of the small Afro-American petty bourgeoisie. From the

1870s to the present, the overwhelming majority of middle class black intellectuals, political leaders and entrepreneurs have opposed socialism. Black Reconstruction politician John R. Lynch, Speaker of the Mississippi legislature in 1872 and a three-term Republican Congressperson, had no sympathy for "socialism" or "anarchism." Blacks, he felt, should strive to join interracial unions, but should repudiate violence.[44] Booker T. Washington made headlines with his caustic criticism of socialism, radicalism and Negro participation in the trade union movement. Even Washington's liberal black critics were committed to his "Black Capitalism" program.

John Edward Bruce, a founder of the first black academic society, the American Negro Academy, was decidedly anti-socialist. After inviting A. Philip Randolph to speak before the Academy on December 30, 1919, Bruce judged the address "a bitter attack on all things not socialistic." Bruce wrote in his diary, "I have no faith in socialism and its propagandists. It has occupied the attention of thinkers for centuries past and no three of them seem to agree as to its efficacy as a solvent for the ills of the body politic. Socialists are themselves divided and there can never be unity in division."[45] On the crucial point of a strategy for black economic development, black nationalists who supported Marcus Garvey and the staunchest of racial integrationists in the NAACP could agree: American capitalism was not structurally racist, and the desperate material condition of blacks could be alleviated through the accumulation of capital in the pockets of black entrepreneurs.[46]

Many prominent leaders of the contemporary black movement continue to "exhibit a simplistic fixation on racism and are unable (or unwilling) to delve any deeper into the American social structure."[47] Although he has since moved to a variety of socialism (Kwame Nkumahist thought), Stokely Carmichael best represented this "fixation" in the black movement during the late 1960s. At an anti-Vietnam War conference in April 1968, for instance, the former SNCC leader claimed that Marxism was "irrelevant to the black struggle because it dealt only with economic questions, not racism." As for Karl Marx, Carmichael said that he refused to "bow down to any white man." On the question of black-white working class coalitions, Carmichael declared, "Poor white people are not fighting for their humanity, they're fighting for more money. There are a lot of poor white people in this country, you ain't seen none of them rebel yet, have you?"[48]

In the 1970s, many cultural nationalists surpassed John E. Bruce in their hostility to Marxism. "Our struggle cannot be defined as a class struggle in the traditional Marxist manner," wrote *Black Books Bulletin* publisher Haki Madhubuti. "As far as skin color is concerned in the United States, if you are black, you are a slave." Cultural nationalist author Shawna Maglangbayan denounced Marxism as a "reactionary and white supremacist ideology whose chief aim is to maintain Aryan world hegemony once capitalism is overthrown. The idea of an 'alliance' with Left-wing white supremacy is a still-born infant which black Marxist fanatics resuscitate each time they muster enough force to rear their heads in the black community."[49] In fairness, it is most accurate to describe the majority of black elected officials as moderate-to-liberal social democrats. They do not take the anti-communist polemics of either the Reagan Administration or black cultural nationalists too seriously. However, few could be viewed historically as socialist, and in only rare instances would they be considered Marxist. The economic programs of Black Congressional Caucus members range from liberal Keynesianism to laissez-faire capitalism. On balance, most tend to agree with DuBois' 1940 statement: "The split between white and black workers was greater than that between white workers and capitalists; and this split depended not simply on economic exploitation but on a racial folklore grounded on centuries of instinct, habit and thought."[50]

Finally, black civil society had been so conditioned by capitalism that it is difficult to find major institutions owned or run by blacks which to any degree advocate socialism. This is particularly true in the area of higher education. Historically, black colleges and universities furnish little valuable information critical of the "free enterprise system." Indeed, what is usually taught in the social sciences could be termed "non-economics": a total lack of any economic analysis critical of capitalism. Reflecting on his own education at Fisk University in Nashville, Tennessee, DuBois wrote that "my formal education had touched on politics and religion, but on the whole had avoided economics." Courses on Afro-American slavery discussed the institution's "moral aspects" but never its economic dynamics. "In class I do not remember ever hearing Karl Marx mentioned nor socialism discussed. We talked about wages and poverty, but little was said of trade unions and that little was unfavorable."[51]

The inevitable result of this process of economic miseducation has been a general tendency among black intellectuals in the social sciences to relegate "class issues" to oblivion. DuBois' series of landmark sociological studies on the Negro in America, published at Atlanta University between 1896 and 1914, illustrate this problem. The annual reports covered widely divergent topics: "The College-Bred Negro," "Notes on Negro Crime," "The American Negro Family." In only two brief volumes, published in 1899 and 1907, did DuBois concentrate on black economic activities, and even then the works espoused no serious criticism of capitalism. A half century later, DuBois would write that his entire "program was weak on its economic side. It did not stress enough the philosophy of Marx and Engels."[52] His scholarship on race relations, without equal at the turn of the century, was seriously flawed. "I [did not know] Marx well enough," DuBois said, "to appreciate the economic foundations of human history."[53] Today, for most black Americans, "class" is perceived purely as a function of personal income. The notions of a "proletariat" and a "capitalist ruling class" are abstrations which have little meaning in everyday language.

The Failure of Leadership

THE ABSENCE OF A VIABLE SOCIALIST PRESENCE within black America has become a critical problem in the 1980s. The election of Ronald Reagan and the electoral successes of conservative Republicans across the US in 1980 threw the black movement into disarray. Black nationalist political organizations on the left were increasingly victimized by federal and local harassment; black elected officials in Congress and in state legislatures fought desperately to maintain the number of black majority districts; civil rights groups endeavored to reverse hundreds of Reagan-sponsored initiatives reducing job training programs, public housing, welfare benefits, and health care. This political assault in the wake of the victory of the right is not limited to black concerns. The early 1980s witnessed the defeat of the Equal Rights Amendment; attacks on affirmative action for women and all minorities; a rapidly expanding federal defense budget at the expense of social programs; more overt restriction of the rights of gays and lesbians, etc. In some respects, at least for blacks, the socio-economic and political terrain of the early 1980s parallels the situation in the mid-to-late 1890s, an era dominated by a severe economic depression, the passage of strict Jim Crow legislation, the loss of black male suffrage in the South, and the growth of white vigilante violence. The movement for racial equality which characterized the period of Reconstruction, from 1865 to 1877, succumbed to the control of capital and a conservative Republican-dominated federal government. Similarly, the optimism and activism that was part of the "Second Reconstruction," 1954 to 1966, has been replaced within the black community by frustration and self-doubt.

During the earlier period, the major black figure was Booker T. Washington, founder of Tuskegee Institute, political boss of the "Tuskegee Machine," and leader of the first association of black entrepreneurs, the Negro Business League. Washington counseled public submission to Jim Crow laws and urged blacks to enter into an "historic compromise" with Northern capital and former Southern slaveholders against white workers. The personification of the tendency toward accommodation within the black community at that time, he believed that no real political gains could be achieved through alignment with the trade unions, Populists or socialists. He accepted the American capitalist system as it existed and urged blacks to take an active role in it. Black capital accumulation was the key element of his program.

Seventy years later, during the Black Power upsurge of the late 1960s, many young nationalists simply revived the Washington strategy and cloaked it in militantly anti-white rhetoric. Speaking for this Black Power tendency, black social critic Harold Cruse debated Marxists in 1967, in the following manner:

> When we speak of Negro social disabilities under capitalism,
> however, we refer to the fact that he does not own anything—
> *even what is ownable in his own community.* Thus to fight for
> black liberation *is to fight for his right to own.* The Negro is
> politically compromised today because he owns nothing. He
> has little voice in the affairs of state because he owns noth-
> ing. . . . Inside his own communities, he does not own the houses
> he lives in, the property he lives on, nor the wholesale and retail
> sources from which he buys his commodities. He does not own
> the edifices in which he enjoys culture and entertainment.[54]

Washington would have embraced Cruse enthusiastically.
"The opportunity to earn a dollar in a factory is worth infinitely
more than the opportunity to spend a dollar in an opera house,"
he told his followers. "No race that has anything to contribute
to the markets of the world is long in any degree ostracized."[55]

The coming of Reaganism has given Booker T. Washington's
"Black Capitalism" new relevance for national black political
leaders. Suffering from historical amnesia, they do not usually
attribute their own political and economic agendas to the Tuskegee accommodationist but since they lack political ties with
the socialist movement, past or present, most have uncritically
readopted the Tuskegee "self-help" philosophy as their *modus
operandi.* Rejecting socialism, and even European-style social
democracy, many now espouse a "bootstraps" program to
counter high black unemployment, plant closings and social
service reductions. The failure of socialism to develop ties to the
black movement has opened the door to the right in the 1980s.

Across the country, interest in black private enterprise strategy increased as the 1982 recession deepened. In Buffalo, New
York, for example, a group of blacks formed the Ferguson and
Rhodes American Business Careers Institute to train blacks in
entrepreneurial skills. The Institute's motto, "to help those who
want to help themselves," clearly evokes the spirit of Tuskegee
and the old Negro Business League.[56] The Rev. Jesse Jackson's
Operation PUSH (People United to Save Humanity) pressured
the Seven Up Corporation to sign a $61 million commitment to
invest capital in black-owned businesses in June 1982. The
Seven Up agreement called for $10 million for the creation of
black-owned Seven-Up beverage wholesalerships, $5 million
invested in black-owned life insurance companies, and another

$4.35 million in advertisements in black-owned newspapers and radio stations. PUSH purchased 100 shares of stock in Chrysler, General Motors, Ford, and American Motors, in order to "assure us the right and the platform to voice our concern," according to Jackson.[57] Other black political leaders joined PUSH in proposing black alliances with capitalists.

In June 1982, New Orleans Mayor Dutch Morial told a US Black Chamber of Commerce meeting in San Francisco that "a strong line of communications with bankers [is] essential for the success of black businessmen." Former aide to Martin Luther King, Jr., and currently Mayor of Atlanta, Andrew Young, suggested that the decisive integration battle of the 1980s would be "the desegregation of the money markets." Jesse Jackson, however, remained unsurpassed in his "evangelical advocacy" of black capitalism. At a gathering of the New Orleans Business League in July 1982, Jackson proclaimed, *"We must move from Civil Rights to Silver Rights and from aid to trade."* He urged black clergy to promote the development of small businesses among their congregations, declaring that "churches are financial institutions as well as soul-saving institutions." Jackson said, "Black America does more business with corporate America than Russia, China and Japan combined. Therefore, we want our share of opportunities for risks and rewards! There's something tricky and vicious about the way we're locked out of the private sector. . . . The marketplace is the arena for our development."[58]

Various civil rights organizations applauded Jackson's initiatives, and also emphasized the necessity for aggressive black economic programs. At the seventy-third national convention of the NAACP in Boston, *Black Enterprise* publisher Earl Graves warned the organization:

> We must learn to be more dependent on ourselves, economically and politically. We know by now that as Black Americans we cannot depend solely on government. We cannot depend on anyone or anything outside ourselves to provide real economic opportunity or justice. We have been standing in the same station waiting for economic opportunity, watching train after train pass us by.[59]

Following Graves' address, NAACP delegates endorsed "Operation Fair Share," a campaign of nationwide boycotts against businesses that resist affirmative action efforts.

With the recessions of 1981 and 1982, NAACP leader Benjamin Hooks authorized the creation of an economics analysis unit and a task force to assist local branches to help black small entrepreneurs and unemployed black workers. In Kokomo, Indiana NAACP members responded to Reagan cutbacks in food stamps by organizing a food cooperative, and in Galloway Township, New Jersey, they pressured local officials to set aside half of all new municipal jobs for blacks, women and handicapped people. In Memphis, NAACP leaders persuaded the Nissan Corporation to buy supplies for its local automobile plant from black vendors.[60]

EVEN WITH ITS NEW "ECONOMIC AGENDA," the NAACP is reluctant to develop a militant black capitalist program. When William Perry, the NAACP president of Miami, Florida, introduced a proposal for a "Black Monday"—a plan to have blacks and whites buy exclusively from black businesses on June 28, 1982, national officers were furious. Local whites in the NAACP strongly opposed the idea, and Earl Shinhoster, Southeastern Regional Director of the NAACP, sent a testy mailgram to Perry on June 23, suspending him "immediately and indefinitely." Perry's explanation that the Black Monday "was not intended to be a boycott, just a campaign to support black businesses" did not satisfy his organizational superiors. Shinhoster argued that "any unit of the NAACP is a subordinate unit to the national organization. Autonomy [of the local branch] only extends to issues that are within the scope of the organization." Hooks gave Perry "five days to explain what happened and why his suspension should not be made permanent." Meanwhile, Perry resigned as president and promptly organized an Operation PUSH chapter in Miami. Perry informed the *Miami Times* that Jesse Jackson and PUSH "provide its local units with more autonomy than the NAACP gives its branches."[61]

The Urban League continued in its role as the rightwing of the black movement. When Reagan was elected, former League director Vernon Jordan made the most pathetic concessions to the conservative trend. Reagan deserved "the benefit of the doubt" and it was "dangerous," in Jordan's words, to criticize him. Jordan was willing to wait and see whether "equality can be achieved by conservative means, to look at conservative approaches to see if they will help black people." Jordan's successor, John E. Jacob, moved the organization only slightly to the left. Jacob denounced the recent draft report of the Department of Housing and Urban Development which called for an end to federal aid to inner cities. He revived a 20-year-old proposal developed by former League director Whitney Young which called for "massive federal efforts" combined with "local public-private sector efforts" to retard unemployment and urban decay. Jacob called for joint Democratic and Republican Party efforts to encourage "investments in human capital, urban infrastructure, and economic resources needed to get the national economy moving again."[62]

In Philadelphia, on June 9, 1982, the "Hire One Youth" program was launched by the Rev. Leon Sullivan, chairperson of the Opportunities Industrialization Centers (OICs). The stated goal of "Hire One Youth" was to encourage the private sector to hire 300,000 "disadvantaged young people" during the summer and an additional 700,000 youths by the middle of 1983. "I am appealing to the patriotism of American companies, large and small, in this critical and urgent time of need to put the youth of America back to work," Sullivan explained to the press. "Immediate bipartisan action on the part of President Reagan, the Congress, and the private sector is necessary." Behind Sullivan's appeal for jobs was an omnipresent threat of urban rebellion. "America must act now to put the unemployed youth in jobs before chaos and disorder erupt in our cities," Sullivan said bluntly. "The unemployed youth problem is social dynamite and it is about to explode." Sullivan reminded corporations that a $3,000 tax credit was available to all employers who hired Vietnam-era veterans, cooperative education students, involuntarily terminated CETA workers, and teenagers from "economically disadvantaged" areas. "If every American corporation, business, school . . . puts just one [youth] to work, we can get idle youth off the streets and into the productive mainstream of the American workforce."

Sullivan's program instantly won the support of a broad

segment of both political parties and corporations. A number of urban mayors, including Andrew Young of Atlanta, Bill Green of Philadelphia, Jane Byrne of Chicago, Coleman Young of Detroit, Marion Barry of Washington, D.C., and Tom Bradley of Los Angeles, endorsed "Hire One Youth." Conservative political forces, including the US Chamber of Commerce, Reagan's "Task Force for Private Sector Initiatives," and Republican Governor James Thompson of Illinois, publicly supported the effort. The Seven-Up Corporation agreed to pay for Sullivan's advertising and public relations costs. For all the media hype and political support, it seems unlikely that the effort will generate more than one-fifth of the number of permanent jobs it seeks. Sullivan's OIC was a product of Lyndon Johnson's Great Society programs. From 1964-1980, the OIC network of job training and industrial education programs received more than $500 million in federal funds. According to one source, only 13 percent of those trained in the Philadelphia OIC were working in training related jobs. Many of the OICs nationwide "suffer from mismanagement and poor program performance." Under heavy criticism since the mid-1970s, Rev. Sullivan authored the so-called "Sullivan Principles" which provide loose guidelines to justify continued US corporate investment in *apartheid* South Africa. Like the Tuskegee accommodationist, Sullivan has been a useful tool for both the Republican Party and US corporate interests in a number of ways. For example, in early 1981, Sullivan testified before the Senate Foreign Relations Committee in support of former Secretary of State Alexander Haig. The anti-communist general was "necessary for America," Sullivan declared. Since the mid-1970s, Gulf Oil and other major corporations have funneled tens of thousands of dollars to Sullivan. It would appear, given Sullivan's checkered history, that "Hire One Youth" was less a strategy to end black joblessness than a program to pacify the black ghetto while maintaining the process of capital accumulation within black America.[63]

In October 1980, two important aides to the late Martin Luther King, Jr. endorsed Reagan—the Rev. Ralph David Abernathy and Georgia State Rep. (D) Hosea Williams. Williams said his support for Reagan was justified because "the mounting KKK's violent activities against blacks all across the country" was indirectly a product of the Carter Administration. Appearing with South Carolina segregationist Strom Thurmond, in December 1980, Williams and Abernathy announced that they were "for the Republican platform" and supported the bizarre suggestion that Thurmond, once a presidential candidate of the Dixiecrat Party, serve as "a liason officer between Republicans *on behalf of minorities*" (emphasis added). As loyal members of what one journalist termed "Strom Thurmond's Black Kitchen Cabinet," Williams and Abernathy received a "letter of introduction" from Reagan for a black trade mission to Japan in June 1982. They met with Prime Minister Zenko Suzuki and Japanese business leaders "to promote Japanese investments in the US by offering tax incentives to businesses that invest in joint Japanese-Afro-American ventures." The 17-day trade mission sparked some "interest and curiosity" among Japanese corporations, which admitted that they had "never considered establishing a joint-venture factory in the US with either black or white businessmen." The entire effort may have been futile, however, because on Williams' return he was sentenced to serve one year in a Georgia pentitentiary for numerous traffic violations and for fleeing the scene of an accident in 1981.[64]

The pro-capitalist economic initiatives of black managers in the private sector have ranged from "conservative" to simply absurd. A good representative of their tendency is Joe Black, a Vice President of the Greyhound Corporation. In July 1982, Black condemned unemployed black youth for not understanding the "thrust of the Civil Rights Movement." "Too many of them have chosen to be guided by emotion and want to believe that it was to prove that Black can beat White or mistakenly thinking that we were to receive something just because we're Black." In Black's opinion, it was time for "Black adults" to "have the intestinal fortitude to tell youthful Blacks that they are spending too much time worrying about the word—'racism.' When we were young, we called it 'prejudice,' 'segregation,' and 'jim crow,' but we did not spend our time worrying about it." Racism was not the reason that black unemployment was at an all-time high: "Too often Black college students select 'sop' courses rather than those studies that will make them competitive in today's labor market." Like Hoover Institution

professor Thomas Sowell and other black conservative economists, Black suggested that blacks' ignorance and inadequate
training were to blame for their lack of employment opportunities.[65]

What almost no civil rights leader, corporate manager or
black politician comprehends is that the current economic
plight of Afro-Americans is an integral part of a worldwide
crisis of capitalism. Reaganism, its British counterpart, That-
cherism, and the conservative fiscal policies of Japan, West
Germany and other capitalist countries have escalated unemployment throughout the West. Total unemployment in all
Western countries has soared from 10 million in 1971-72 to a
projected 31 million by the end of 1982. Reagan's July 1, 1982,
"tax cut" did not increase US corporate investment or consumer spending. Conversely, European basic industries, such as
shipbuilding, steel, and petrochemicals are "all in deep trouble," according to the *Wall Street Journal*. British unemployment exceeds 13 percent, and even Japanese unemployment is
at a post-WW II record. The Western crisis in capital accumulation has forced pay cuts in workers' salaries in virtually every
nation. In 1980, the average West German worker, for example,
received $12.26 an hour; last year, the average salary was
$10.47. In the US a similar process of capitalist austerity has
occurred. Average wage increases in the first contract year for
settlements made by unions covering plants of at least 1,000
workers declined from 11.8 percent in April-June 1981 to 2.2
percent in January-March 1982. The result for US black
workers was entirely predictable: official adult unemployment
above 18 percent; black youth unemployment, 58 percent; the
projected failure of over 30 percent of all black-owned businesses *in 1982 alone.*[66]

The recession of 1982 illustrates with painful clarity the
essential political bankruptcy of black middle class "leaders"
and organizations. Unable and unwilling to advance a socialist reorganization of America's political economy, they rely on
corporate paternalism and "self-help efforts" which have all
been tried previously without success. Responding to the economic desperation of the black working class and poor, they
offer rhetoric more suitable to the age of Washington. Without a
coherent anti-capitalist alternative, it appears likely that no

meaningful solution to the long-term crisis of black underde-velopment will be achieved. The distance between the black movement and the socialist vison has actually widened and may continue to do so for the next period.

*　　*　　*

NONE OF THE POLITICAL PROBLEMS posed here can be resolved quickly. White democratic socialists still seldom respect or even comprehend the Afro-American's legitimate claim to a unique national identity, culture, and tradition of struggle. White Marxists often tend to idealize the black community, ignoring tendencies toward compromise and accommodation found not only among the black elite but also within the working class. White social democrats seem to ignore racism entirely, or simply reduce it solely to a question of class. On the other side of the color line, many blacks from different classes and for var-ious reasons of self-interest oppose socialist politics within the black community. Narrow nationalists hate Marxism because they don't trust radical whites; black entrepreneurs hate Marx-ism because it threatens black private capital accumulation; black politicians hate Marxism because they are committed to some form of liberal Keynesianism-to-conservative capitalism; and black preachers hate Marxism because it is atheistic. All of these anti-socialist sentiments are reinforced by conservative tendencies within black civil society and by the continued manifestations of racism by white workers, labor unions and white "progressives."

We need to understand the theoretical and practical relation-ship between race and class. The place to begin, I believe, is with black revolutionary socialist C.L.R. James. In his truly wonderful account of the San Domingo Revolution, *The Black Jacobins,* James makes a comment which strikes me as the initial step toward resolving the paradox: "The race question is subsidiary to the class question in politics, and to think of imperialism in terms of race is disastrous. But to neglect the racial factor as merely incidental is an error only less grave than to make it fundamental."[67]

Footnotes

1. W.E.B. DuBois, "Problem Literature," *Crisis* 8 (August 1914): 195-196.
2. Angela Davis, *Women, Race and Class* (New York: Random House, 1981), p. 51.
3. *Ibid.*, pp. 70-71.
4. *Ibid.*, pp. 212-215.
5. David Herreshoff, *The Origins of American Marxism: From the Transcendentalists to De Leon* (New York: Monad, 1973), pp. 17-18, 31-32, 39-47. Also see Arthur M. Schlesinger, "Orestes Brownson, American Marxist before Marx," *Sewanee Review* 47 (July-September 1939): 317-323.
6. The classical statement of American economic determinist thought is Charles A. Beard's *An Economic Interpretation of the Constitution of the United States* (New York: MacMillan, 1913). Of some interest is Beard's introduction to the 1935 edition of his seminal study. Beard admitted that he was "interested in Marx when I discovered in his works the ideas which had been cogently expressed by outstanding thinkers and statesmen." However, he denounced the widely-held view that his writing was influenced by Marx. Of Marxist views, he declared, "have I the least concern. I have never believed that 'all history' can or must be 'explained' in economic terms, or any other terms."
7. Albert Fried, ed., *Socialism in America* (Garden City: Anchor, 1970), p. 387.
8. Herreshoff, *The Origins of American Marxism*, pp. 159, 168-169.
9. *Ibid.*, pp. 127, 148, 159, 169.
10. DuBois, "The Socialists," *Crisis* 1 (March 1911): 15.
11. DuBois, "A Field for Socialists," *New Review* 1 (January 11, 1913): 54-57. Also see DuBois, "Socialism and the Negro Problem," *New Review* 1 (February 1, 1913): 138-141.
12. DuBois, *The Autobiography of W.E.B. DuBois* (New York: International Publishers, 1968), pp. 218, 260. Mary White Ovington was among the few white socialists in the early 1900s to make the cause of racial equality central to their vision of a socialist society. See Ovington, "Vacation Days on San Juan Hill—A New York Negro Colony," *Southern Workman* 38 (November 1909): 627-634; Ovington, "The Negro in the Trade Unions in New York," *Annals of the American Academy of Political and Social Science* 27 (June 1906): 551-558; Ovington, "The National Association for the Advancement of Colored People," *Journal of Negro History* 9 (April 1924): 107-116.
13. Fried, ed., *Socialism in America*, p. 386.
14. Milton Cantor, *The Divided Left: American Radicalism, 1900-1975* (New York: Hill and Wang, 1978), p. 14.
15. Philip S. Foner, *Organized Labor and the Black Worker, 1619-1973* (New York: International Publishers, 1974), pp. 175-176. DuBois denounced Frey's "awkward and insincere defense of the color line in the A.F. of L." in "Postscript," *Crisis* 36 (July 1929): 242.
16. *Ibid.*, pp. 162, 191-195, 209; and Cantor, *The Divided Left*, pp. 15, 122. A valuable source on the rise of black participation in the US Communist Party is Mark I. Solomon, "Red and Black: Negroes and Communism, 1929-1932," Ph.D. dissertation, Harvard University, 1972.

17. Foner, *Organized Labor and the Black Worker*, pp. 278-280.
18. DuBois, "The Negro Mind Reaches Out," in *The New Negro*, ed. Alain Locke (New York: Atheneum, 1977, reprint of 1925 edition), p. 407.
19. Foner, *Organized Labor and the Black Worker*, pp. 52, 53, 103.
20. August Meier, *Negro Thought in America, 1880-1915* (Ann Arbor: University of Michigan Press, 1963), pp. 46-47; Seth M. Scheiner, "Early Career of T. Thomas Fortune, 1879-1890," *Negro History Bulletin* 28 (April 1964): 170-172. Fortune eventually came under the hegemony of Booker T. Washington's "Tuskegee Machine," renounced many of his leftist views, and quietly receded into political oblivion. See Emma Lou Thornbrough, "More Light on Booker T. Washington and the *New York Age*," *Journal of Negro History* 43 (January 1958): 34-49; and August Meier, "Booker T. Washington and the Negro Press," *Journal of Negro History* 38 (January 1953): 68-82.
21. Albert Fried describes Lucy Parsons as "a dark-skinned Mexican" in the collection he edited, *Socialism in America*, p. 187.
22. See Carolyn Asbaugh, *Lucy Parsons: American Revolutionary* (Chicago: Charles H. Kerr, 1976).
23. Meier, *Negro Thought in America, 1880-1915*, pp. 142, 180, 186-187.
24. Wilfred D. Samuels, "Hubert H. Harrison and 'The New Negro Manhood Movement,' " *Afro-Americans in New York Life and History* 5 (January 1981): 29-41; Manning Marable, *From the Grassroots: Social and Political Essays Towards Afro-American Liberation* (Boston: South End Press, 1980), pp. 59-85.
25. Angelo Herndon, *Let me Live* (New York: Arno Press, 1969, reprint of the 1937 edition), pp. iii-x, 77, 80, 82-83, 186-187.
26. Meier, *Negro Thought in America, 1880-1915*, pp. 203-204.
27. DuBois, "To Black Voters," *Horizon* 3 (February 1908): 17-18. Also see DuBois' 1911 editorial, "Christmas Gift," *Crisis* 3 (December 1911). DuBois repeats the assertion that the Socialist Party "is the only party which openly recognizes Negro manhood. Is it not time for black voters to carefully consider the claims of this party?"
28. DuBois, "Along the Color Line," *Crisis* 2 (October 1911): 227-233.
29. DuBois, "Postscript," *Crisis* 34 (August 1927): 203-204.
30. DuBois, "The Battle of Europe," *Crisis* 12 (September 1916): 217-218
31. DuBois, "The World Last Month," *Crisis* 13 (March 1917).
32. DuBois, "The Negro and Radical Thought," *Crisis* 22 (July 1921): 204.
33. DuBois, *Autobiography*, pp. 29-30.
34. DuBois, "Russia, 1926," *Crisis* 33 (November 1926).
35. DuBois, "Forward," *Crisis* 18 (September 1919): 235.
36. DuBois, "Postscript," *Crisis* 39 (June 1932): 191.
37. DuBois, *Autobiography*, pp. 31-32.
38. Isaac Deutscher, *Stalin: A Political Biography* (New York: Oxford University Press, 1949), pp. 345-385.
39. See Robert C. Tucker, ed., *Stalinism: Essays in Historical Interpretation* (New York: W.W. Norton, 1977).
40. W.E.B. DuBois, "Colonialism and the Russian Revolution," *New World Review* (November 1956): 18-22; DuBois, "The Stalin Era," *Masses and*

Mainstream 10 (January 1957): 1-5; DuBois, "The Dream of Socialism," *New World Review* (November 1959): 14-17.

41. A representative sample of literature by recent black revolutionary nationalists, Marxist-Leninists, and democratic socialists includes: Angela Davis, *Angela Davis: An Autobiography* (New York: Random House, 1974); Davis, *Women, Race and Class*; Robert Allen, *Black Awakening in Capitalist America: An Analytic History* (Garden City: Anchor, 1969); James Foreman, *The Making of Black Revolutionaries* (New York: MacMillan, 1972); Wiliam Sales, "New York City: Prototype of the Urban Crisis," *Black Scholar* 7 (November 1975): 20-39; William Strickland, "Whatever Happened to the Politics of Black Liberation?" *Black Scholar* 7 (October 1975): 20-26; Damu I. Smith, "The Upsurge of Police Repression: An Analysis," *Black Scholar* 12 (January/February 1981): 35-57; John Conyers, "The Economy is the Issue, Planning for Full Employment," *Freedomways* 17 (Spring 1977): 71-78; Ronald Dellums, "Black Leadership: For Change or For Status Quo?" *Black Scholar* 8 (January-February 1977): 2-5; Julian Bond, *A Time to Speak, a Time to Act* (New York: Simon and Schuster, 1972).

42. Herndon, *Let me Live*, pp. 80, 114-115. Herndon's own writing is also filled with religious symbols and overtones. On pages 82-83, he denounces DuBois, who was not yet a Communist, and black Chicago Congressperson Oscar De Priest as "the tools and the lickspittles of the white ruling class. They speak with the sweet voice of Jacob, but they extend the hairy hand of Esau."

43. Nell Irvin Painter, *The Narrative of Hosea Hudson: His Life as a Negro Communist in the South* (Cambridge: Harvard University Press, 1979), pp. xiii, 23, 24, 133-135. Also see Hosea Hudson, *Black Worker in the Deep South* (New York: International Publishers, 1972).

44. John Hope Franklin, *From Slavery to Freedom* (New York: Random House, 1969), pp. 318, 321; Meier, *Negro Thought in America, 1880-1915*, p. 46.

45. Alfred A. Moss, Jr., *The American Negro Academy: Voice of the Talented Tenth* (Baton Rouge: Louisiana State University Press, 1981), pp. 145-146.

46. Allen, *Black Awakening in Capitalist America*, pp. 100-101. As Allen puts it, "Garvey took Washington's economic program, clothed it in militant nationalist rhetoric, and built an organization which in its heyday enjoyed the active support of millions of black people."

47. *Ibid.*, p. 250.

48. *Ibid.*, pp. 250-251.

49. Manning Marable, *Blackwater: Historical Studies in Race, Class Consciousness and Revolution* (Dayton: Black Praxis Press, 1981), p. 110.

50. DuBois, *Dusk of Dawn*, p. 205.

51. DuBois, *Autobiography*, p. 126.

52. *Ibid.*, pp. 215-217.

53. *Ibid.*, p. 228.

54. Harold Cruse, *Rebellion or Revolution* (New York: William Morrow, 1968), pp. 238-239.

55. Meier, *Negro Thought in America, 1880-1915*, p. 101.

56. "Area's First Minority-Owned Business Institute Established," *Buffalo Challenger*, 28 July 1982.

57. "PUSH Scores Again: 7-Up Agrees to Invest Money in Black Business: Auto Industries Next!" *Buffalo Challenger*, 21 July 1982. The major corporations are, of course, eager to provide token amounts of capital to the black middle class, if in doing so they increase their respective shares of the $125 billion black consumer market. In June 1982, Anheuser-Busch announced that it would spend $1 million in black-owned newspaper advertising. A black vice president of Anheuser-Busch made the pledge before a meeting of black publishers in Baltimore. "We are committed to the economic development of those companies which are owned and operated by minorities. [We] will expand the number of minority suppliers and contractors with whom we do business. Blacks support our products," he stated, "and [we] need to communicate to [black] consumers how much we appreciate their support." "Anheuser-Busch to spend $1 million with black newspapers," *San Antonio Register*, 1 July 1982.

58. "PUSH Leader Says We Must Move to Silver Rights and to Trade," *Omaha Star*, 22 July 1982.

59. Tony Brown, "Kennedy: Trumped-Up White Liberal," *Buffalo Challenger*, 21 July 1982.

60. Diane E. Lewis, "Is the NAACP in Step or Out?" *Boston Globe*, 28 June 1982; "NAACP Attacks Reagan, Backs Liberal Democrats," *Guardian*, 21 July 1982.

61. "William Perry Suspended from NAACP," *Miami Times*, 15 July 1982; Marable, *Blackwater*, p. 160.

62. John E. Jacob, "Formulating Urban Policy," Fort Lauderdale *Westside Gazette*, 8 July 1982; Sheila Rule, "Urban League Asks for U.S. Jobs Plan," *New York Times*, 2 August 1982.

63. Marable, *Blackwater*, pp. 154, 165; "OIC Announces Youth Hiring Program," Fort Lauderdale *Westside Gazette*, 8 July 1982.

64. Marable, *Blackwater*, pp. 156-157, 160; "Black Trade Mission to Japan Successful," *Pensacola Voice*, 19-25 June 1982.

65. Joe Black, "By the Way . . . ," *Buffalo Challenger*, 14 July 1982.

66. "Unemployment on the Rise across the Western World," *San Francisco Chronicle*, 11 May 1982; Anthony Mazzocchi, "It's Time for Management Concessions," *New York Times*, 27 June 1982; Daniel Yergin, "Unemployment: The Outlook Is Grim," *New York Times*, 13 July 1982; Lauri McGinley, "Joblessness Rise Shows Economy Is Getting Worse," *Wall Street Journal*, 10 May 1982; Art Pine, "Europeans Pessimistic As Recession Appears Deep, Hard to Reverse," *Wall Street Journal*, 10 May 1982.

67. C.L.R. James, *The Black Jacobins: Toussaint L'Ouverture and the San Domingo Revolution* (New York: Vintage, 1963), p. 283.

The Current State of the Feminist Movement

LYNN CHANCER

"It was the closest feminism has come to directly allying itself with the Nazis and the Ku Klux Klan." So said a participant in a feminist conference on sexuality held at Barnard College in New York. "A truly liberating experience," said another. Such radically divergent responses are indicative of some of the problems facing the feminist movement today. While it is not unusual for such gatherings to be characterized by severe disagreements, or the occasional antic behavior of some "charismatic" superstar, this conference was unique for the absence of shared understandings and common premises.

It was organized by a group of feminists who called themselves, in the words of conference planner Ellen Willis, "sexual libertarians." Among the speakers was a representative of SAMOIS (named for the Lesbian dominatrix in the sado-masochist classic *The Story of O*), a lesbian group advocating sado-masochistic relationships, which sought to distribute a leaflet showing a razor between a woman's spread legs but was prevented from doing so by the Barnard administration. While SAMOIS's views were not necessarily those of the planning group, the notion that feminism should no longer be prescriptive in the area of sexuality was an underlying theme. As one of

---

LYNN CHANCER, *who has been active in feminist causes, is studying for her Ph.D. in sociology and women's studies at the City University Graduate Center. She is doing her thesis on feminist theory.*

the speakers told me, the time has come for feminists to stop thinking that "sexuality can be made obedient to political imperatives. . . . We should be criticizing people on the basis of their politics, not what they do in the bedroom."

Feminists may, in practice, have engendered a sense of guilt and hostility in women who are married or are masochistic or have other characteristics which have been viewed critically. To the extent that women have been made to feel guilty or excluded, feminism has failed as a general movement and Barnard was correct in expressing concern about this problem. But it neglected to make emphatically clear that practical failures are not equivalent to theoretical apologias. All social movements must retain their right to vision and evaluative judgment. Without the ability to imagine a world where sado-masochism does not exist as a psychological correlative to power, where there is an end to abusive behavior by man to woman, woman to woman or man to man, feminists would not have devoted themselves to radical change. Our goal was and remains compassion and change. Any theoretical position which justifies interpersonal violence is utterly irreconcilable with a feminist politics.

Much of the fervor behind the rise of contemporary feminism came from the recognition that male leftists gave lip service to "political" equality while "personally" oppressing their female sexual partners. To dissociate political and bedroom behavior is to nullify protests against battering, rape and other forms of interpersonal sexism. To sanction sadism by women in the name of feminist sexual liberation is to approve the notion that what we find reprehensible in male sexual violence is acceptable, even benevolent, when practiced by women; it is to endorse the status quo sexuality which reigns in male-dominated culture.

A woman at the Barnard conference asked, at one point, why these views were surfacing at a time of Reaganism and right-wing reaction. Is it a coincidence, she wondered? The answer she received was that this is a time when people need to express themselves. But express themselves how? And why in a form which implies acceptance of sado-masochism and questioning the personal as political, the fountainhead of feminist theory? What has led feminism to this pass? Perhaps an examination and analysis of the trends in the feminist movement will stimulate debate aimed at returning feminism to a firmer footing.

Radical Feminism and the
Rise of the Feminist Movement

MANY RADICAL WOMEN, previously involved in socialist, New Left or anti-war activism, date their feminist conversion to the now-famous 1969 anti-inaugural demonstration against Nixon at which men hooted sexual epithets at women speakers who were told to leave the platform "for their own good."

In a broad sense, material conditions, such as reliable contraception, the post-WW II entry of women into the labor force in large numbers, and improved household technology aided in the rise of contemporary feminism. But it was women's participation in the civil rights and anti-war movements that made them most aware of the need to fight directly for their own liberation.

This is not the first wave of American feminism to emerge after women's participation in other movements for social justice but merely the latest episode in a pattern yet to be broken. In the first wave, women came to suffrage after finding the Abolitionists loathe to support their fight for equality. Similarly, the second wave—pre-WW I to the attainment of suffrage in 1920—was fueled by women's involvement in reform movements of the Progressive Era. Participation in movements highlighting inequalities applicable to their own position led women to struggle on their own behalf. Ironically, they encountered blatant sexism in these movements, but in the course of their activity these women acquired new political and organizational skills. All three of these factors played a part in the origins of "radical feminism."

Most important in the development of radical feminism, aside from demonstrations for abortion rights, demands for space in "women's magazines," consciousness raising groups, etc., was the publication of theoretical works. Revolutionary in impact, they form the basis of feminist theory from which almost all currents have drawn their ideas.

Simone de Beauvoir's *The Second Sex*, published in the United States in 1952, is the only masterpiece of feminist theory yet produced. It did for feminism what *Capital* did for the socialist movement: it clearly diagnosed a condition, traced its historical development and described in detail its present mode of operation. Works that followed have contributed major theoretical expansions of de Beauvoir's pioneering work. This is not to underestimate the political significance of the later books. Betty Friedan's 1963 *The Feminine Mystique* was like Bellamy's *Looking Backward* in effect: it galvanized thousands of housewives into feminist activity to escape the malaise so accurately described by Friedan and to help change their own lives. In 1969, Kate Millet's *Sexual Politics* spelled out a theory of patriarchy initially developed by de Beauvoir. It was followed in rapid succession by a flurry of books further elaborating feminist theory—in 1970, Shulamith Firestone's *The Dialectic of Sex*, 1971, Juliet Mitchell's *Women's Estate*, 1974, Ti-Grace Atkinson's *Amazon Odyssey*.

The content of radical feminist thought is even more vital than its history. The concept of "patriarchy" was introduced to signify the range of power relationships through which men dominate women. As Millet argued in *Sexual Politics*, whether a state once existed that was not patriarchal is unprovable and irrelevant. What matters is that all known societies, in different cultures and time periods, exhibit this oppressor-oppressed relationship. While the concept of patriarchy is fairly well known today and accepted by many, the detailed account of it given by radical feminists in the early seventies was revelatory and sobering. For many women, there was a sense of discovery in finding suddenly illuminated and explained a condition they had always known. They also came to the realization that the rule of men over women had persisted through feudal, capitalist and "socialist" upheavals. In contrast to the emphasis later placed by socialist feminists on historical specificity, it was precisely this universality of patriarchy that interested the early feminists and became the core of their theory.

In addition to the elaboration of patriarchy was the demystification of gender. Under patriarchy, arbitrary gender characteristics were superimposed on the neutral facts of sex. Women were supposedly passive by nature, men active; to the world of the former belong emotion, to the latter rationality. These "subjective" categories corresponded to the divisions made in the "objective" environment between the inessential and the essential, the private and the public, the "personal" world of the housewife and the "political" world of men. But if gender and sex were not equivalent, as radical feminists realized, what of the complex systems which stemmed from this false premise? Demystifying gender led to the discovery that the personal had been kept separate from the political in the interests of male power. Like gender, it was an arbitrary arrangement, a patriarchal construction. That the personal should equate to the political—that people's personal behavior has political implications and vice versa—was and is feminism's most essential insight.

The implications of the personal as political in the family were thoroughly explored by radical feminists. Marriage and the family had, until then, been largely ignored by male writers who dismissed "woman's world" as not worthy of study. Yet, it was in the family that sex-role stereotyping and the psychology needed to perpetuate it were instilled. Women learned to think of themselves as objects, and to gear themselves toward motherhood rather than careers. If they wanted to break away and enter the "public" sphere, they were expected to do double work. The customs of patriarchy protected marriage by law. Even now, in many places a husband can legally rape or beat his wife, adultery is taboo for women and deviations from the heterosexual norm are punished. But if a woman chose not to marry, she faced few socially acceptable alternatives.

Although patriarchy was legally well equipped to insist on marriage, it also employed gentler ideological means. Through its glorification of permanence, the union of individuals who needed each other for life to be complete, the ideology of romantic love maintained the illusion that marriage was a blissful panacea. It worked so well that the old adage was more or less borne out: for a man, his wife is part of his life; for a woman he is the world.

While the feminist movement is responsible for a change in the way that many, if not most, women view themselves today, as individuals in their own right with talents and careers outside of marriage, ancient customs die hard. The patriarchal structure may be shaken but it certainly is not dead.

RADICAL FEMINISM WAS NOT MERELY theoretical; it had political views that remain valid. The early feminists, like other radicals, knew that women had to be the agents of their own liberation. It was clear from historical experience that women's issues should not be subordinated to other problems. Elizabeth Cady Stanton predicted that the attainment of suffrage would take 100 years more if it was not granted concurrently with the vote for black men; in fact, it took 50. Later, the radical Women's Party was asked to put aside the fight for the vote in order to support WW I. The same pattern occurred over and over again, and persists to this day. The war must come first, the class struggle, the anti-nuclear movement takes precedence. But since the personal is political, the radical feminists insisted that women must act independently, that their own struggle had to be the core of their organizational involvements. And since they wanted their own organizations to be different than those in which they had participated previously, most feminist groups experimented with non-hierarchical, more communal structures. With these goals in mind, radical feminists created an autonomous movement based on the idea of women as a class. This theme, although implicit in most radical feminist thought, was made explicit in Atkinson's *Amazon Odyssey*, in which the political grouping, women, was treated with the same legitimacy and respect that socialists give to the proletariat.

What about working class and economic issues? Women both were and were not a class in the Marxist sense. United by a large number of political, social and psychological characteristics, they were nonetheless divided by class, race and status. The radical feminists were by no means completely unaware of the difficulties raised by this view of class. They simply assumed a kind of anti-capitalism as part of their ideology. For example, whether or not one agrees with her thesis, Firestone's argument for sex as a more inclusive category than class assumed the downfall of capitalism in the course of a feminist revolution. Both de Beauvoir and Millet assumed the necessity of socialism to improve the condition of women and to end economic exploitation. The assumption was that radical feminism sought an end not only to sexual but to all forms of oppression. However, the relationship between feminism and other movements was not developed until socialist feminist theory made its appearance.

Faced with the sexism of the patriarchal Leviathan they had identified, the radical feminists chose what might be called in Marxist terminology, a bourgeois stage of development. (Whether it could have been skipped is a pointless debate. It is certainly logical that it happened as it did.) Elementary as it may seem now, little more than 15 years later, it had to be established that women were capable of undertaking a variety of professions, that they were entitled to equal pay for equal work and that they should be granted full access to educational institutions. These and other issues like abortion and day care were interrelated. In practice, radical feminists became involved in battles on many fronts. They took on affirmative action, university tenure for women, battering, rape, abortion rights, credit for women, employment discrimination and much more.

No matter what remains to be achieved—and a great deal does—it was a brilliant beginning and an enormous accomplishment. It led to the proliferation in the last decade of innumerable feminist groups, caucuses, women's centers and women's studies programs. The fact that the media adopted more and more feminist rhetoric was a certain sign of success in the coopting world of American culture. But it also meant trouble by the late seventies; for the media's genius is its ability to separate parts of an ideology, to isolate carefully what can be accommodated within the system from its more revolutionary context. The illusion created was that radical feminist goals had been realized when in fact only a small group of middle class women had been affected. Some women dropped out of the movement, feeling they had obtained all they needed; others joined the reform-oriented National Organization for Women (NOW).

As economic conditions worsened, right-wing reaction gained ground. Worried by the social changes in society, by both black and feminist demands, right-wing forces took the offensive on the sanctity of marriage and the family and the "right to life." This, too, took its toll on radical feminism. Some women became exhausted, worn out by protracted battles not all of which were won. Others may have felt that feminism demanded greater endurance and sacrifice than they had originally expected. For whatever individual reasons, what resulted was a turning inward, away from the political, a part defiant, part resigned decision to create their own culture. Symptomatic, perhaps, is that Kate Millet did not go on to further theorizing after *Sexual Politics* but created literary works like *Flying* and *Sita*. The impulse is vaguely reminiscent of the one which motivated the nineteenth century utopian socialists, and it suffers the same fatal flaw. As Marx observed, such communities try to escape the outer world of which they are a part, but the world tends to engulf them nonetheless.

THE MOST TROUBLING FORM the inward turn took was the development of cultural feminism, an assertion of women's superiority to men rather than their equality. Radical feminists had argued passionately that there was no such thing as an "essence" of masculine or feminine; they rejected any association of the feminine with inherent traits like passivity or dependence, or the masculine with strength and assertiveness. Cultural feminists like Mary Daly in her book *Gyn Ecology* or Adrienne Rich in *Of Woman Born* moved away from the radical feminist rejection of inherent traits to embrace the belief which grew increasingly popular both within and outside lesbian feminist circles, that women are innately kinder, more compassionate and more elevated than men. The correlate to this, of course, is that men are, *by nature*, unkind, unfeeling and base. It is this very belief in "essences" that feminism strongly contested from the start. (Phyllis Schlafly also believes women to be kinder and more compassionate, which is why she thinks they should stay home and raise children.) This aspect of cultural feminism is a dangerous departure from radical feminist ideas. To the extent that notions of "essences" have entered feminist politics, speakers at the Barnard conference did have a point in criticizing cultural feminism.

Some tendency toward the mythification of women has always been latent in the movement: as early as 1971, anthropologist Elizabeth Gould Davis was searching for women's "roots" in her book *The First Sex*. But it was in the later seventies, interestingly enough around the same time feminism began to decline, that cultural feminism became a divisive ideology within the movement. A major cause was the "Jane

Alpert incident," which split the radical feminist community into two opposing camps. Alpert had been active in the anti-war movement and had gone into hiding after being involved in acts of violence for which she and others were indicted. She surfaced years later and turned herself in to the federal authorities. As part of a plea bargain, she divulged critical information about the underground. On one side of the feminist community were those who supported Alpert's actions despite her betrayal because she was a woman. On the other, there were those who did not believe that sex could be used to absolve individuals from all personal responsibility. The incident was divisive and caused a good deal of hostility. Such cultural feminist attitudes, combined with external problems (such as media cooptation and reaction) and the failure of the movement to develop its potential, both theoretically and politically, seriously undermined the political thrust of the feminist movement.

A number of theoretical problems raised by de Beauvoir, Millet, Mitchell and others, such as the nature of oppression in all its forms, have not been explored. Engels' assumption that the elimination of class oppression would spell the elimination of sexism can neither be proved nor disproved on the basis of the societies which call themselves "socialist" today. They are marked by both class oppression and sexism, but then, none is a socialist society. However, there is no reason to believe that sexism would automatically be eliminated under socialism. In *The Second Sex*, de Beauvoir devoted a section to an analysis of why people oppress others and Atkinson mentions the same problem in passing. In existential terms, they spoke of a "tendency" to oppress which has remained more or less uniform over time and which represents a response to anxiety and ultimately to death. But a fully developed theory of oppression and ways to alleviate it have not been produced by feminists. In addition, radical feminism has not produced its own theory of history. How has sexual oppression changed over time and by what dynamics? There is no analogue to the Marxist theory of history which predicts general processes that might lead to revolutionary change. Feminism has not yet formulated rigorous hypotheses about why patriarchy is strong in some periods as opposed to others, or whether it contains internal contradictions that might lead to its demise.

Aside from theory, radical feminism has failed to develop a political program which might form the basis for the creation of an organization. Simone de Beauvoir may have given feminism its only *Capital* to date, but its *What Is To Be Done?* remains to be written.

One reason why radical feminism may not have become more political was its insistence on avoiding hierarchical and centralized organizations. In *Beyond the Fragments*, Sheila Rowbotham said that feminism's ability to grow as a movement without reproducing oppressive power structures should be noted by male leftists. But she cautioned that this decentralization might be harmful if carried to extremes. Radical feminists needed an organizational structure to maintain continuity between its more and less active periods. Unlike previous waves of feminism when one group alone represented the radical branch of the movement (Susan B. Anthony's National, for example, or the Woman's Party), the current wave lacks a radical center. A lack of continuity is responsible. The earlier groups failed to sustain themselves after the twenties so that from the thirties through the fifties there was no organized feminist movement. Continuity, essential for growth and stability, continues to be elusive.

Radical feminism, past and present, was and is essentially a middle and upper class movement, concentrating primarily on such issues as professional education and careers. Only in recent years, with the appearance of socialist feminism, has the movement addressed itself to working class concerns. The failure of radical feminism to become a multi-class movement deprived it of a large number of potential adherents, divided women against each other and fed anti-feminist sentiment. More than that, the middle class politics of radical feminism made it difficult to distinguish between the radical and reform branches of the movement. As the illusion spread that reform goals were being realized, many women felt that these aims were the same for both groups. Yet, in fact, as we shall see, reform and radical feminism are in many ways antithetical. The feminism of Kate Millet's *Sexual Politics* is negated by Betty Friedan's *The Second Stage*.

Reform Feminism
and the Second Stage

IN HER BOOK, *Women in Modern America*, historian Lois Banner notes that contemporary feminism "may be one of the few liberal movements in modern American history that has been so completely permeated by the tactics and ideology of [its own] left." It is an accurate perception since the reform branch of feminism sprang Athena-like from the forehead of the radical wing. The reformers selectively borrowed ideas from their radical sisters, and these ideas then became the basis upon which they built their own organization.

With the exception of books, specific in nature, like *The Feminine Mystique*, the theory behind reform feminism was the old radical exposé of patriarchal society. The reformers, also predominantly middle class women, were naturally attracted to the idea of equal pay for equal work, women's control over their own bodies and equal access to education and job titles. Many of them were, or aspired to be, professionals—doctors, lawyers or academics—and knew that sexism prevented women from having satisfying lives and careers. Others were housewives who attended "consciousness raising" meetings where they learned that their individual experiences were far from unique and that they would be more fulfilled if they worked and shared household responsibilities with their husbands. These women supported a reform version of feminism which culminated in 1966 with the founding of NOW, Betty Friedan's conception of a mass women's organization, dedicated to changing laws and cultural practices inimical to women.

Like any reform movement, NOW was not concerned with revolutionary transformations. It wanted a "new deal" and, reminiscent of earlier reform feminists, often harked back to constitutional documents to argue that when "liberty and justice for all" excluded women, it was a sham. Generally career oriented and attuned to marriage, the reformers were not interested in exploring alternatives to the nuclear family. A dispute over such a question in 1973, when the New York chapter of NOW refused to support lesbian women's struggle against discrimination, abruptly separated reform from radical feminists. Even more important, NOW was in no way an anti-capitalist organization. On the contrary, it was purposefully silent about issues of economic exploitation, since socialism was of no interest to women who wanted to enter business and the professions, i.e., to become a part of the system.

The membership of NOW skyrocketed from a fairly small number in 1966 to 30,000 in 1973 and over 200,000 by 1982. In contrast to radical feminist groups, NOW's structure was much more conventional; it had elections, chapter presidents, dues and task forces. It was "political" in the manner of a good pressure group or lobbying organization. Like earlier reform groups, it developed a one-issue orientation. Whereas the National Women's Suffrage Organization had focused singularly on the vote, NOW came to devote itself almost entirely to passage of the Equal Rights Amendment (ERA).

ERA, interestingly enough, was most successful in the years immediately after its introduction, concurrent with the ascendance of radical feminism. As Banner observes, the theoretical focus and political aggressiveness of radical feminism probably compelled the reform movement to remain on the offensive. The rapid growth and influence of the women's liberation movement led some thirty states to endorse the ERA within a relatively short period. But the media cooptation and conservative backlash responsible in large measure for the decline of radical feminism, affected the reformers as well, and eventually sealed the fate of the ERA.

Yet, while the ERA was defeated in June 1982, NOW's power as a political interest group is greater today than it was in the past. In the frenetic final days before the deadline, NOW managed to raise an astonishing $1.3 million per month to blitz the three states that had held out. The sum was larger than the monthly funds raised by the Democratic National Committee and, according to New York NOW president Denise Fuge, has led mainstream politicians to come courting. For the first time, she said, there is the perception of a "women's vote," analagous to a "black vote" or a "Jewish vote." Women have become a financial and an electoral force. While, at the time of NOW's formation, its members had to fight to become lawyers or professors, those who "made it" boast of their own "old girls' network" sixteen years later.

But ERA *was* defeated, abortion rights are far from secure

and the movement as a whole suffers from inertia. Why else did Betty Friedan, founding mother of reform feminism, feel the need to write *The Second Stage* a year ago if not to revitalize the movement she helped to initiate? Unhappily, if implemented, her recommendations would have the opposite result. For, in *The Second Stage*, Friedan says that feminists should not have been so critical of marriage, men or the family. In so doing, they alienated people who otherwise would have been sympathetic. The second stage, then, suggests that women work more closely with men and corporations to meet their home and career needs. One problem with Friedan's argument is that by proposing a second stage, she assumes the first has been completed. But many of the goals of the first stage, such as day care and shelters for battered women have not been met, while accomplishments like affirmative action and abortion rights are now in jeopardy.

How can women retract their criticism of the family without jettisoning feminist ideology itself? That feminist theory may have appeared threatening, that it might have been presented with greater political skill, is not to say that it is wrong. Friedan proposes the classic reformist solution in the face of momentary adversity: retreat; become more "respectable"; accommodate to traditional views. The truth is that the movement's greatest successes were achieved when women rejected accommodation and demanded redress in straightforward political terms. If reforms were as easily attained as Friedan suggests, the feminist movement would never have been born. Radical feminism with its "excesses" is responsible for many of the victories achieved by the reformers. Worried by the movement's left, the establishment acceded to many of the reformist feminist demands.

Actually, Friedan's "second stage" is to reform feminism what the Barnard conference is to radical feminism; each in its respective way hints at potential peril. Both have deviated from feminism's original premises; both are expressions of self-doubt. The conference questioned the link between politics and sexuality; Friedan is troubled by women's autonomy and attacks on the family. Neither tackles the basic question of strategy: how can feminism steer a better course to its goals, in times of depression and reaction as well as in times of prosperity? With the defeat of the ERA, the reform wing must assess its concentration on that single issue to the exclusion of all others. Substituting one issue for an entire philosophy raises the problem of what to do when that issue, either as a result of success or failure, can no longer serve as a rallying point. Given its own decline, the left is familiar with that dilemma in the aftermath of the Vietnam War.

The reformers have an additional problem. They represent only one class of women and, as a result, have not raised economic issues which would attract working class and minority women. Support for capitalism, after all, is not necessarily in reform feminism's best interest. If radical feminism failed to develop class connections, the reformers never even considered the question. It is only with the rise of socialist feminism that questions of class entered the feminist movement.

Socialist Feminism: The Unhappy Marriage

BARBARA EHRENREICH, IN A NEW AMERICAN MOVEMENT pamphlet, quipped that a socialist feminist is a socialist who goes to twice as many meetings. But, no matter where the emphasis is placed, socialist feminism significantly widened the scope of feminist concerns by adding questions of class to those of sex.

In July 1975, over 1,500 women attended the first large socialist feminist conference in Yellow Springs, Ohio. Some were already active feminists, others were Marxists of one variety or another who were dissatisfied with the Marxist analysis of women's oppression. They no longer believed that economic transformation would automatically lead to women's liberation. Earlier, during the heyday of the civil rights and anti-war movements, feminists had called attention to the sexism of socialist men. These feminists must have empathized with Sheila Rowbothom, who provides vivid descriptions of her problems in the British Trotskyist movement in her book, *Woman's Consciousness, Man's World.* For example, there is the "man from Militant who solemnly told everyone that drugs, drink and women were a capitalist plot to seduce the workers from Marxism." Perhaps socialist women discovered that they were doing far more typing or coffee making than discussing or leading, that socialist boyfriends could be as brutally sexist as non-socialist ones. Reality proved that feminism had much to offer socialist women.

Since radical feminism omitted an explicit class analysis, it was unsatisfactory. Thus, the Yellow Springs conference incorporated into its principles of unity not only support for an autonomous women's movement but a commitment to fight capitalism along with patriarchy. In developing their own political analysis, socialist feminists borrowed the strengths and abandoned the weaknesses of their radical feminist predecessors. They agreed, for example, that radical feminism's treatment of patriarchy was ahistorical since it failed to distinguish variation from one society to another. Unless the interaction between capitalism and patriarchy was better understood, they felt, there was little hope for change.

In addition, socialist feminists challenged Engels' theory of the origins of the family. According to Engels, the origin of women's oppression coincided with the emergence of private property. Socialism would therefore eliminate sexual oppression by bringing women into the productive process. But why was it that women rather than men were the oppressed in the first division of labor "between man and woman for childbearing?" What was the division based on? Certainly not private property which could have accommodated itself to other social arrangements. If, however, the division was based on sexual power, the male's physical power to control women and their child bearing, then private property was not the only factor; sex played a distinct role. In socialist feminist terms, both relations of production and reproduction were relevant to women's particular oppression.

Seeking a new theoretical outlook, socialist feminism attempted to synthesize capitalism and patriarchy and to study the way in which capitalist patriarchy specifically affected women. Kinship patterns in different societies were reviewed, along with women's labor history and the dual housewife/reserve labor role played by working class women. The role of race was explored and led to writing on the interrelationship of class, sex and race. Perhaps the best developed studies related to an understanding of housework from a capitalist patriarchal perspective. Such questions as whether women, as house-workers, create surplus value, whether they should be paid, their role in maintaining and stabilizing the capitalist econ-omy and in reproducing the labor force materially, and their availability as a marginal labor force, all were investigated.

Political activity was a natural by-product of these innova-tive theoretical contributions. A substantial number of study groups and caucuses have proliferated since the seventies, and several issue-oriented organizations have been affected by socialist feminist theory. In particular, the Committee for Abortion Rights and Against Sterilization Abuse (CARASA) and the National Network for Reproductive Rights (N2 R2) have linked class and sex by supporting abortion rights and opposing sterilization abuse whose victims are overwhelm-ingly poor and minority women. These groups fought the Hyde Amendment to eliminate federally funded abortions, with the same combativeness that NOW brought to the ERA battle. But CARASA contrasted sharply with reform feminist groups which tended to downplay or ignore sterilization abuse. With a pro-choice position crossing class boundaries, CARASA is a good illustration of the political difference between socialist, as opposed to reform and even radical, feminism.

In spite of these political activities and shared principles, major controversies within socialist feminism remain to be resolved. Politically, some women distinguish between "social-ist" and "Marxist" feminists. Socialist feminists are those who believe the concept of patriarchy has some validity and are likely to work in both feminist and socialist organizations. Marxist feminists, on the other hand, tend to dismiss patri-archy altogether and concentrate solely on women's relation to capital. They are active only in Marxist organizations where they urge women to play an expanded role in formulating Marxist theory.

Corresponding to this "socialist"/"Marxist" split is a serious theoretical dilemma: has Marxism taken precedence to femi-nism in socialist feminist analyses? Heidi Hartmann, in *Women and Revolution: The Unhappy Marriage of Marxism and Feminism,* argues that socialist feminism is in fact more socialist than feminist. Other essays in the same volume express dissatisfaction with the way feminism and marxism (with a lower case m) have been wed. Hartmann suggests that socialist feminism is like English common law marriage—husband and wife are one, and that one is Marxism. That feminists who are generally critical of marriage use this institution to describe the relationship of feminism and Marxism is itself a sign of discontent. A problem area of the "marriage" is Marxism's relatively greater power as an older, more established theoretical tradition, resistant to radical change of its basic tenets, particularly when that might involve a challenge to the power arrogated by male Marxists, consciously or unconsciously, to themselves.

Even more pertinent to the unhappiness of the marriage may be the danger of socialist feminism internalizing the ideology of the "oppressor," so to speak; in this case Marxist subordination of sex to economics. Socialist feminism tends, in more subtle form, to repeat Engels' error by reducing women's oppression to a function of capital, suggesting that capitalism "needs" or "requires" it. But does capitalism actually require women's oppression? Capitalism structurally only needs labor power, a proletariat. The nature of that labor power in which men play the leading role and women are marginal, and thereby doubly oppressed, is a socially constructed variable. Under pressure from a strong feminist movement, couldn't capitalism exhibit greater flexibility and allow women equality of oppression? Couldn't it attempt to find another marginal labor force if it had to? Possibly. But to do so would entail an enormous degree of reorganization and, alas, the feminist movement is not yet strong enough to put capitalism to that test, so the question is somewhat academic. One writer who has faced the problem is Michele Barrett. In her interesting book, *Women's Oppression Today*, she criticizes "functionalist" and "reductionist" aspects of socialist feminism. But even Barrett will not make a complete break with the economic tradition. It is as if some Marxist superego were at work, enabling her to grant only "relative" autonomy to patriarchy. Ironically, after rebuking radical feminism for assigning too great a degree of autonomy to patriarchy, she awards the almost synonymous expression, "ideology of gender," a similarly independent role. However, the consequence of subordinating sex to economics is serious enough in two important respects to go beyond academic hairsplitting.

For one, it diverts attention from the political implications of sex as independent of class. For the present and foreseeable future, women must have autonomous organizations regardless of whether they live in capitalist, socialist or other societies. Second, and crucial to the future of feminist theory, is that making sexism a function of capital tends to reduce feminist support for socialism simply to self-interest, i.e., because women cannot be sexually liberated under capitalism. But what if they could? Should they no longer be anti-capitalist? Theoretically speaking, women's support for socialism must stem both from self-interest and the moral conviction that all oppression is wrong, no matter what its manifestation. Both feminists and Marxists should creatively explore the nature and philosophy of oppression to learn whether those previously oppressed will oppress others once they achieve power, a particularly relevant question for feminists who should be suspicious of equating power with purely material or economic motives.

Despite reservations, socialist feminists cannot abandon some version of "patriarchy" or concept of sexual power as independent of economic class, a "patriarchy" that has both universal and specific characteristics. (To admit that something is universal should not lead to a feeling of hopelessness, any more than the Marxist observation that all societies have been class societies precludes revolutionary change.)

It is interesting that socialist feminism borrows more from the concepts and language of Marxism than it challenges or lends in return. How many male Marxists have read *The Second Sex* compared to the number of feminists who have read *The Communist Manifesto*? With the exception of Rowbotham's discussion of decentralized politics in *Beyond the Fragments*, the relationship is usually what Marxism can do for feminism rather than what feminism can do for Marxism.

Socialist feminism plays an important role for its insistence on the inclusion of class analysis. It has also emphasized the need for historically specific as well as general descriptions of patriarchal traits. These contributions extend, modify and refine the framework of feminist thought. In and of itself, however, socialist feminism does not constitute a distinct theory separable from the ideas of radical feminism. In simple terms, socialist feminism must by nature be more feminist than socialist. Were it not for the problems specifically faced by women, why else would it exist? Forget talk of unhappy marriages and divorce. For some time to come, feminism must have a room of its own.

Socialist feminism embraces three major convictions: 1) women, necessarily the agents of their own liberation, must have autonomous organizations; 2) women are a class, united by certain characteristics and divided by others; and 3) feminism is a philosophy that seeks to eliminate all forms of human oppression. Doesn't radical feminism embrace identical principles? If so, socialist and radical feminism have much more in common politically than is generally recognized. Efforts toward creation of socialist-radical unity are more in keeping with the political objectives of a feminist movement than a socialist feminist "marriage" with Marxism.

*   *   *

How can we best unify and revitalize the movement? Although radical and reform feminists hold many beliefs in common about sexism, the reformers neither seek alternatives to the nuclear family nor do they share the radicals' opposition to capitalism. In general, radical feminism has a broader vision of feminism than reform feminism and seeks more sweeping social changes.

Consequently, although NOW is the largest feminist organization and has recently demonstrated its newly acquired political power, it does not offer an attractive option to radical feminists. Although sizable, the number of women actually active within NOW is a small proportion of the dues paying membership. Therefore, even if radicals were to join NOW and try to change it from within, they would not find a participating "mass" membership any more than socialists would find loyal millions within the amorphous organization called the Democratic Party. Both notions are based on a view of parties and organizations in the European sense. The reality is that these groups function more in terms of leadership and committees than membership participation. Difficulties in changing NOW were encountered by radical feminists in the late sixties and by sectarian groups in the seventies. More recently, many feminists have been frustrated by NOW's unwillingness to focus attention on abortion rights and sterilization abuse, in contrast to the National Abortion Rights Action League (NARAL) or CARASA (which also deals with sterilization abuse).

More important, however, just as socialists need to have their own organizational place in the American political spectrum (and ought not to be content simply to work within the Democratic Party or Americans for Democratic Action), radical and socialist feminists must have an alternative group. A new feminist organization is badly needed at present. Joining with those socialist feminists who share their ideas and want to rejuvenate the movement, radical feminists could give women another organizational option. Such an arrangement would coalesce the myriad radical and socialist feminist study groups, task forces, women's centers and caucuses into a more politically coherent entity. The result would be a new "umbrella" organization that would take a multi-faceted and multi-issued approach to feminism. Hopefully, it would encourage the development of fresh and innovative theories and explore the possibilities of community and trade union organizations of women. A flexible and decentralized structure would allow for local autonomy while maintaining the benefits of a large organization. The proposed group would in no way preclude cooperation and coalition with NOW or other reform groups on a variety of specific issues. On the contrary, cooperation would be sought and encouraged wherever possible.

The effect of this alternative, it should be emphasized, would be to revitalize and energize the movement as a whole. As Banner and others have noted, feminism, like other progressive social movements, has always benefited from the existence of a strong left wing within its ranks. The main goal of the organization would be to put feminism back on a firmer footing. Given the conservative reaction and the confusion within the radical, reform and socialist branches of feminism, a different strategy for building a movement of all women is an urgent priority.

Selected Bibliography

Atkinson, Ti-Grace, *Amazon Odyssey* (New York: Link Books, 1974).

Banner, Lois, *Women in Modern America: A Brief History* (New York: Harcourt, Brace, Jovanovich, 1974).

Barrett, Michele, *Women's Oppression Today: Problems in Marxist Feminist Analysis* (London: Verso Editions, 1980).

Daly, Mary, *Gyn Ecology* (Boston: Beacon Press, 1978).

Davis, Elizabeth Gould, *The First Sex* (New York: G.P. Putnam, 1971).

De Beauvoir, Simone, *The Second Sex* (Harmondsworth: Penguin, 1974).

Eisenstein, Zillah, ed., *Capitalist Patriarchy and the Case for Socialist Feminism* (New York: Monthly Review Press, 1979).

Firestone, Shulamith, *The Dialectic of Sex* (New York: Bantam, 1971).

Friedan, Betty, *The Feminine Mystique* (New York: Norton, 1963).

The Second Stage (New York: Summit Books, 1981).

Hartmann, Heidi, "The Unhappy Marriage of Marxism and Feminism," in *Women and Revolution: The Unhappy Marriage of Marxism and Feminism*, ed. Lydia Sargent (Boston: South End Press, 1981).

Kuhn, Annette, and AnnMarie Wolpe, eds., *Feminism and Materialism* (London: Routledge and Kegan Paul, 1978).

Millett, Kate, *Sexual Politics* (London: Sphere, 1970).

Mitchell, Juliet, *Women's Estate* (New York: Bantam, 1976).

Rowbotham, Sheila, *Woman's Consciousness, Man's World* (Middlesex: Penguin Books, 1973).

Rowbotham, Sheila, Lynne Segal and Hilary Wainright, *Beyond the Fragments: Feminism and the Making of Socialism* (London: Merlin, 1979).

Rubin, Gayle, "The Traffic in Women: Notes on the 'Political Economy' of Sex," in *Toward an Anthropology of Women*, ed. R. Reiter (New York: Monthly Review Press, 1975).

Sargent, Lydia, ed., *Women and Revolution: The Unhappy Marriage of Marxism and Feminism* (Boston: South End Press, 1981).

Reflections on Fascism and Communism

JULIUS JACOBSON

"STALINISM IS THE MOST SUCCESSFUL VARIANT OF FASCISM." With that pronunciamento, made at the American Workers and Artists for Solidarity rally, Susan Sontag became the eye of a political storm. Oscillating between the penitential and accusatorial, which charged the atmosphere and added a touch of theater to the event, her mea culpas and belated revelations about the unrelieved malevolence of Communist societies met with boos and hisses from a good part of the audience at Town Hall. And hardly had the meeting been adjourned when dozens took to their typewriters, providing several publications with an editorial glut. Unfortunately, the polemical torrent has been reduced to a trickle, which is both telling and sad because Sontag's concerns are neither trivial nor arcane. They involve basic evaluations (re-evaluations for Sontag) of myth and reality in the Communist world past and present; questions of history, politics, social and moral values relevant to the fate of us all and of special significance for those who consider themselves of the left.

It was not only declared at the meeting but made explicit in many of the letters to various editors (at least a majority of those published) that Sontag's equation of Communism and fascism was prima facie evidence that she had defected from

---

JULIUS JACOBSON *edited* Anvil *and the Marxist Journal,* The New International. *He is an associate author of* The American Communist Party: A Critical History *(1919-1957), Beacon Press, 1957, and edited* The Negro and the American Labor Movement, *Anchor Books, 1968 and* Soviet Communism and the Socialist Vision, *Transaction Books, 1972. He was the editor of* New Politics, *a journal of socialist thought, in which many of his articles appeared.*

the left to join forces with the neo-conservative right. Jessica Mitford, for example, found that "the logical conclusion implicit in Susan Sontag's speech" is "first strike, anyone?" Gary Wills didn't go so far as suggesting that Sontag's equation implies nuclear holocaust but was content to charge her with borrowing from the anti-Communist arguments of the *Readers Digest* and of having become a sort of latter-day McCarthyite: she aims "to shame the Left for having believed in the authenticity of anti-colonial movements, the untenability of Chiang's position, the nationalist tensions between China and Russia, and the fictive character of Senator McCarthy's 'investigation.' " Another letter writer shot from the hip: if Sontag visits Miami's "little Havana" she will be "flanked by ex-National Guardsmen from Anastasio Somoza's regime; and that they will give her a cocktail party funded from the drug money that also feeds the Cuban terrorists." A Chicago union functionary rebuked *The Nation* for printing Sontag at all, advising that weekly to "leave anti-communism and Soviet-baiting in the paws of yahoo scribblers for ultraright magazines." An equally elegant indictment was handed down by another moralist, Abby Hoffman, who believes that "Sontag's song would have been best sung in chorus with Bob Hope and Frank Sinatra, not from the stage of Town Hall." And again we have the image of Sontag as a one-person-nuclear-threat from another correspondent, who didn't like "reviving the rhetoric of the Cold War, escalating the military budget" and warned that "increasing nuclear tensions do nothing to help the people of Poland, Afghanistan, etc." and concludes: "Why not give peace a chance?" An irate black woman delivered the following low blow: "I would opt for Joseph Stalin over a Strom Thurmond or a Jesse Helms any day. Under Stalin I could only vote for one 'president.' Under Thurmond or Helms, none." (Of course, under Stalin she might be dead.)

Thus for many, Sontag, through her equation, becomes a nuclear menace, spiritual heir of the infamous Wisconsin McCarthy, consort of American racists and Latin American killers, perhaps even a scribbler. To be fair, not all the critical responses were on this primitive level; some were better reasoned. There were also letters of support, only a few of which were interesting. However, a splendid article-length comment by Jacobo Timmerman, titled "Moral Symmetry," appeared in the March 6, 1982 issue of *The Nation*. And in her moving essay on life in South Africa, "Living in the Interregnum" (*New York Review of Books,* January 20, 1983), Nadine Gordimer concludes with a thoughtful discussion of the issues raised by Sontag.

Special mention must be reserved for Alexander Cockburn in whose *Village Voice* columns muddied political waters were so roiled that they occasionally emitted a whiff of old fashioned Stalinist villification. In a discussion of the Costa Gavras film, *Missing,* he gratuitously entered Susan Sontag's name and formulation:

> Is it so much the spirit of our times that the unspeakable or the unjust can never be faced: that the US contrived the overthrow of Arbenz; promoted the execution of a million Indonesian communists; murdered Vietnamese by the hundreds of thousands; tolerated and sustained torture and butchery in Latin America?
>
> All is *forgiven,* because all is forgotten. *A la Sontag, communism becomes fascism and vice versa.* [Emphasis added.] Between the two goes the US, treading the middle way, supporting El Salvador generals for a half-century and then feeling especially virtuous for forcing some National Guardsmen into the dock for murdering the nuns. It doesn't take much to purge the imperial conscience.

Note the insidious weaving, à la Vyshinsky, of Sontag's name and point of view with moods, tendencies, even culpable regimes, prepared to tolerate, forgive, forget, perhaps be complicitous in, the torture, execution, butchery of millions in Indonesia, Vietnam and Latin America. At least there are no "fascist mad-dogs."*

---

* In the finest tradition of Stalinist amalgams, Cockburn recently (*Village Voice,* January 4, 1983) linked Norman Podhoretz and George Orwell, "As far as I'm concerned, Podhoretz and Orwell deserve each other." What moves Cockburn to couple a Reaganite reactionary with the author of *Homage to Catalonia* who fought alongside the revolutionary POUM in Spain? The answer might be found in his "From Brezhnev to Andropov—Yuri-Communism: What Is Its Future?" (*Village Voice,* November 23, 1983). From it one might conclude that it is Cockburn and Andropov who deserve each other.

If the equation Communism equals fascism implies that "all is forgiven, because all is forgotten" vis-à-vis the crimes of American imperialism, the formula must also imply that where the crimes of Stalinism have been forgotten, as in Hungary and Czechoslovakia, there, too, "all is forgiven, because all is forgotten." The Communism equals fascism formula would then be transformed from an intended equivalency of evil to an apologia for both Communism and capitalism, with Susan Sontag thereby becoming less a convert to the right than an unmitigated fool.

HAS SONTAG MOVED TO THE RIGHT? Is she the latest recruit to the French "New Philosophers" as Cockburn also intimated? Little in her remarks per sé supports the charge. On the contrary, Sontag clearly separated herself from the Janus-faced right which laments the plight of the Polish people and simultaneously supports or rationalizes oppression and terror in rightist dictatorships. The meeting, she noted, was not only being held to support the "democratic workers' movement in Poland" but "to stake out a different kind of support for Poland than that tendered by, say, Reagan, Haig and Thatcher." Answering her critics in *The Nation*, she wrote of the "democratic movement in El Salvador whose struggle to overthrow the tyranny backed by the American government I passionately support."

For many of her critics, this is not enough to validate her democratic credentials. All they heard was her now total renunciation of the Stalinist church and that remains an unforgivable political heresy for those to whom unambiguous opposition to totalitarianism *as a social system* becomes a confession of rightwing guilt. It is to commit the sin of "fanatical anti-Communism" (no one ever speaks disparagingly of "fanatical anti-fascism"), as if to pin such labels on accused heretics absolves the accuser from the responsibility to answer arguments rationally or to review one's past allegiances and present commitments in the light of history.

Perhaps, when all is said and done, Sontag will move to the right. It is certainly true that many who discard all illusions about Stalinism are so traumatized by their new awareness that they lose the ability to distinguish between the perverse "false consciousness" of Stalinism (or "Communism")* and the political and moral values of authentic radical and socialist movements; not only is Communism now evil but the whole notion of socialism becomes utopian at best or criminal at worst.

In any case, Sontag's political evolution is of far less interest and importance than the respective merits of the *two* contradictory formulations made at the Solidarity rally—the first, of course, is Sontag's view that Communism is successful fascism; the second formulation, made by her most vigorous critics, places an equal sign between Sontag's position and capitulation to the right. The latter position is indefensible, and what it suggests will be discussed later. But if many of Sontag's critics reject her view unfairly, that does not make her position, as presented at the meeting, unimpeachable. Sontag, or others who accept her equation, are obliged to make clear, at some point, on what level the equivalency of fascism and Communism is made. Is it an assertion of an ideological and class affinity of Communist and fascist societies? Or is it only intended to summarize, in an immediate descriptive and human sense, the similar levels of violence and oppression both use to achieve and retain power?

The Equation Viewed Sociologically

ANYONE WHO TRIES TO IDENTIFY Communism and fascism in a precise sociological sense would be hard-pressed to make a

---

* The terms "Communism" and "Stalinism" are used interchangeably in this article. Russia, China, Cuba, Vietnam, etc., are all Stalinist countries in that they share the basic socio-economic class character of Russian society as it emerged under Stalin's rule. However, the term "Stalinist" is so closely associated in the public consciousness with the extraordinary violence of Stalin's dictatorship that there is an understandable resistance to using "Stalinism" as a generic descriptive term. As difficult as it is for a communist to surrender the term "Communist" to the Stalinist enemy, it is best to do so for the sake of clarity.

My own descriptive preference is for the term, bureaucratic collectivism, convincing case. On that level, differences and contradictions do exist that are serious and politically relevant.

Historically, fascism is the brutal response of a beleaguered capitalist class threatened by a profound economic and social crisis and menaced by a rebellious working class. Seeking stability, fearful for its very existence, the ruling class can no longer tolerate even the limited freedoms of bourgeois democracy. It seeks salvation, instead, in a semi-autonomous state which supresses traditional liberties, tames the working class and even circumscribes the rights of the capitalist class as a whole, as it continues to protect much of the power and privileges of private capital.

"Communism" (or bureaucratic collectivism, i.e., Stalinism as a social system), on the other hand, can be defined as a society in which politics transcends economics; where the means of production are owned and controlled by the state and the state is owned and controlled by a single party. The viability of this society depends on its ability to destroy the owners of private capital as an economic class and a political force (possibly permitting agrarian and minor vestiges of a market economy), to suppress all opposition and, above all else, to prevent or contain any manifestation of economic or political independence by its working class. Democratic rights, cultural autonomy and intellectual freedom are inimical to a ruling class which consists not of representatives of the working class or of bankers and industrialists but of the leading luminaries of the all powerful Communist Party and its subordinate government administrative and military bureaucracies.

THESE DIFFERENT CLASS STRUCTURES imply differences in social cohesiveness and suggest the theoretical limits to internal change in each society. Take Spain and Russia as prototypical systems. Franco's mission in the thirties was to preserve the Spanish bourgeoisie from the threat of godlessness, anarchy and socialism. He serviced his class well. But neither the

---

which sums up the view that Russia is neither socialist nor communist nor capitalist but a society where social control of the "collectivized" means of production is exercised by a new exploitative ruling class whose "executive committee" consists of the Communist Party's top bureaucrats.

Falange in particular nor fascism in general had a quintessential, permanent relationship to capitalism. Without capitalism there can be no fascism, but the converse is not true. In Spain, in Germany, in Italy, capitalism has survived and, arguably, benefited from the fall of fascism.

In Russia—and Communist societies in general—the same dichotomy between class and governing authority could not exist for any extended period, for there the Communist Party is the counterpart of *both* the bourgeois *class* and the fascist *state*. To challenge the Party is to challenge the ruling class and the converse *is* true.

In Russia the politically organized ruling class operates on a sophisticated level of class consciousness. It sees more clearly than many of Sontag's critics that any attempt to deprive the Party of its authority is at the same time, consciously or not, an attempt to undermine Communism as a social system. The Party can ease its terror but it cannot surrender what it euphemistically calls its "leading role." In all economic planning and state organs, in the military, in the judicial system, in the state-owned company "unions," etc. the Party must be eternally (sometimes murderously) vigilant in guarding and enhancing its supremacy.

There was not the same class rooted compulsion for Franco to weave Spain's social fabric so tightly. The fact is that after 35 years of fascist rule, the Falange was not able either to absorb or fully neutralize other potentially competitive institutions, bureaucracies and political tendencies—e.g., the church, state sponsored "unions," monarchists. This looser social organization of fascism compared to totalitarian Communism left Franco comparatively vulnerable to lateral pressures as well as to more basic resistance from below. By the seventies many a Spanish bourgeois had come to view fascism as an economic encumbrance and a political liability.

Spanish fascism, its power eroded for decades by internal stress and resistance, was toppled in a massive popular upheaval which raised the specter of socialist revolution but, unfortunately, fell short of achieving a fundamental change in class rule. A parallel move to dispossess the ruling Party in Russia, unlike in Spain, would automatically raise the level of confrontation from one evoking the mere specter of socialism to a social revolutionary struggle aimed at expropriating the ruling class.

(Here it best be noted, at least parenthetically, that to describe Communism as more total in its social controls than fascism is not to picture the latter as benign. A particular fascist society can be more loosely controlled from above than a particular Communist state and, at the same time, be more cruel.)

THE NOTION OF COMMUNISM AS NOT MERELY a variant of fascism but the "most successful" variant, when permitted to stand by itself, is also flawed in that it suggestively imputes to Communism a homogeneity and invincibility that is simply not the case. Just as Spanish, Italian and German fascism rarely operated as a single unified force, Communism in power reveals anything but a spirit of mutual accommodation and dedication to an internationalist ideal. The historical circumstances (e.g., national and cultural traditions, internal opposition, unique economic needs, etc.) of the rise to power vary from one Communist country to another, leading to antagonisms and sometimes combustible contradictions within the Communist world.

Even a brief look at the different sources of power in Russia, Poland and China shows that on a meaningful historical level, Sontag's formula has more shock value than educational merit.

In Russia, the Stalinist ruling class emerged out of the ashes of the Russian revolution, not as a mythic phoenix, but as a brutal form of historical retribution for the inability of Russian socialism to withstand the corrosive and corrupting impact of years of civil war, hunger and isolation. In the twenties, Stalin, and the Communist Party he already dominated, instinctively moved to fill a threatening void. And fill it they did, with terror, slave labor and graves. Factories were also built but the foundations for this industrialization (and collectivization) were the bones and blood of millions upon millions of victims. (It was an industrialization that was about as "socially progressive" as the growth of German industry from 1933-1939. Hitler, too, reduced unemployment.)

The current Russian ruling class, then, emerged from *within* at a time when no traditional class appeared to have the vigor and resources for reorganizing society.

Poland was different. There, without a mass base, with a large percentage of its cadres systematically murdered by Stalin and Hitler during the war years, the Kremlim picked up the Polish Communist Party by its emaciated neck and returned it in Russian tanks to Warsaw, where it was enthroned as a new ruling class before whom the Polish masses were ordered to kneel and say their Hail Josephs. But potential discord is built into the ambiguous relationship between an imperialist power and its colonial compradores, torn between dependence on and fear of their foreign benefactors, on the one hand, and allegiance to their own national class and personal ambitions on the other. And Poland provided excellent soil for the seeds of discontent to germinate. In addition to the Poles' traditional animus toward things Russian, there were the more recent bitter memories: the Nazi-Soviet pact, which gave the green light for the Wehrmacht's blitzkrieg; the Russian massacre of 10-15,000 Polish officers in the Katyn forest in 1941; the enslavement and physical liquidation of countless thousands of Polish socialists, Communists, Bundists, of nationalists and of Jews; the slaughter of Poles by Germans in the 1944 Warsaw uprising under the watchful eyes of a nearby Russian army led by Marshal Rokossovsky who was ordered to allow Warsaw and its citizens to burn before launching a Red Army assault to "liberate" the city.

While the Polish ruling class is a feeble and unreliable ally for the Russians, in other Communist countries the Kremlin has deadly enemies, above all, in China. There, the Communist Party did not move in to fill a threatening social vacuum as in Russia and it was not artificially imposed as in Poland. It was a genuine mass movement which conquered a strong foe (a foe backed by the most powerful country in the world, the US) after 20 years of civil war. Mao used Stalin's techniques—bloody purges, genocide, gulags—to consolidate the rule of the Party, but emulation is not obeisance. The Chinese Party could afford to and does operate independently of the Kremlin, motivated more by its own national class interests, including territorial ambitions, than by concern for long range international, ideological and class concerns.

The similarities, then, in class rule in Poland, Russia and China provide no greater impetus for collaboration than the common class denominator in capitalist counties has served to save mankind from the slaughter of capitalist wars.

Had Sontag coupled her formulation with an acknowledgment of this diversity and rivalry within the Communist world, some of her critics might have been a bit less indignant. Her failure to do so created the impression that Communism is a massive international conspiracy, which conjured up a rerun of McCarthyite hysteria.

This disorder and disarray within the Communist world also suggests that Communism is not quite as "successful" as Sontag might have us believe. Volcanic pressures from below have erupted throughout Eastern Europe and exist within the mother country as well.

*　　*　　*

SONTAG'S COMMUNISM-EQUALS-SUCCESSFUL-FASCISM FORMULA seemed confined to an equivalency between the two as *state powers*. How does one compare fascism and Communism *ideologically* when out of power? Can *Communists* be equated with *fascists*? Can Communist and fascist controlled organizations be coupled and is there an identity between fascist and Communist parties as opposition movements? The answers provide clues to understanding the essence of each movement and how radicals and socialists can most effectively counter the influence of both.

To present Communism as simply a variant of fascism runs the risk of obscuring important ideological distinctions. Fascism occasionally borrows some of the terminology of populism, even of socialism: it is against the "Big Bankers," "the monied interests," etc., but its propaganda is more heavily weighted with appeals that are blatantly primitive and base. It plays on and promotes racial prejudices and chauvinism. It is the force of "national salvation" committed to a holy war against Communism and Marxism.

The ideological trappings of bureaucratic collectivism are another matter. Stalinist barbarism is adorned with a human face; a mask it must wear. Brezhnev cannot burn socialist libraries in Red Square; he can only choose selectively what appears on Party bookshelves, censor others and consign the rest to oblivion.

The zeal with which Stalinism strives to preserve its false socialist image flows from its efforts to seek a popular mass base in the working class and, generally, among poor and exploited peoples. It also seeks a special place of respect and authority among intellectuals. Here, Sontag's equation, when offered without qualifications, can be misleading and dangerous for those of us who are committed to fighting Stalinism not only on an intellectual level but in real political life. For the endemic need of Communism to find a mass base in the working class, particularly where it is not in power, and to present itself as a force for social justice, puts Communist organizations into direct competition with authentic socialists and radicals. (The armies of fascism also seek proletarian recruits but not in the same way and seldom with any degree of success; their cadres come primarily from the middle class and the military, with shock troops provided by declassed and marginal elements.)

Thus, in trade unions, civil rights organizations, the feminist and peace movements, etc., where our paths cross with Communists and their sympathizers, it behooves the socialist left to reach out to those activists whose acceptance of or sympathy with Communism may be subjectively motivated by idealistic sentiments and passions similar to those that move radicals and socialists to an uncompromising rejection of Communist totalitarianism. This paradoxical relationship of the anti-Stalinist (or anti-Communist) left to Communists was properly understood and acted upon in decades past, when Communist parties were even more intransigent than they are today.

A nostalgic example, at least for this writer: on the agenda of local leftwing socialist meetings, there was often the quaintly worded subject of "opponents work." This never referred to work among or within fascist organizations—what could be accomplished there?—but most often to efforts made to win over Communists and their sympathizers within Communist front organizations and sometimes to more clandestine operations within the Communist Party itself or its youth affiliate. It was understood that for all the moral equivalency and political symmetry that could be drawn between Communist and fascist *societies*, on an individual, human level fascism and Stalinism were not equal. The recruits that the socialist left found in Stalinist parties and their peripheral organizations could never have been drawn from the Silver Shirts, Coughlinites, the Liberty League or the KKK.

WE HAVE NOTED THE DIFFERENCE between Communists and fascists as *individuals*. But what does it mean to sum up Communism as "successful fascism" with respect to *organizations* controlled by Communists? It is inconceivable that any radical or socialist would suggest a positive approach to, say, some component part of the Moral Majority. It is, or should be, no less far fetched for the same radical or socialist to reject dogmatically involvement in any organization controlled by Communists, presumably agents of "successful fascism."

Communism draws on the terminology and traditions of Marxism (at the same time violating both); it speaks of peace and social justice (as it mass produces nuclear weapons and jails peace activists); its manifestos reject imperialism and denounce racism (as it overruns weaker nations and practices genocide). But it is the surface propaganda and appeal of Communism which concern us at the moment. What counts here, as has been noted before, is that Communism, when operating as an opposition force in bourgeois society, is driven by an inner dynamic to win the allegiance of the broad mass of people. It is driven, above all, to establish itself as a force *within* the organized labor movement—the trade unions. Consequently, Communists, when out of power, can be responsive to the needs and interests of workers in given situations up to the point where working class gains might conflict with Communist political objectives. By contrast, fascism lacks this incentive of its allegedly successful twin and operates *outside* of and in violent opposition to the union movement.

The Equation Viewed
on the Human Level

I HAVE NOTED A FEW OF THE theoretical and practical political problems raised by the fascist-Communist equation when offered as a precise, historical equivalency. But how does one determine in human, moral terms if Hitler(ism) was more/less evil or more/less inhuman than Stalin(ism)? By numbers killed? Hitler destroyed 6 million Jews and millions of others in the death camps, and the figure would soar if we added all the others murdered in the 12 year history of the Third Reich. What about Stalin's toll? In the decade after Stalin emerged ascendant in the late twenties, there was the forced collectivization in the Ukraine with death as its major harvest. Additional millions were killed in the purges and in an unprecedented concentration camp system. All in all, it is cautiously estimated that in the longer span of Stalin's rule there were 15 million corpses to testify to the achievements of a man and a Party speaking in the name of socialist brotherhood and singing the *Internationale*.

Are we to measure the humanity or inhumanity of each system by an average-per-year body count?

Is it a matter of comparing the techniques of mass murder? Hitler used the unimaginably grisly method of the gas chamber and the ovens. Stalin relied on more traditional techniques of starvation, torture, executions. Is there a basic moral difference?

Is there a moral choice to be made between the imperialist ambitions of a Hitler that turned to dust and the reality of Stalin's expansionism? Through the use of military force, sometimes "legitimized" by fraudulent elections, Russia subjugated Eastern Europe and the Balkans. (The three culturally distinct Baltic nations had been absorbed in 1941 as an integral part of Imperial Stalinist Russia.)

The level of cruelty that Hitler would have used to contain liberation movements had he succeeded in subjugating Europe is not difficult to imagine. But the methods by which Stalin and his successors crushed national resistance movements is a matter of record—armed intervention and unleashing the terror apparatus of Quisling parties. There were Communist tanks against the rebellious stone throwing workers of East Berlin in 1953. The Hungarian socialist revolution of 1956 drowned in blood by Russian storm troopers. The tragic repetition of Hungary in Czechoslovakia 12 years later. There was Poland 1956 and 1970 and 1976 and 1982.

On this count, are the sins of Stalinism to be viewed tolerantly relative to what one might imagine would have occurred under the reign of a triumphant Nazi Germany?

131

We need not limit ourselves to comparisons of Hitlerism and Stalinism. How does the Russian invasion of Hungary measure up to Mussolini's bombs dropped on Ethiopian villages? (Let us not forget that the Italian army at the time was fueled, in part, by Russian oil.) Which act was more acceptable in its perfidy? What of Stalinist Cuba, where the state jails its critics, has executed opponents when it felt the need to do so, denies workers the right to strike, prohibits the formation of opposition parties, supports every imperialist outrage committed by the Russian bureaucratic ruling class? Is a Cuban gendarme, humiliating homosexuals as he herds them through public avenues en route to a "rehabilitation" center, more acceptable than his fascist counterpart because he is decked out in a Guevara beret? The poet, Armando Valladares, was imprisoned for 22 years (the last six on a starvation diet that crippled him) because he criticized the Maximum Leader. Is that more moral than the barbaric treatment of opponents in Spanish prisons during El Caudillo's reign?

What about the horrors of Maoism? Its persecution of an entire nation, the widespread use of torture and public executions by "cultural" killers? And isn't the evidence there, for all willing to see, that while Mao's successors have reduced the deceased Chairman from god to fallible, even miserable, human dimensions, the Chinese people remain the victims of a totalitarian ruling Party that cannot abide political liberties? Is Communist China's denial of basic human rights a lesser or greater evil than the outrages that were committed in, say, Franco's dungeons?

What are the comparative grades for the Cambodian Khmer Rouge and the Chilean dictatorship? In Cambodia the Communists beat, stoned and shot to death a significant portion of their own population. The Chilean dictatorship tortured and killed thousands upon thousands of opponents real and alleged. Is one preferable to the other? To be sure, the Reagan "intellectuals" make a choice. They prefer the Chilean, Salvadoran and other rightwing dictatorships, especially those, no matter how barbaric, that are allies of the US. No one on the left should succumb to the same immoral approach by apologizing for, or minimizing, the venality of Communist dictatorships.

The simple human realities of each system make it impossible to decide which is more, or less, brutal. There can be no scorecard. Let us say that, on balance, it is a draw, that on this level fascism and Stalinism meet as *equals* in the inferno of authoritarian/totalitarian repression.

IN SEVERAL OTHER RESPECTS—political, cultural and psychological—there is more than a modicum of merit in the Communism-fascism equation. They share common enemies and deeply rooted phobias. Neither fascism nor Stalinism can coexist internally with any institutional manifestation of working class independence, neither can permit genuine trade unions, nor can they tolerate an uncensored press, legal opposition parties, freedom of speech or any of the civil and political rights to which all are entitled and which are the very soul of socialism. Sexism is an essential feature of fascism; similarly, there is no Communist state that has overcome sexual repression, or is interested in doing so. (Women in Russia are allowed the right to hard labor for meager wages, along with their domestic duties. But a list of women holding important positions in what are, at least theoretically, decision-making bodies, would hardly fill a 3 x 5 index card.)

Also freedom of cultural expression and experimentation are clearly unacceptable to any modern ruling class which demands absolute political obedience. Instead, "art" is put into the service of the state and what emerges as a substitute are heroic novels, odes to leaders, lifeless romantic portraits, posters of muscular workers fulfilling production quotas, hideous totalitarian architecture (to borrow Norman Mailer's term). Modernism and innovation are "decadent" or "bourgeois" or "antisocial," always dangerous and, as genuine artistic expression, driven underground in Communist as well as fascist societies.

Finally, psychologically, the impact of Communist Party rule on the individual can hardly be less devastating than it is in fascist societies. A quantitative comparison of the extent to which individuals are alienated in authoritarian and totalitarian states is obviously impossible. On the other hand, one need not be a trained sociologist or psychologist or Marxologist to understand that in fascist and Communist societies, where the individual is deprived of any authority at the point of production or on any level of the political process, where self-expression is repressed, sometimes criminalized, where work is hard, luxuries scarce, where the state attempts to regulate personal lives from thought processes to sensual pursuits, that in both societies, more or less equally, the individual is beset by a degree of loneliness, frustration and fear that many in the Western left fail to grasp.

*　　*　　*

NEITHER SONTAG NOR MANY OF THOSE who booed her may be aware that comparisons of fascism and Communism have a long and interesting history, as old as the anti-Stalinist left. In the thirties and forties it was all part of the larger "Russian Question," the nature of Stalinism in and out of power, debated by social democrats, anarchists, revolutionary Marxists. Some came to the conclusion that Russia was a form of "industrial feudalism," others thought it "state capitalist," there were those who believed Russia was dominated by a new reactionary "bureaucratic collectivist" class and still others who clung to the notion that Russia was a "degenerated workers state." In the course of those polemics, parallels between fascism and Stalinism were debated with considerable vigor. Norman Thomas wrote a book, *Red Fascism*, Trotsky found a political symmetry between fascism and Stalinism, Franz Neumann discussed in depth what he believed to be their similarities, yet they and other radicals, some of whom saw an identity of the two systems, not mere parallels, were not therefore expelled from the radical community, cast into the nether world of reaction, by those who disagreed.

Why, then, should Sontag's borrowed use of an old, if controversial, concept within the socialist movement have so shaken her audience? Obviously it was a political response. But more than that, it was also a response to Sontag's "style," a reaction to someone who came to address the rally with hostile intent.

Here was a meeting to support Solidarity, not to apologize to the Russians, yet the manner in which Sontag addressed the gathering smacked of a prosecutor holding her listeners complicitous in the crimes of Communism. If there was any doubt that Sontag meant her formula to provoke, not influence, it was put to rest by Sontag herself in an interview with Charles Ruas

(*N.Y. Times Book Review*, 24 October 1982) when, referring to her role at the Solidarity rally, she recognized that "I said something I wasn't supposed to say, and I knew what I was doing. I knew I would be booed and I would make some enemies there. The idea of it is you were supposed to be a good guy and be mobilized for the pro-Poland rally on February 6 and the anti-nuclear rally on June 12. I didn't want to do that anymore."

If Sontag didn't want to be a "good guy" any more where Poland is concerned, why did she accept the invitation to speak in support of Solidarity? She clearly had no intention of seeking any rapport with her audience. The torch of her new-found enlightenment was used as a club, its flame emitting more smoke than illumination. Her presentation was predicated on a total misunderstanding of the current state of the left. There was not the slightest suggestion of awareness that the audience at the Solidarity rally was representative of an American left far more conscious of the nature of Stalinism than earlier left-wing movements, as evidenced by its readiness to rally *against* Communist oppression.*

Consider that, in the late thirties, the American Communist Party had perhaps 100,000 members and controlled a vast net-

---

* The overall "left," which I believe has moved closer to an awareness of Communist realities compared to the attitudes of decades past, is neither homogeneous nor organizationally identifiable. Some are members of pacifist organizations, others are affiliated to the Democratic Socialists of America, but the left as a whole is manifest more in a "literary" sense, revolving around radical publications such as *The Nation, In These Times, Radical America, Working Papers, Mother Jones, Monthly Review* and books published by South End Press and Monthly Review Press.

While the readership of these journals and books represents the large majority of the political left, moving in an anti-Stalinist direction, I am also aware of the smaller counter-tendency represented by the proliferation of tiny sects that have moved into the camp of Stalinism and neo-Stalinism. My argument is not with them for they strike me as impervious to reason, frozen in a state of intellectual rigor mortis for which I know no cure. Between these sects and the broad left there is the school of "official Trotskyism," which I place in quotation marks, for it, too, is part of the counter-tendency, in my opinion, adopting positions which have as little relationship to the anti-Stalinist spirit and politics of Trotsky as the chauvinism of Stalin in the twenties had to the revolutionary politics of Lenin. Can one imagine a Trotsky wooing a Castro today?

It is with the broader "literary" left that I am primarily concerned here.

work of social, cultural and political peripheral organizations. Its influence in the trade union movement was strong and on the rise. If Stalinism did not look like the wave of the American future, it nonetheless made more than ripples in political waters. Its members not only enjoyed the sense of belonging to a Party that could make a practical difference at home, there was also the psychological uplift provided by the reality of power in the Soviet Union of which they were all made to feel somehow a part.

In contrast, the anti-Stalinist left was pathetically weak in numbers and influence. The Socialist Party was little more than a sect, and the revolutionary anti-Stalinist left—the Trotskyists—was a sect. I can bear witness that to be in the latter was a lonely existence. For it was a sect with the towering mission of building the vanguard party that would lead the masses in struggle against the bourgeois state, with the simultaneous task of destroying the influence of Stalinism, an ideology Trotsky aptly called the cancer of the labor movement. Thus a puny David taking on two Goliaths. To survive politically and psychologically, idealism had to be reinforced with a powerful sense of history and tempered by a sense of irony and good humor, since, while we may have had the correct program, they—the Stalinists—at least in comparison to us, had the masses.

It was a time when the Stalinists could fill Madison Square Garden while the forces of revolutionary socialism had to settle for a New York City-wide rally drawing, at best, 300 friends, relatives and "contacts" to Irving Plaza.

And now? While radicals today cannot fill the Garden, they did manage to fill Town Hall in defense of Solidarity. How large a hall can the Communist enemies of Solidarity fill in New York? How many will demonstrate in the streets on behalf of the Polish junta? Reflect for a moment that in New York City, the bastion of American Stalinism in its halcyon days, Communism as a conscious, organized political force has been reduced to virtual nothingness. Now *they* are immobilized. And it will not do to ascribe this impotence to fear of exposure, persecution, repression, etc. It reflects a profound crisis in a Communist world that would still like all to see it as far more "successful" than it is. There is no reason to help it out in the image-making department.

Compare the attitudes of the left today with those of the New Left in the late sixties and early seventies. Neither the Prague spring of 1968 nor the summer roll of Russian tanks which overwhelmed it aroused more than a desultory note of disapproval in the left. Bear in mind that during those epic events Dubcek never kneeled before a Pope, nor were there ties to a Catholic Church for Stalinist apologists to exploit propagandistically. The Revolution was not avowedly anti-Communist; it was actually led by a wing of the Party and it aspired to "Socialism with a Human Face." Thus, whatever liabilities the New Left of that period might have found in the equivalent of a Polish revolution were absent in the Czechoslovakian. Still the New Leftists offered little support.

In 1982, there was an outpouring of radicals to demonstrate solidarity with Solidarity, and the leftwing press took up its cause despite the fact that socialism is not inscribed on its banners and the revolution is clearly anti-Communist. Moreover, the role of the Catholic Church and the image of Walesa genuflecting before the Pope has not proved to be the liability it would most certainly have been for a potential radical audience in the sixties. Here, too, the differences are instructive, revealing a left today that is more mature, with wider concerns and fewer illusions about the nature of Communism than the New Left of the earlier decade, again indicating a degree of failure, not success, of Communism. This represents an historic shift whose significance and worth are apparently lost on someone determined to let the world know that she will no longer be a "good guy."

*   *   *

BUT THE OVERT HOSTILITY TO SONTAG and to the notion that Communism can be equated to fascism was more than a backlash against brusquely presented, uncongenial views. The intensity of the resentment and the political content it was given show that old barriers, although lowered, have yet to be scaled by the left on the road toward the full realization that the Polish people are the victims of a *social system* (call it Communist or Stalinist or bureaucratic collectivist) that is totally retrograde. One might have hoped that the cracks in the Communist world would prove wide enough for all on the left to see that in these totalitarian animal farms, freedom is terror and

Communism is anti-communism. Yet, there are those who, even while deploring the Kremlin's role in Poland and the anti-dissident campaign in Russia, continue to talk about basic reform "from above" in Communist states whose rulers "above" are preoccupied with the task of smashing recalcitrants "below." Above all, what clouds the perception of this segment of the left is the somewhat less than grand illusion that somewhere, somehow, even if only remotely, there is something fundamentally progressive about Communist societies. At the very least, they are more progressive than capitalism. Called into play by some is a ritualistic reliance on "nationalized economy" to give weight to shibboleths about Russia being "socially progressive." But a "nationalized economy" divorced from popular control and under the aegis of a political tyranny should have no greater charm for a socialist than a privately owned General Motors.

In and of itself, a nationalized economy is neither reactionary nor progressive; it depends on who controls the state. Nor can a nationalized economy determine the methods and the pace of industrialization. Where the economy is nationalized, only the state—whether controlled from above or, democratically, from below—can decide when and how to accelerate economic growth. This is crucial to our discussion because it is in Russia's forced industrialization in the thirties and its aftermath that so many seek validation of the "socially progressive" credentials of the Stalinist economic system. By attributing industrial growth to the imperatives of the nationalized economy rather than to the Communist Party's conscious policy of consolidating its supreme political-economic hegemony, the horrors of Russia's forced industrialization are minimized in favor of a dazzling display of economic growth statistics. Behind the statistical curtain can be seen:

• An upheavel that inflicted more suffering than any bourgeois industrial revolution, with millions of peasants, workers, and kulaks the *inevitable* victims of *Stalinist* industrialization.

• An upheaval in which the primary target was not the "remnants of capitalism" but the "remnants of socialism." The leaders of the Bolshevik revolution, its cadres, and all socialist and anarchist tendencies had to be liquidated and the road closed to any revival of Soviet democracy.

• An upheaval in which the beneficiaries were: *the Party*, whose totalitarian supremacy, under the aegis of Stalin, was established by the industrial counterrevolution and which became a new exploitative, economically privileged class that knew how to enjoy the perquisites of power (today, the Stalinist nouveaux riches have their dachas, chauffeur-driven limousines, the finest food from special commissaries where they do not have to queue up, and enough pocket money left to buy wardrobes of designer jeans on the black market); *the military*, for which the planned economy allocates whatever is necessary—at the expense of the consuming public (as in the US)—to build enough nuclear warheads to end all debate in all places for all times. For *the masses*, the benefits of Stalinist industrialization are more visible in the euphoria of some in the Western left than in their cupboards.

Homage is paid to Stalinist nationalization and industrialization for having raised Russia out of the cultural darkness of tsarism. Since no nation can reach modern industrial status if its workforce can neither read nor write, illiteracy had to be, and was, overcome. That was good. But how do we factor into our judgments the quality of that education—what the newly literate are *permitted* to read and *allowed* to write? And how are interpretations and evaluations affected by the fact that while the Party-state was obliged to raise literacy rates, the same state in the interests of the same nationalized economy was methodically fulfilling its parallel historic mission of jailing, torturing, and murdering countless thousands of the most literate and educated members of society—its poets, novelists, journalists, historians, teachers, philosophers. This massacre of the intelligentsia had nothing to do with an abstraction called "Nationalized Economy." It had everything to do with a particular nationalized economy in the service of a concrete totalitarian state which fears and despises the most literate and intellectual beneficiaries of its own compelling need to improve educational and technical skills. Extermination of vast numbers of the intelligentsia was a *precondition* for Stalinization of the nationalized economy.

This war against the intellectuals, though less bloody than in the past, exists in permanence in totalitarian systems. For those who grow too educated, read too much, write too much, the labor camps will never be closed and psychiatric cells have been opened.

Another pseudo-Marxological boast: Russia's nationalized economy is free of capitalist "anarchy of production," "irrationality" and "internal contradictions," etc. etc. Of course, Russia is not plagued by capitalist contradictions and crises. Neither were paleolithic cultures nor slavocracies in antiquity nor feudal societies in the Middle Ages. How could it be otherwise where there are neither private owners of large-scale industry and capital nor a market in the bourgeois sense? No capitalism, no *capitalist* crises. That is not to say that totalitarian economies are free of built-in contradictions. Basic to socialist theory, a nationalized economy requires conscious democratic control and planning to realize its maximum social and economic potential. This socialist conception has never been tested. But it has won negative confirmation in the abundant evidence that totalitarian economic planning inexorably leads to mismanagement, inefficiency, imbalances, fraud, corruption, waste, shortages, demoralization, and loss of incentives; for the workers, denied any voice in economic planning, there is the certainty of alienation, exploitation and depressed wage levels.

TO ACCEPT THE NOTION THAT A SOCIALIST ECONOMY can coexist with political dictatorship is to deny the centrality of democracy to socialism. Yet, for Marx, "the first step in the revolution by the working class is to raise the proletariat to the position of the ruling class, to establish democracy." For Engels, it is after "the proletariat seizes political power" that it "turns the means of production into state power." And it would be good if all in the left accepted Lenin's stricture that "whoever wants to approach socialism by any means other than that of political democracy will inevitably arrive at absurd and reactionary conclusions."

These pithy declarations of democratic socialist principles are unacceptable to some in the left. An editorial in *In These Times* (December 22-January 11, 1983) is proof of Lenin's warning that those who deny the indivisibility of democracy and socialism will arrive at conclusions that are "absurd" and "reactionary." The editors note their "more than deep embarrassment" caused by the denial of civil liberties in "Eastern European Communist countries and in Third World socialist nations." Never mind for the moment that "deep embarrassment" is a rather feeble term of compassion for the victims of totalitarianism. The editors proceed to prove that they are not really *that* embarrassed:

> Some democratic socialists attempt to resolve the contradiction by insisting that any regime that denies the right of free speech, free assembly, the right to form unions and strike, and the right to form political parties and freely contest for power is not socialist. We understand the motivation for this denial, but it doesn't make sense to us.

From this inventory of freedoms denied in Communist countries, one might think that the conclusion would be: Communism is fascism, à la Susan Sontag. But, no, the Communist countries are socialist despite the lengthy list of derelictions. Why? Because they, the Communist leaders, say so. Even the head of the Polish Junta is taken at his word:

> Whether we like it or not, Poland's General Wojciech Jaruzelski talks about "the great collective duty" of "strengthening the Socialist state." We may say, no, that's no socialist state, but the words ring hollow in most people's ears. The Communists can no more be denied their connection to socialism than can we. And because they have actually taken power, they appear in many people's eyes to have a better claim to it than we.

There is something unreal about all this. It is as if a hardened criminal—we'll call him Yuri—had just been found guilty of the following crimes: he garrotted his grandparents, slaughtered his mother and father, strangled his children, terrorized his neighborhood and hired thugs to invade adjacent turfs. Brought before the judge, he is asked if he has anything to say before sentence is passed. Yuri looks directly into the eyes of the judge and speaks: "Your Honor, my grandparents were socialists, my parents were socialists, my children were Komsomols and I am a Communist. And it was my collective duty to..." Fortunately for Yuri, the judge is no ordinary bourgeois jurist. He, the judge, is also a socialist! He even writes theoretical tomes reconciling socialism and despotism. Yuri is chastised by an embarrassed judge. But Yuri, who cannot be denied his socialism merely because of his criminal record, is freed. How can one socialist confine another, especially Yuri, who, given his socialist ancestry, may even have a better claim to socialism than we?

The editors have a simple way of overcoming their embarrassment about the denial of freedom in Communist countries:

> We can no longer rely simply on the equation of the principles of freedom and equality with socialism, because any fool can see that "real, existing socialism," [the current Kremlin jargon for its system] while achieving a greater degree of equality, has stopped far short of the degree of freedom now possible.

Any fool should see the absurdity of trying to reconcile the embarrassing realities of the Communist world with socialism by simply redefining socialism to include all who say "We are Communist" or "We are socialist." One may come to the conclusion that socialism has proved to be a utopian dream—there are many neo-conservatives who would agree—but to say that a society that cannot abide democracy can still be socialist makes as much sense as saying that a wooden object that has neither roots, nor trunk nor branches, is a tree. A truncheon, perhaps, but not a tree.

MUCH OF THE IN THESE TIMES EDITORIAL is a poor echo of the sophisticated apologia for Stalinism advanced by the prolific Isaac Deutscher, who argued with great polemical skill that the dictatorship and much of its terror were historically necessary to consolidate the "social conquests" of the October Revolution. There is this important difference. Deutscher accepted the implication of his views. He defended Stalinism in its post-war expansionism, and with few tears and no equivocation he supported the Communist suppression of every major effort by the oppressed people in the empire to free themselves of the Stalinist yoke. In post-war Europe, he saw the Russians bringing socialism to Eastern Europe "in the turrets of their tanks." In Hungary 1956, he wrote, the Russian invaders tried to "wind up with the bayonet, or rather with the tank, the broken clock of the Hungarian Communist revolution."

By contrast, today in the left, even among those who hold to Deutscherite conceptions, the cruel logic of ideology has been overwhelmed by a deeper sense of decency, given the mounting evidence of the repressive nature of the Communist regimes. Nevertheless, the dilemma persists for those on the left who support Solidarity, on the one hand, and on the other perceive Russia as an imperfect socialist society.

It is barely conceivable that the editors of *In These Times*— perhaps the most widely circulated, influential publication on the left—would support the Russian-dictated suppression of democratic resistance movements in Eastern Europe. There can be no question however that these definitions and redefinitions of socialism have the potential of undermining the support they have given to Solidarity. The editorial in *In These Times* reflects these contradictory pressures.*

Inhibiting many on the left from acknowledging the reactionary character of the Communist systems is the fear that to reject Stalinism totally means, at best, to join the camp of capitalism as a liberal reformer or, at worst, to become an apologist for or supporter of the reactionary anti-Communism of the Reagans and Thatchers. (Nobel Prize winner Garcia Marquez admitted in a recent interview that he voices his criticism of "communistoids"—the term is his—only privately so as "not to play into the hands of the Right.") This assumption is reinforced by the political and moral devolution of so many theoreticians and intellectual luminaries of the anti-Stalinist left of years past. Sidney Hook, Irving Kristol, James Burnham, Max Shachtman are only a few names that come to mind of former leftwing and revolutionary socialist opponents of totalitarianism whose radicalism succumbed to their anti-Stalinism. They threw in their lot with "the West"—capitalism—as the only force capable of stemming the Communist

---

* While the editors of *In These Times* have taken a position that in its clear implication is a retreat from support of Solirarity, that is not necessarily reflective of the majority of its readers or all its editors. In its January 19-25 issue, there is a number of very effective criticisms of the editorial, including a sharp rebuttal by dissenting Associate Editor, John B. Judis.

tide in Vietnam, El Salvador, Chile. But it was not anti-Stalinism that proved to be sufficient cause for their capitulation to the West; the causal link between what they were and what they became was their abandonment of an independent socialist perspective. For some, socialism had become a force for evil, for others it was simply irrelevant to the struggle between East and West.

Those on the left who are persuaded that uncompromising anti-Communism leads to reaction have more in common with the League of ex-Bolsheviks for Nixon and Reagan than they realize. Coming from opposite ends of the spectrum, they join in a mutually shared pessimism: a frozen conception of a world divided between just two camps—Communist and capitalist. Implicitly and explicitly, they deny the historical viability of socialism.

It is awe for "nationalized economy," misdirected fear of aiding the right and the downplaying of democracy which lead so many in the left, including enthusiastic supporters of Solidarity, to adopt positions on questions of peace, political strategy and, most recently, the historic role of American Communism which are inimical to the cause of peace, of socialism and of the historical truth.

Peace

One of the more commonplace and sophomoric arguments is that for the sake of peace we must show prudence and judiciousness in our criticisms of Communism lest we play into the hands of Cold Warriors in Washington and arouse the ire of the Kremlin. Seldom has so urgent a cause been so abused as by those who continue to pluck at these time worn strings. Would those who orchestrate or sing this tune not be jarred if the lyrics were revised to read: for the sake of peace we must show judiciousness and prudence in our criticisms of capitalism lest we play into the hands of the Cold Warriors in the Kremlin and incite the wrath of the Reagan Administration?

It is impermissible to dismiss negative accounts about Communists per sé as just so much grist for the Cold War mill. Anti-Communists become Cold Warriors when their revelations about Communism are used to serve reactionary domestic and global objectives. When Jeane Kirkpatrick and her right-wing advisors from Social-Democrats USA decry Communist practices it is invariably for the larger purpose of presenting a Pinochet as a worthy ally or of justifying the sending of arms and military "advisors" to the Salvadoran junta. In this context, anti-totalitarianism becomes transparently hypocritical and fraudulent. On the other hand, to speak the truth about Communism and to be as forthright in exposing the crimes of capitalism provides the basis for the most effective struggle against the militarism and imperialist ambitions of both power blocs.

By the same token, it is wrong to dismiss Communist criticisms of Western capitalism or American foreign policy solely on the ground that they are always presented in the service of reactionary Communist interests. But, if to recognize that an Andropov, for his own reasons, can tell the truth or part of the truth at least some of the time about economic and social conditions in the West does not make one an apologist for Stalinism, why do so many in the the left assume that whoever does not automatically dismiss rightwing motivated accounts of the unbearable quality of life in Communist countries is an apologist for the bourgeois right or a "fanatical anti-Communist"? It is a disturbing double standard.

If, in this country the left is urged, even by friends of Solidarity, to guard against militant anti-Communism for the sake of peace, should the same advice be given to dissidents in Communist countries with respect to their governments? In Russia, too, Cold Warriors hold rather high positions. Should dissidents limit *their* struggle against totalitarianism for the sake of peace? Remember, the Polish upheaval has provided the Reagan Administration with obvious propaganda advantages and a pretext for demanding a huge increase in the US nuclear arsenal (which the Kremlin claims to be just cause for expanding its nuclear weaponry). Therefore, if in the West the cause of peace requires toning down anti-Communism, in the East it suggests abandoning struggles for human rights and national independence. Put another way: if the cause of freedom in Poland upsets detente, arouses Cold Warriors in the White House, incites the Kremlin, escalates the dangers of nuclear holocaust, then, for caution's sake and in the interests of human survival, is it not better to have the Jaruzelski solution to the Polish crisis than to have Solidarity pursue a life-threatening struggle for justice? This logical construct is vulnerable only in that its premise falsely denies the indivisibility of truth, peace and opposition to both power blocs.

Strategy

Sontag's harsh retrospective and current judgments clearly upset those who still cling to the notion that Communism should not be attacked as vigorously as capitalism because "the enemy of my enemy is my friend or ally." This strategy is commonplace in bourgeois diplomacy, openly stated by Reaganite neo-conservative ideologues who refuse to mount attacks on rightist dictatorships—from Argentina to South Africa—because "the enemy of my enemy is my friend and/or ally." Guided by the same opportunism-cum-strategy, some of Sontag's critics, even among those prepared to denounce the Kremlin for its role in Poland, remain chary of fundamental attacks on Communism as a social system for fear of providing aid and comfort to the immediate enemy, American capitalism. Apply this thought process to Poland and we wind up with bizarre conclusions. There, the immediate enemy is the Soviet Communist Party; the Reagan Administration is also the enemy of the Soviet Communist party; ergo, Solidarity must be urged to seek ties to the Reagan Administration or, at the very least, to maintain a cynical silence about US supported violations of human rights in other parts of the world (exactly what Kristol, Podhoretz & Co. urge).

Compassion

One also senses that compassion for the Communist victims of McCarthyism and the haunting memories of such outrages as the execution of the Rosenbergs clouds the objectivity of many radicals, inhibiting them from making the necessary distinction between a Communist as victim of bourgeois reaction and, simultaneously, proponent of a social system as vicious and repressive as fascism.

American Communism: The Search for Roots

For the New Left of the sixties and early seventies, at least for a number of its more articulate and sometimes outrageous spokesmen, history was garbage and all those over 30 suspect. If history is garbage there was no need to study it and if all over 30 were to be discounted, there was no incentive to seek ancestral roots. The defiant symbolic act inevitably grew in importance at the expense of developing theoretical conceptions, historical discoveries or visions of the future. As a result, a movement with marvelous potential that reached its peak strength during the soul-searing horror of the Vietnam War foundered on the rocks of its own intellectual limitations. Repression took its toll, true enough, but its bloodiest wounds were self-inflicted, a lack of theoretical motivation and clarity—not the least of which was its failure to take a clear stand against all oppressive societies.

By contrast, the left today has taken a stand on Poland in healthy contrast to the New Left's relative quiescence vis-à-vis the Prague Spring. And consistent with its concern for theory and history many in today's left are trying to find a place for themselves in the continuum of American radicalism. It is a splendid quest that deserves far better than what it has thus far produced.

In their genealogical excavations, a number of radicals exploring the past have dug up the old American Communist Party. It is not being put on display as the most inspiring ancestral find but, it is argued, how unworthy of affection and emulation could the old Communist Party have been if its members participated in the great sit-down strikes of the thirties and the formation of the CIO? There was Gastonia, Angelo Herndon, rent strikes, the Scottsboro "Boys," the Abraham Lincoln Brigade. There was pain, suffering, martyrdom; the human aspects of the Communist past no historian can overlook. All true, but in the hands of some leftwing historians and researchers, the political role of the Party in its "heroic" period has been so misstated and misunderstood that what emerges at times are not historical evaluations but silly, sentimental romances. (Perhaps the most hilarious example is Vivian Gornick's 250-page caricature, *The Romance of American Com-*

147

munism, which appeared a number of years ago and received plaudits from some surprising sources.)

Any party or movement, present or past, must be judged by its ideology, its choice of models, its internal life, its relation to other parties, how its activities affect class consciousness. Certainly, one cannot find sustenance or make an historical generalization about the early Communist party on the basis of isolated party activities, divorced from a wider and deeper political context. "Loyalty" and "courage" may be, in the abstract, splendid virtues. And a militant strike moves all socialists. But the "loyal" and "courageous" Communist cadres sent to Harlan County by the Party in the thirties to promote class struggle activities (and the Party) could be the *same* comrades instructed by the *same* Party to break strikes in the coal mines in the forties, after the Wehrmacht attacked Russia. It is that reality which should clue us in to the basic role of American Communism. The *same* Party which declared that "The Yanks Are Not Coming" during the Nazi-Soviet Pact berated the Allies with equal vigor for not opening a Second Front immediately after Hitler unilaterally dissolved the treaty.

The Party which demanded self-determination for the American black belt in the early thirties was the *same* Party that, a decade later, denounced black and white civil rights leaders as tools and agents of fascism for trying to organize a March on Washington to protest discriminatory practices in the armed forces and in industry. In the early thirties the chant at Party-organized May Day parades was "Free Tom Mooney and the Scottsboro Boys"; ten years later, the same Party beamed with pleasure when the US government sent Trotskyists to prison under the Smith Act and interned Japanese Americans in prison camps. The Party of the thirties which damned the crimes of American capitalism was the *same* party whose leader, ten years later, wrote: "I extend the hand of friendship to J.P. Morgan." The Party that tried to establish its credibility in the early organizing days of the CIO was the *same* organization which raised strikebreaking to an organizational and ideological art as it worked feverishly to force the trade union movement to surrender its precious hard-won gains on the altar of super-patriotism during WW II, on behalf of its Russian masters.

The Party that today decries America's nuclear buildup (not the Russian, naturally) is the *same* party that applauded the most heinous war crime of WW II—the US's atomic bombing of Hiroshima and Nagasaki. It was the *same* Party and had the *same* mission. In all those twists and turns, the Party remained consistent to what American Communism was all about. And what this movement was all about historically is something that so many on the left cannot accept. Its function is revealed by the one unifying, consistent thread in the Party's maze-like history: an inflexible and absolute loyalty to the Soviet Communist Party from the late twenties until Khrushchev's shattering revelations and the Hungarian Revolution in 1956. A subservience that was total. The American Party responded to American life (and to the international scene, of course) *only* as it was permitted or ordered to by the Soviet Party. It operated in the monolithic image of its Russian role model and mentor and brooked no public disagreement or internal debate.

Even in the early twenties, when there were interesting factional disputes, everything was finally settled by Comintern appointed "American Commissions." As far back as 1926 the legendary Communist leader, William Z. Foster, said it all: "If the Comintern finds itself criss-cross with my opinions, there is only one thing to do and that is to change my opinions to fit the policy of the Comintern." In 1929, the internal totalitarian lid was shut tight when the Soviet Party ordered the expulsion of the leadership of one Party faction led by Jay Lovestone. Although Lovestone had the support of at least three-fourths of the Party rank-and-file just months before his excommunication, only a handful left the party with him, testifying to the degree to which—even at that early date—ideological principles and independence of mind were overwhelmed by the "persuasive" force of the Moscow behemoth.*

---

* In the dark days of McCarthyism this subservience of the American Communist Party to its Russian overlords was cleverly and demagogically used by the Cold War philosopher, Sidney Hook, as the basis for his argument that Communism here was more a "conspiracy" than a "heretical" political movement. It was a clever twist of words and concepts that provided an intellectual rationale for repression, such as firing Communist teachers. Subservience, however, is not conspiracy; and to be a dupe is not to be a spy. Individuals were

In all the tumultuous events, here and abroad, from that year, 1929, until 1956, I have not seen or heard of a single article, a mere paragraph, not even one lonely word in any American Communist publication that took exception to or even remotely and tentatively questioned a single position or reversal of position adopted by the Soviet Party, neither in its public nor internal press. Now there's Romance for you! The mathematical beauty of the precise meeting of minds, a unity of purpose delayed only for the time it took to make a transatlantic phone call or deliver a telegram from Moscow to New York.

Was not this need and talent of Stalinism to crush individuality, to build around its papal center an aura of infallibility, to hold real, potential or invented deviationists in line with the threat of eternal damnation, to substitute rituals and slogans for study and reflection, to wed idealism to obedience and sacrifice to the cause of oppression all reminiscent of the techniques and psychology of fascist parties? Even where physical violence is concerned there are appreciable similarities between the two. Particularly during the Romantic thirties the anti-Stalinist left had to contend with Communist Party goon squads as well as the violence of fascist Coughlinite thugs.

THERE ARE OTHER MEASURES FOR JUDGING the American Communist movement—the effect it had on its own members and sympathizers, and its impact on American radicalism as a whole.

From virtually year one of the Party (or Parties—there were two at the beginning) its ideological gymnastics turned the organization into a revolving door:

• The agrarian radical of the early twenties attracted by the Party's initially sane and positive approach to midwest progressivism ran as from a disturbed nest of hornets when Moscow ordered a servile party to turn on LaFollette and his labor allies.

• The Western copper miner, the Mesabi Range ironworker,

---

not forced to join the Party, membership was voluntary; and it is a strange conspiracy where thousands of alleged conspirators defected regularly.

the Detroit lathe operator, the New York garment cutter—
thousands of them—deserted the Party that shifted from dual
unionism to the opposite tactic of "boring from within" and
then went back to "revolutionary" union antics only to revert
to participation in the official labor movement (soon, as
strikebreakers)—somersaults that had nothing to do with
American conditions or the needs and interests of the working
class.

• Party propagandists ordered to pen mash notes to Socialists and union leaders who they had denounced only yesterday
as "social fascists" and "labor fakers" eventually took their
literary skills elsewhere, often to write their memoirs.

• Activists who deified Stalin as the anti-fascist saviour
joined the apostasy when anti-Nazi cartoons in the *Daily
Worker* gave way to realistic depictions of Russian emissaries
hugging Nazi dignitaries.

• Thousands of faithful, seemingly unshakable in their belief
in His infinite wisdom—whatever He did was good for Russia
and whatever was good for Russia was good for the American
people—fled the temple when Stalin's pallbearers soon revealed
that what they buried was more Satanic than godly; defections
that swelled to a mass exodus when the Russian Wehrmacht
blitzkrieged the Hungarian nation.

The above, of course, is only a random sampling of the reasons for disillusionment, but it is sufficient to illustrate that the
history of American Communism, far from being a Romance,
was a tragedy in that it exhausted the energies of vast numbers
in a cause that was unjust and destructive.

The contradiction between the personal hopes and beliefs of
so many caring men and women and the reality of what they
were doing could not withstand the historical evidence indefinitely and when the shock of recognition came it was often with
stunning finality. Literally hundreds of thousands of militant
workers, intellectuals and young people were permanently
scarred, politically and sometimes psychologically, by their
association with the Party. A few who left moved in a socialist
direction. Others, well trained by the Party, became prominent
union bureaucrats. (Joseph Curran, for example, head of the
National Maritime Union, was rewarded with the Stalin Peace

Prize, in recognition of his special talent for cracking the skulls of union dissidents. A few years later, he applied those skills to breaking the heads of Communist and anti-Communist oppositionists in the same NMU.) Others remained politically alive in liberal causes. More than a few shifted to political conservatism. But the vast majority, given over to weariness or cynicism, were lost to organized radicalism forever.

In any meaningful historical sense, then, American Communism was a major obstacle to the emergence of a significant socialist movement in this country, and it was a disaster for the broad labor movement and even for its own members and sympathizers. It was not a movement of the American left but a totalitarian incubus that fed on labor and progressive organizations, functioning *in* the left and *against* it.

AND WHAT IS TRUE OF AMERICAN COMMUNISM, past and present, can be more emphatically asserted about societies where the Communist parties hold state power. They do have characteristics paralleling fascism. They are systems, call them what you will, which can be defined first of all by what they are not: neither socialist nor left in even the broadest sense of the term.

For if words, concepts, traditions and history have any meaning, to be "left" is to acknowledge the right to organized political opposition—socialist, Communist, anarchist, liberal, conservative—something that is anathema to Communist parties in power. To be "left" is to recognize and resist economic inequities; yet, in Communist countries, gross wage differentials between workers and bureaucrats rival those of capitalism. To be "left" is to fight racial bigotry and sexual exploitation; yet, anti-Semitism is semi-official policy in Communist countries, and women have less responsibility and power than they do in Western capitalist states. To be "left" is to fight for the right of working people to form independent class organizations known in the West as unions; such independent organizations are denied even the right to exist (let alone the right to strike) in Communist countries. To be "left" is to demonstrate against the imperialist adventures of one's own country; to demonstrate against anything advocated by the ruling Party in a Communist country is an act of heroism—to resist Russian imperialist occupation, domination or outright absorption of

weaker states can mean imprisonment, psychiatric punishment, even death. And on it goes: freedom versus anti-freedom,
culture versus anti-culture, self-determination versus imperialism—the left versus the Communist right.

Certainly, "the left" is not a narrowly defined category, but
neither is it so all-embracing as to include hardened tendencies,
organizations or ruling powers committed to a denial of fundamental human rights. Someone who identifies with Solidarity but fails to see the basic similarities between a Jaruzelski
and an idealized Castro is different from the person with a
firmer and wider commitment to totalitarian ideologies and
regimes. What is important, though, and this is the responsibility above all of the thinking, intellectual left, is to show that
simultaneous support for Solidarity and for Castro is inconsistent, that even minimal endorsement of the latter (who supports the Polish junta and martial law, denies Cuban workers
independent unions and denies the populace as a whole the
democratic rights for which Solidarity still carries on its heroic
struggle) undercuts the cause of freedom in Poland. To view a
Castro, a Pol Pot, the Kim Il Sung dynasty, Chinese despotism
or any Communist tyranny in a favorable light is about as
politically "left" a stance as Irving Kristol's embrace of the
Chilean and South Korean dictators.

*   *   *

FOR THE SOCIALIST LEFT, Stalinism must be fought as vigorously as capitalism. The anti-Communism of the left has
nothing in common with the attitudes of a Reagan or Kirkpatrick. Their purpose is the defense of capitalism, relying on
military postures, and their alternative is a Latin American
dictator, a Turkish tyrant or an Iranian Shah. *Their* anti-
Communism has no place for a working class Poland. For
them, the Jaruzelskis are the lesser evil to the Walesas. *Their*
anti-Communism provides a diet on which Communism thrives;
if rightwing anti-Communists did not exist, the Communists
would invent them.

The anti-Communism of the socialist left is inseparable from
its anti-capitalism. It is not only antithetical to everything the
Cold Warrior stands for, it is also potentially more effective

because it stems from an affirmation of peace, freedom, democracy, national rights—not only when it is convenient or for the sake of appearance—but genuinely and universally: in Poland and El Salvador, Cuba and Chile, Russia and the US.

The New York Intellectuals in Retreat

ALAN WALD

> *What would happen if men remained faithful to the ideals of their youth?*
> Pietro Spina in *Bread and Wine*, Ignazio Silone.

WILLIAM BARRETT'S *The Truants: Adventures Among the Intellectuals* (New York: Doubleday, 1982) is the latest and most substantial addition to what is rapidly becoming a distinct sub-genre in American intellectual history. Since the late 1960s there has been a steady stream, now swelling to a torrent, of books and articles about a group of writers known as the "New York Intellectuals" or the "New York Family." The terms refer to a loose circle of politicized writers, critics, and academicians whose preeminent literary forums have been *Partisan Review, Commentary* and *Dissent*. Members of the group who were old enough to be politically active in the 1930s tended to become not only anti-Stalinists but also revolutionary Marxists of one persuasion or another. Today, quite a few—including such former Trotskyists and Trotskyist sympathizers as Lionel Abel, Saul Bellow, Sidney Hook, Irving Kristol, Melvin Lasky,

---

ALAN WALD, *Associate Professor of English Literature at the University of Michigan, is the author of* James T. Farrell: The Revolutionary Socialist Years *(New York University Press, 1978) and* The Revolutionary Imagination: The Poetry and Politics of John Wheelwright and Sherry Mangan *(to be published in April 1983 by University of North Carolina Press). He has had articles in* Antioch Review, Marxist Perspectives, The Nation *and other journals and is presently writing a political and cultural history of the anti-Stalinist left in New York from the 1930s to the present.*

and Seymour Martin Lipset—are associated with the reactionary "Committee for the Free World" led by *Commentary* editor Norman Podhoretz. This is a predominantly pro-Reagan organization which, among other activities, sponsored an April 6, 1981 *New York Times* advertisement to "applaud American policy in El Salvador." Many of the other surviving New York intellectuals identify with the Democratic Party.

Appraisals have been made of the New York intellectuals by Bert Cochran, James Gilbert, David Hollinger, Mark Krupnick, Christopher Lasch, S. A. Longstaff, Philip Nobile, Mark Shechner, and Grant Webster (see Bibliography at the end of this article). In addition to numerous literary analyses of the work of Saul Bellow and Edmund Wilson, there have been three biographical and critical studies each of Hannah Arendt, Mary McCarthy, and Lionel Trilling, two of Max Eastman, James T. Farrell, and Delmore Schwartz, and one of Clement Greenberg. Even more striking has been the production of semi-autobiographical works such as the one by Barrett, who had been a member of the *Partisan Review* editorial board for some years after WW II and is currently a Reagan supporter as well as a member of the Board of Directors of the Committee for the Free World. Such memoirs include not only the several best-sellers by Alfred Kazin and Norman Podhoretz, and the ironic political "confessions" published by Mary McCarthy and Dwight Macdonald in the 1950s, but also numerous autobiographical pieces by Lionel Abel, Daniel Bell, Leslie Fiedler, Sidney Hook, Irving Howe, Irving Kristol, George Novack, William Phillips, Harry Roskolenko, Diana Trilling, Lionel Trilling, and Bernard Wolfe.

The widespread and continuing interest in the New York group by students and scholars of radical political and cultural history—not to mention those sections of the reading public fascinated by intimate revelations about the lives of the literary mandarins of our time—obviously stems from the mark these writers have made on American culture. The *New York Times Book Review* described *Partisan Review* as "the best literary magazine in America" when its founder, Philip Rahv, died in 1974. Further evidence of the power and importance of the New York intellectuals on the national scene during recent decades has been provided by such political and sociological studies as Philip Green's *The Pursuit of Inequality*, Charles Kadushin's *The American Intellectual Elite*, and Peter Steinfels' *The Neo-Conservatives*. Barrett's *The Truants* received a front-page laudatory notice in the February 7, 1982 *New York Times Book Review* in which the reviewer, Hilton Kramer, also a member of the Committee for the Free World, offered not a single criticism, disagreement, or demurrer.

What does Barrett's *The Truants* add to our knowledge of the history of the New York intellectuals? In terms of the formation and evolution of *Partisan Review*, the basic story has been told so many times that Barrett can supply only a few new details about internal squabbles. Here are some tidbits of his gossip. We learn that the eventual break-up between chief editors Phillips and Rahv in the late 1960s actually began as far back as 1945-46 with a quarrel over Rahv's having made unflattering remarks about his fellow editors to people outside the *Partisan Review* circle; that Alfred Kazin was always regarded with suspicion by members of the inner circle, who recalled Diana Trilling's characterization of him as a "starry-eyed opportunist"; that creative writers had so much difficulty with the ingrown and self-devouring atmosphere of the *Partisan Review* circle that James Agee intentionally broke from it, that Elizabeth Hardwick lost her ability to write the simple and direct kind of fiction with which she began her career, and Saul Bellow developed a complicated strategy of self-protection; that Delmore Schwartz had an inexplicable "consuming hostility" toward Lionel Trilling and jumped at the chance to write an attack on him ("The Duchess's Red Shoes" in 1953) after convincing Rahv that Trilling was using *Partisan Review* to "protect his left flank." Given all of the petty feuds, faction fights, and splits recounted by Barrett, it is difficult to understand how any of the *Partisan Review* intellectuals could be as contemptuous as they were of the "sectarian infighting" of some of the small groups on the left.

Perhaps Barrett's greatest contribution is his set of vivid portraits of the various personalities in the *Partisan Review* circle. For the most part his characterizations seem judicious, although there are moments when his anti-radical bias comes through. For example, he says that the "black and white simplifications" that marred James Burnham's conservative thought "may have been a legacy Marxism left with Burnham," forgetting to mention that Burnham had been a neo-Thomist before becoming radicalized, a fact well-known to the *Partisan Review* circle. Barrett often searches for some key to a writer's personality. In the case of William Phillips, the "essential tragedy" of Phillips' life was the creative block he suffered after leaving academe to become a full-time writer. Barrett suggests that the block was caused by Phillips' brilliantly quick and dialectical mind, enabling him to argue "either side of a question." The result was a "certain quality of detachment and sterile skepticism" without "any strong beliefs generally," beyond his attachment to his circle of friends. One exception: his hatred of Stalin was so intense that, when Stalin died, Phillips reportedly felt "strangely empty—almost as if something central to his life had gone."

But if Phillips was, on the whole, "an essentially kind" man, Rahv is depicted as the opposite. Barrett calls him a "menacing and angry person" who was also an extraordinary "physical coward," fearful, for example, of getting into an argument with Clement Greenberg, who had the reputation of someone "who goes around socking people." Like Phillips, Rahv was obsessed by Stalin, but the obsession only periodically overshadowed his original view that the Stalinists "had distorted the whole meaning and nature of Marxism." Further, he had a second bête noir that kept his Marxism alive in the cultural field while he was politically withdrawn and silent: he was antagonistic to the school of New Criticism associated with the *Kenyon Review*, which he felt "tried to escape the broad claim of Marxism that the literary work cannot be torn from its social and historical context."

BARRETT ALSO PROVIDES A DETAILED RECOLLECTION of the degeneration of Delmore Schwartz from literary genius to paranoid derelict. It is a moving story, but, as Mark Shechner pointed out in *The Nation*, 27 February 1982, it is one already familiar to readers of James Atlas's biography of Schwartz and Saul Bellow's roman-à-clef, *Humboldt's Gift*. Shechner also noted that the personality sketches are usually made memorable by the use of clever nicknames and catchy phrases coined by either Barrett or some other member of the *Partisan Review* coterie. For example, Edmund Wilson, who used to refer to the magazine as the "Partisansky Review" and to its editors Potash and Perlmutter (two Jewish tailors in a Broadway play who picker constantly), is said to have taught Barrett "the meaning of waddle . . . or rather the possible varieties and nuances of a waddle," from the way Wilson walked among the ruins of Rome. Schwartz described Meyer Schapiro as "a mouth in search of an ear," Hannah Arendt as a "Weimar Republic flapper," and Lionel Trilling as "the Matthew Arnold of Morningside Heights." Barrett calls Sidney Hook a "Johnny One-note" on the question of anti-Stalinism, but then adds that "the one note at which he was perpetually hammering away was a momentous one."

However, the wit of these caustic characterizations is frequently undercut by Barrett's insistence on using superlatives to praise the intelligence and importance of his friends. Mary McCarthy is described as "one of the most brilliant women and formidable intellectuals of her time," and her 1940 short story, "The Man in the Brooks Brothers Shirt," is said to be superior in "class and caliber" to any feminist writing since. Clement Greenberg is quoted approvingly as saying that "William Phillips and Philip Rahv are two of the most intelligent people in the country." James Agee and Delmore Schwartz are described as "the two best literary talents of their generation." Barrett himself says that Lionel Trilling was "the most intelligent man of his generation." In unison, such unrestrained judgments did not deter Hilton Kramer from proclaiming Barrett "one of our best critics."

Kramer also praises *The Truants* for Barrett's ability to examine "governing ideas with an unusual degree of intimacy, intelligence, and candor," and for his "penetrating analysis of the intellectual life of its period." Unfortunately, the book is replete with errors about Marxism, Trotskyism, and Communism. This erodes the self-glorifying sub-theme that Barrett and his neo-conservative friends are the repository of wisdom regarding these matters, thus eminently qualified for political leadership of the American intelligentsia.

For example, Barrett explains why he had "mixed feelings" about Trotsky's theory of Permanent Revolution even when he was a self-proclaimed Marxist: "If the revolution is permanent and unceasing, then next week you reverse what you have revolutionized last week." To anyone who has the slightest familiarity with Trotsky's most famous theoretical contribution, this statement will be astounding. Trotsky, like all Marxists, believed that social relations and institutions would continue to evolve after the working class took power, but the essence of the theory of Permanent Revolution, derived in part from Marx, involved an analysis of the dynamic of social change in economically underdeveloped countries. In such countries, Trotsky theorized that in the age of imperialism the proletariat was the only class capable of carrying out political and social tasks earlier associated with the radical bourgeoisie (such as land reform and national unification). What Barrett is describing in this passage is something more akin to Mao's "Cultural Revolution" in the 1960s, or, worse, to Stalin's slanders against Trotsky's internationalist policies in the 1920s.

It is also doubtful that Barrett understands, or ever understood, the basic Trotskyist critique of Stalinism, since he writes that socialism is no longer an option for him because he realizes that "the dictatorial course of socialist revolution can no longer be dismissed as an aberration due to the personality of Stalin." Trotsky, of course, took into account Stalin's individual role but never claimed that Stalin's personality was what transformed the political character of the Russian revolution. In *The Revolution Betrayed*, he clearly describes the encircling conditions and economic class forces that precipitated the crystallization of a bureaucratic caste in the USSR, for which Stalin served as chief spokesman.

These blunders undermine Barrett's repeated references to himself as having been a Marxist since the early thirties—indeed, as one who was "passionately arguing Marxist theory" even in the 1940s. In a May 24, 1982 *New York Times* interview with Michiko Kakutani, Barrett even refers to himself as having been in his *Partisan Review* days "a Marxist with a Trotskyist orientation." Apparently this fanfare about his Marxist expertise is necessary to give credibility to the familiar premise stated early in the book that only former Marxists can understand the truly pernicious nature of Marxism and the Soviet Union. During the Cold War many of these types made lucrative careers based on an equally shallow expertise. Nonetheless, Barrett's frank testimony about the Marxist and Trotsky-ist origins of the New York intellectuals does serve as a useful antidote to those who tend to minimize the group's original commitment to revolutionary communism.

Otherwise, it is difficult to find much that Barrett gets right in his book in regard to either Marxist political or cultural matters. Nineteen thirty-seven is given as the year of "the last of Stalin's purges," even though the sensational Bukharin trial did not begin until 1938. When *Partisan Review* was relaunched in 1937, we are told that the Communist Party advocated "a cultural doctrine of social realism and proletarian culture," even though this line had been discarded two years earlier for the People's Front, with its Hollywood and Broadway stars, one of the reasons why Phillips and Rahv became disen-chanted with the Party. He describes the Communists' and fellow-travelers' view of the USSR in the late 1940s as a "Worker's State," even though their official doctrine was that such a stage had been superseded by "socialism" a decade earlier.

Alerted by these errors, the readers of *The Truants* will find that the more Barrett tries to elaborate, the more he tends to distort. Regarding WW II, Barrett describes the debate in *Partisan Review* as follows: "Rahv and Phillips, though Marxists, were willing to bend principle and support the Allies because Hitler and the Nazis represented a break with Western Civiliza-tion that had to be opposed. But Macdonald, then a Trotskyist, insisted on being a purist: The War was essentially a struggle of capitalist powers and we should stay aloof and watch the dis-ease take its course." Yet, in the "Ten Propositions on the War" that Macdonald and Clement Greenberg published in *Partisan Review* in 1941, they clearly state that Hitler's victory *would* mean a "break" in our civilization, that "isolationism is pro-vincial inanity," and that they were continuing to advocate a socialist revolution in America during war-time because a socialist victory would actually intensify the war effort, mak-ing "a more efficient, energetic and uncompromising fight against Hitler." Obviously Barrett's understanding of the real meaning of a revolutionary opposition to WW II is about as adequate as his understanding of the theory of Permanent Revolution.

Barrett's description of the deradicalization of James Burnham is also somewhat skewed. He tells us that in the late 1930s Burnham reached the conclusion that socialism should not be theorized as "inevitable" but only as a "moral idea." According to Barrett, Burnham published these views in the "Trotskyist organ" and Trotsky "thundered furiously" from Mexico that people who worried about "moral ideas" had succumbed to "petty-bourgeois revision." At this point "Burnham was promptly read out of the party," and responded with an essay called "Lenin's Heir" that "appeared in *Partisan Review* in 1939." Barrett has the facts so jumbled here that it would take several pages to set them straight, but the essential points are that: 1) Burnham acknowledged that he had never agreed with dialectical and historical materialism, but considered the matter unimportant until a dispute broke out in the Trotskyist movement over the correct policy toward the USSR in the early days of WW II; 2) Burnham was never "read out" of any party but joined a faction in the Trotskyist movement that split to form the Workers Party, from which he speedily resigned of his own volition; 3) "Lenin's Heir" was published in 1945, so it hardly could have been part of a factional polemic with Trotsky who was assassinated in 1940.

In addition to such factual errors, readers of *The Truants* will have to have a strong stomach for many of Barrett's politically outrageous opinions. Barrett maintains that when French revolutionary intellectuals of 1789 first spoke of "The People," they took "the first step toward the Gulag"; that the USSR alone is to be blamed for the start of the Cold War; that corporations in the US "bow before Washington"; that "free will and the moral reality of the individual who makes his free choice" are "anathema to the Marxist mind"; and that Stalin was an "active and conscious agent of evil." In addition, there are derogatory remarks about the struggle for homosexual rights and sexual freedom ("What was so bad about the closet anyway? It was warm and cozy there") and open admissions to colleges for minority students.

EVEN MORE ASTOUNDING, BARRETT APPENDS to his account a summer 1946 *Partisan Review* editorial he wrote, "The Liberal Fifth Column," in which American liberals are excoriated for being too soft on the USSR and a more belligerent US foreign policy is urged. Barrett believes that such a message needs to be repeated to the intellectual community and to American rulers today. However, he ignores the responses provoked earlier by this mistaken attitude, such as Irving Howe's in the April 1947 *New International*. At that time Howe pointed out that obsessive anti-Communism only obscures the question of which forces one allies oneself with to wage this battle, and that it "can only render impossible an effective struggle against Stalinism—not to mention making hopeless any sort of positive socialist aim." Howe explained that by rejecting "the method of analysis which characterizes the basic aspects of American foreign policy in class terms," *Partisan Review* "has succumbed to *Stalinphobia*, a disease common among intellectuals who were once radicals; its major symptom is that regular tired feeling. *Stalinphobia* takes the form of bitter and quite justified denunciations of Stalinism without any corresponding effort to develop a sociological understanding of it. Hatred for Stalinism becomes an emotional block to its political analysis." Howe further identified Barrett's *Partisan Review* editorial with the "vulgar articles" contained in the rightwing Social Democratic *New Leader*, "which always lead to support of one or another reactionary imperialism solely because of its conjunctural opposition to Russia." The prophetic nature of these remarks is confirmed by the fact that every time a contingent of New York intellectuals has moved to the right in the past four decades, it has used anti-Communism as its excuse—whether directly referring to the threat of Soviet aggression, or in denouncing domestic movements for social change as being "Stalinist" in methods or style.

Finally, there is irony in the fact that Barrett's book is dedicated to Delmore Schwartz and Philp Rahv. They appear to be invoked as a warning to the reader about the terrible fate of alienated rebels more than as the subjects of any tribute by Barrett. Throughout his discussion of Schwartz, the impression is given that if the poet had rebelled less against the mainstream of American culture (for example, if he had worked in an insurance office like Wallace Stevens), he might have found "more peace and in the end more time for his poetry." The treatment of Rahv is more important, because he is explicitly ridiculed as an example of an intellectual who fails to grow up and entirely repudiate his radical past.

Barrett claims that with the death of Stalin in 1953, Rahv suddenly reverted to what Barrett takes to be Trotsky's original view of the contradictory nature of the Soviet Union: "The Revolution of 1918 [sic] had abolished the capitalists and established the collective ownership of the economy, the people now owned the means of production; that was progress, indeed it was the great step forward toward which the whole of humanity aspired; then had come that wicked man Stalin who had imposed his own political dictatorship on top of this new economic structure; that was regress." Barrett was astounded that at the end of his life Rahv was talking about the necessity of a "political revolution" in the USSR: "[Rahv] seems never to have imagined that such a revolution, if it were indeed to bring about liberty, would not so much have to complete as to sweep away the work of the October Revolution."

What galls Barrett most about Rahv is that the more secure he became—in 1958 he was appointed professor at Brandeis University although he had never attended college—the more radical he became. Truly this was a case of biting the hand that fed him: "He was like those children of affluence during the 1960s who found their middle-class advantages a further reason for hostility toward American society. Rahv, in fact, was one of those intellectuals of the 1950s who was preparing the way for the radical outbursts of the 1960s; and when these came, he was ready to receive them with open arms. All in all, it was to be a strange turn in the career of a man who had always been an outsider: hitherto, in the 1930s and 1940s, he had fought against the dominant trend, but now in the 1960s he had turned about and was running with the pack." Hilton Kramer quoted this entire passage in *The New York Times Book Review*, calling it "quite the best thing in Barrett's book." Kramer is as incredulous as Barrett that "the more he [Rahv] prospered, the more violently did he denounce the system that had brought him success."

Whatever one may conclude about Rahv, these remarks reveal a good deal about his adversaries, the contemporary neo-conservatives. What is so reprehensible about a self-made intellectual, or for that matter a disaffected member of the ruling elite, who allies himself or herself with working people and other social rebels in their struggle for a society in which all can enjoy the privileges now enjoyed only by a few? Do Barrett and Kramer think that Rahv should have fallen on his knees in gratitude before America's rulers for having saved him from the pit of poverty and a life of meaningless work? Their views are confirmation that the neo-conservatives, rather than having completely abandoned their quondam Marxist analysis of capitalist society as a struggle of the haves against the have-nots, have actually retained central portions of the analysis; the difference, however, is that they now align themselves with the haves instead of the have-nots.

Having become reconciled in their old age (for some, like Podhoretz, it is a premature old age) to the exploitative system they once abhorred, it is tempting to predict that at least some of the rightwing New York intellectuals will continue on a course analogous to the one selected by the proverbial Irish atheist who undergoes a deathbed conversion to Catholicism. Such a conjecture isn't as far-fetched as it may seem. One of Barrett's more recent contributions to *Commentary* was called "On Returning to Religion."

A Radical or a Reactionary Tradition?

ALL THIS NOTICE BY BARRETT AND OTHERS leaves one wondering what lessons a new generation of Marxist intellectuals, concerned with forging links to a usable past as well as avoiding the mistakes of its predecessors, can extract from the experience of this group which, with only a few exceptions, has allied itself with the most reactionary forces in American society. Certainly Barrett's book leaves the impression that for radicals, especially for Trotskyists and other anti-Stalinist Marxists, the early careers of the New York intellectuals are an embarrassment and might best be forgotten. The theme of the book scarcely touches upon the efforts of intellectuals to devote their special skills to supporting working class struggles, fighting racism, campaigning against political repression during the McCarthy era, protesting imperialist domination, or understanding and enhancing the cultural life of the working class and other oppressed sects. Indeed, such concerns are never mentioned. Instead, the book is structured to communicate a very specific political message: leftwing anti-Stalinism was and continues to be a chimera, a forum of truancy from one's responsibility to face up to the truth that the intellectual's "own continued existence as a dissenter depends on the survival of the United States as a free nation in a world going increasingly totalitarian."

In other words, Barrett holds that the only true form of anti-Stalinism is identical with pro-capitalism, a political position shared for different reasons by the brutal rulers of the USSR. But this notion is too ingenuous to be taken seriously. In addition to the fact that American foreign policy historically has abetted the gangster-like rule of many countries in the "free world," there is the obvious point that, if one refrains from criticism of American capitalism in the belief that one's freedom to dissent depends on capitalism's existence and perpetuation, one is simply helping to create, by voluntary means, a society without meaningful and deep-going dissent.

IN LIGHT OF THE REACTIONARY SELF-IMAGE being created by Barrett and some of his fellow New York intellectuals, it is not surprising that many young intellectuals in search of an alternative radical tradition have turned elsewhere. This accounts for the current infatuation with the history of American Communism, particularly during the Popular Front era, reflected by the many favorable references in radical journals to the work of Paul Buhle, Vivian Gornick, Maurice Isserman, Mark Naison, and others. The New York intellectuals are often dismissed with scorn by contemporary radicals. Even when they are treated with some sympathy and understanding, the legacy is so confused that what is most relevant, worthwhile, and enduring in their tradition is sometimes missed. (See, for example, the most recent scholarly study of *Partisan Review* ["Cosmopolitan Values and the Identification of Reaction: *Partisan Review* in the 1930s," by Terry A. Cooney], which depicts the political trajectory of the magazine's editors as evolving from pro-Communism prior to 1936 to "anti-Stalinism" after 1937, without clearly explaining that the specific content of their "anti-Stalinism" went through marked changes as well.)

The political evolution of the New York intellectuals has

made it extremely difficult to convince young radicals that their leftwing anti-Stalinist politico-cultural contributions in the 1930s should be critically assimilated as one of the more useful components of a rich Marxist heritage. Barrett is an authentic representative of one of the ultimate but less savory results of that tradition. There are certain obvious continuities between his present reactionary posture and some of the positions taken by the New York intellectuals in their previous incarnations. But if one understands the changes in political orientation on the part of many of them just prior to, during, and especially after WW II, the years *The Truants* focuses upon, it becomes clear that their evolution was not the only one possible. In fact, only by understanding the profound nature of these changes can one come to grips with the contradictory aspect of the New York intellectuals that confuses most people: that a group of individuals who began their careers as revolutionary communists during the 1930s could become an institutionalized and even hegemonic component of American culture during the reactionary 1950s, while maintaining a high degree of collective continuity. This particular evolution for so many in the group might incorrectly suggest that their politics were tainted from the beginning. Thus, it is crucial to demonstrate that the group's political and cultural anti-Stalinism meant different things at different times. Politically oriented members of the generation of the sixties and seventies find it hard to believe that the more reactionary figures among the surviving New York intellectuals, such as Sidney Hook and Irving Kristol, once functioned as genuine Marxist revolutionaries at the same time as they expressed uncompromising opposition to Stalinism. The left of this later generation fails to understand that it was not the anti-Stalinism *per sé* that was responsible for the metamorphosis of these intellectuals into neo-conservatives but a host of social and historical factors, which put an end to their socialist perspective.

By successive stages the New York intellectuals moved from a distinct current of communism in the 1930s to a distinct current of liberalism by the 1950s, and, in political allegiance, they moved from advocacy of socialist revolution to a mildly critical support of American capitalism. At the beginning, most of the intellectuals were anti-Stalinist communists; by the 1950s most had become anti-communist liberals. Individuals who were not members of the original core joined the group at various points, but what the newcomers were assimilated into was a group drifting in a conservative direction.

This shift—in which certain doctrinal components appear to remain the same in form while being utterly transformed in content—represents the most significant bond between such disparate members of the group as Lionel Trilling, who was of immigrant Jewish parentage, a devoted professor, and rather evasive in his political pronouncements, and James T. Farrell, who was an Irish-American, generally hostile to academe, and at times abrasively aggressive in his political declarations. In fact, the appellation "New York intellectuals" arose as a somewhat mystifying euphemism for a group originally called "Trotskyist intellectuals" (for example, in James Burnham and Max Shactman's 1939 essay, "Intellectuals in Retreat"). After all, many in this group came from cities other than New York (Farrell, Saul Bellow, Harold Rosenberg, and Isaac Rosenfeld were from Chicago), and others would be classified by most cultural historians as journalists rather than intellectuals (such as Benjamin Stolberg and James Rorty).

One reason for coming into the name of the "New York intellectuals" has to do with a change of status. During the 1930s, when they coalesced as a distinct set, most had not gained the prominence acquired in later years. Sidney Hook, James T. Farrell, Louis Hacker, Lewis Corey, and Edmund Wilson had developed national reputations at that time, but Lionel Trilling did not publish *Matthew Arnold* until 1939 and Meyer Schapiro, Philip Rahv, Mary McCarthy, Harold Rosenberg, Lionel Abel, and other aspirants had yet to publish a book. Fame and influence came only after they had excised their anti-Stalinism from the context of revolutionary Marxism and quasi-Trotskyist politics in which it had been fashioned. It was precisely this political transformation that constituted the binding moment in their evolution and signaled their entrance as a significant current into American intellectual history.

WHEN AND HOW DID THIS POLITICAL EVOLUTION HAPPEN? The Moscow Trials and the relentless growth of fascism caused some in the group to become shaken and demoralized in the late 1930s; then came WW II, a complex event that disoriented many of the intellectuals and caused some to repudiate long-held positions; finally, the atmosphere of the postwar and Cold War years—filled with disappointments and fear as well as opportunities for new careers in publishing and academe—brought about the final stage in their collective change of political allegiance. Remarkably, even though they made this shift in different groupings—each denouncing the other for its apostasy before following suit—they remained a coherent and distinguishable politico-cultural current. Despite broad variations in political orientation, ranging from the affiliation of Max Eastman and James Burnham with *National Review* to the social democratic views of Irving Howe, Meyer Schapiro, and others grouped around *Dissent*,* the tradition of the New York intellectuals had become such a specific ideological current that Norman Podhoretz and others of his generation could assimilate it second-hand and perpetuate some of its features in the decades that followed the war.

The main lines of the group's ideological evolution before, during, and after WW II can be traced in several key documents produced during the thirties, forties, and fifties. From what may be considered their founding statement of May 1933—in which Lionel Trilling, Elliot Cohen (a former editor of the *Menorah Journal*† who later founded *Commentary*), and oth-

---

* The New York intellectuals were called a "herd of independent minds" by Harold Rosenberg, correctly reminding us that all generalizations about them must be subject to certain qualifications. For example, *Dissent* editor Irving Howe, 15 years younger than the original core, began his intellectual career as a harsh critic of the group. By the 1950s he had abandoned his revolutionism and, as a regular contributor to *Partisan Review* and *Commentary,* he was assimilated into the group as its leftwing. During that period, unlike so many in the group, he refused to join the American Committee for Cultural Freedom. Today he is a member of Democratic Socialists for America.

† One of the earliest manifestations of the New York intellectuals can be found in a circle of friends and contributors to the Jewish humanist magazine *Menorah Journal* in the 1920s, several of whom

ers announced their rupture with the Communist Party—it is clear that their initial disagreements with the Party were only tactical and strategic ones within a Marxist framework. They contended that the Party, through its method of operating in the National Committee for the Defense of Political Prisoners, to which they had belonged, was retarding rather than promoting the struggle for communism. Nine months later, when Elliot Cohen, Lionel Trilling, Diana Trilling, Clifton Fadiman, Edmund Wilson, John dos Passos, and others published an "Open Letter" in the *New Masses* condemning the Communist Party's February 1934 disruption of a Socialist Party meeting in Madison Square Garden called in solidarity with the Viennese workers massacred by the rightwing government of Austria, the intellectuals' perspective remained explicitly anticapitalist. It included an attack on social democracy for being too passive in the struggle against fascism and having "suspicious ties" to the capitalist status quo. The main objection, once more, was that the ultra-left tactics of the Communist Party impeded progress toward the Party's professed goal of working class revolution.

A similar position was promulgated by Sidney Hook a year later in a symposium in V. F. Calverton's journal *Modern Monthly*. In an essay called "Why I am a Communist: Communism Without Dogmas," Hook differentiated himself from the liberal and social democratic views of the other contributors, John Dewey, Bertrand Russell, and Morris Cohen. His anti-Stalinist criticisms of the Communist Party were matched by equally fierce denunciations of the reformism and class collaboration which characterized the Socialist Party of Germany and the Labor Party of England. These parties, he said, "be

---

were students at Columbia University. By isolating this sub-group, we can see some of the formative influences, preoccupations and attitudes of the larger group. These include a sympathy for modernism in literature, a universalist outlook despite (or in some cases because of) their Jewish upbringing, an aspiration to reconcile pragmatism and Marxism, and a youthful attraction to Leon Trotsky who, for some, is eventually displaced by Freud.

came the instrumentalities by which the dictatorship of finance-capital lowered the standards of living, strengthened the national defense, continued the old shell game of diplomacy in foreign affairs and restricted, in the interest of national unity, militant working class agitation." Hook's unambiguous political allegiance is revealed in his final sentences: "It seems to me that only communism can save the world from its social evils; it seems to me to be just as evident that the official Communist Party or any of its subsidiary organizations cannot be regarded as a Marxist, critical or revolutionary party today. The conclusion is, therefore, clear: *the time has come to build a new communist party and a new communist international*" (emphasis in original). He intended to implement this call—very similar to the one issued by Leon Trotsky a year earlier—through the activities of the newly-formed American Workers Party headed by A. J. Muste.

This is the clearest programmatic statement documenting the anti-Stalinist Marxism of the New York intellectuals in their formative phase. Differences among the group on certain subsidiary theoretical matters and in degrees of personal commitment already existed. But the group's original impulse was to condemtn Stalinism for its reformist politics, to reject Stalinism not because it was bolshevism—but precisely because it *wasn't.* Certainly this was the view of Calverton's *Modern Monthly*, which had only recently come under fire from the Communist Party. It had already been expressed by two members of the *Modern Monthly* editorial board in 1934: Max Eastman, who considered himself a Trotskyist though he was organizationally unaffiliated, and Edmund Wilson, who in 1931 declared in the *New Republic* his desire to "take communism away from the Communists." During this period Hook served as the main theoretician of *Modern Monthly*, Lionel Trilling began contributing book reviews, and six of Trilling's associates from the old *Menorah Journal* circle were published in the magazine—Elliot Cohen, Louis Berg, Herbert Solow, Felix Morrow, Anita Brenner, and Tess Slesinger (who would shortly find her way back to collaboration with the Communists).

Following the Communist Party's explicit embrace of reformism, signaled by the Popular Front turn in 1935, the first

Moscow Trials a year later and growing awareness of the Party's counter-revolutionary role in Spain, this anti-Stalinist left began to broaden. When *Partisan Review* was relaunched in December 1937, after breaking with the Communist Party, the editors essentially agreed with Hook, the former *Menorah Journal* writers, and the *Modern Monthly* editorial board. Although they professed freedom from political bias in matters of artistic preference, and eschewed organizational affiliation, they declared their adherence to a revolutionary, communist, working-class program: "Our program is the program of Marxism, which in general terms means being for the revolutionary overthrow of capitalist society, for a workers' government, and for international socialism. In contemporary terms it implies the struggle against capitalism in all its modern guises and disguises, including bourgeois democracy, fascism, and reformism (social democracy, Stalinism)."

This last affirmation, that both social democracy and Stalinism are reformist vehicles for sustaining the rule of world capitalism, is crucial. It is the key to understanding the New York intellectuals' critique of the Popular Front. In later years some of the New York intellectuals retrospectively criticized the Popular Front as a means by which the evil genius of Communism manipulated innocents and fellow-travelers. But the cutting edge of their original criticism was that the Popular Front truncated the struggle for communism by accommodation to the continued rule of imperialism because it was the instrument by which the Communist International hoped to stabilize an alliance between the Soviet Union and the democratic capitalist regimes in the West. In a 1939 *Partisan Review* article, "Anatomy of the Popular Front," Hook argued that "a socialist who supports a Popular Front government may find that as a result of its program of defense of capitalism, it may open the gates to Fascists who are even more resolute defenders of capitalism."

DURING AND AFTER WW II, most of the New York intellectuals abandoned the revolutionary pro-working class perspective they had previously defended. For many, like Hook and Rahv, signs of their later transformation first appeared in a startling reversal of one of the most fundamental positions that they had previously held—that capitalist America's entrance into WW II would not be to defend democracy or to fight fascism on principle, but to attain domination of the world's economy. Until 1940, the New York intellectuals frequently argued that the war must be politically opposed as an imperialist war, and that the working class, oppressed minorities, and colonial nations should continue their struggle for a socialist world that would eradicate fascism, permanently, by eliminating its capitalist roots.

In April 1936, Hook debated Popular Front supporter Ludwig Lore in the pages of *Modern Monthly* on the issue of whether to support the League of Nations' sanctions against Italy for invading Ethiopia. Hook argued that these sanctions would simply serve as an instrument in the hands of the great capitalist powers, England and France, to strengthen their imperialist grip over newer rivals. He adamantly argued that the United States, France, and England should not be portrayed as good or progressive in contrast to rival capitalist nations such as Italy and Germany, because this would obscure the imperialist economic foundations they had in common. "Notice that bourgeois democratic France is doing in Indo-China, bourgeois democratic Belgium is doing in the Congo, bourgeois democratic England is doing in Egypt precisely the same thing which Italy wants to do in Ethiopia," admonished Hook.

Hook also insisted that it was false to depict the coming war as a "choice between fascism and bourgeois democracy." He argued that "politically, economically and culturally the real choice is between *socialism* and fascism. Those who look for a lesser evil to escape the struggle for socialism will always find one at hand, relegating socialism . . . to the land of pipe dreams...." Hood maintained that the first enemy of any oppressed class is its own ruling class: "From the point of view of the working class any measure which strengthens the military arm of the State power weakens the workers in their struggle for socialism. Was this not the lesson of the social-democratic debacle in Germany [in 1914] where the socialists voted military appropriations as 'defense' against the enemies of Kultur ... only to discover that the military machine would countenance no socialist agitation, and was used most ruthlessly against the working-class?" Hook concluded his polemic with a memorable prophecy: "Those who are diverting the labor movement from the struggle for socialism to a support for nationalist sanctions and imperialist war may live to see the suicidal consequences of their policy, i.e., the destruction of the militant working-class movement."

What happened four years later is that many of the New York intellectuals carried out what Hook had explicitly characterized as a "suicidal" policy: Under the pressure of popular support for the war they lost sight of the overriding class character of the war, ironically emulating the Communist Party's Popular Front line. What remained at root an inter-imperialist conflict between the Anglo-American and Axis powers became reduced in their view to but one of its facets—a war against fascism. The monster of British imperialism—once described as the brutal master of India, much of Africa and the Mideast, and as "perfidious Albion," betrayer of the Spanish Republic—was now blotted out almost entirely by the image of the heroic English at the Battle of Britain.

The position taken by many of the New York intellectuals (among the exceptions for various reasons, Wilson, McCarthy, Greenberg, Schapiro, Macdonald, and Farrell) was rooted in the reality of the times, especially in the mass pressure to conform to American ruling class propaganda about the war. Much has been written about the need felt by American intellectuals to conform during the McCarthy era, but less often discussed is the pressure to line up with Washington during WW II.

WW II WAS AN IMMENSELY POPULAR WAR. The entire American left, with the exception of miniscule groups of pacifists and Trotskyists, enthusiastically supported it. After all, the revelations of fascist atrocities were hideous beyond belief, involving the destruction of entire peoples. And after Germany's attack on the Soviet Union in June 1941, the issue of the USSR's survival loomed large for those who felt that it still retained some progressive features. Radicals, above all, understand that in real world conflicts there is no room for fence-sitters; either one fought fascism in the concrete, militarily, or one did not. These were very powerful arguments for not viewing WW II in a routine manner—from a Leninist or Luxemburgian point of view—simply as a replica of WW I.

Yet to change one's characterization of the war from being fundamentally inter-imperialist to fundamentally anti-fascist had a logic of its own. In retrospect, there is evidence that even those who claimed to give the war no more than "critical" support were unable to act in any meaningful way to aid working class and anti-racist struggles at home and support movements for national liberation in the colonies such as India. In practice, political support for the war meant to subordinate the working class to the ruling class, and thus to succumb ultimately to the same myth of the "sacred union," based on a supra-class "national unity," that had discredited and virtually destroyed the Second International at the advent of WW I.

The clearest evidence that political support for the government's war effort meant halting the struggle for socialism in the United States and placing the liberation of oppressed minorities on the back burner can be seen in the actions of the Communist Party. As documented in Irving Howe and Lewis Coser's *The American Communist Party* and elsewhere, the Party dubbed all war-time strikes "treacherous"; it applauded the government's imprisonment of Socialist Workers Party leaders under the Smith "Gag" Act; it denounced the "Double V" campaign of Afro-Americans for civil rights at home in conjunction with victory abroad as disruptive; it called Norman Thomas an "accomplice of fascism" for his concern with civil liberties on the home front, particularly his criticism of the internment of the Japanese-American population; and it opposed the movements for national independence in the colonies of the Allies.

What was required, to be consistent with the original anti-imperialist analysis of Hook and the other New York intellectuals, was a program of military struggle against fascism that also fostered the class independence of the workers from the ruling class. The "revolutionary defeatism" proposed by Lenin never implied a willingness to be subjugated by oppressive regimes. An appropriate extension of Hook's original analysis might have been based on the principle that the workers themselves had to take charge of the war effort, expressed through demands for trade union control of the military, and consistent propaganda explaining that the real war aims of the American ruling class were unambiguously imperialist despite the demagogy of Roosevelt's "Four Freedoms." On such a basis the battle for socialism could have been continued during the war; but apart from the intellectuals in Trotskyist parties, only Schapiro, Farrell, Greenberg, and Macdonald (in his early phase) shared this perspective.

In the summer of 1940, Hook wrote in the *New Leader* that WW II was not an imperialist war but a progressive one that warranted the political support of every socialist. In 1943, in the latter part of a major article appearing in two issues of *Partisan Review*, he made his famous charge that those of his former associates who still adhered to a revolutionary working class position on the war, such as Schapiro and Farrell, had exhibited a "failure of nerve." Writing under the pseudonym David Merian, Meyer Schapiro responded that, confronted with the reality of war, it was Hook who had lost his nerve and embraced the same perspective he had excoriated in previous days.

The result of abandoning an anti-imperialist position during WW II, coupled with the decline of working class militancy and the beginnings of the Cold War, was that many New York intellectuals dismissed the reality of American imperialism in the postwar period. This view was explicitly expressed in a 1948 statement by Philip Rahv that "American 'imperialism' is the bogey of people who have not yet succeeded in getting rid of their Stalinist hangover." In various forms most of the New York intellectuals eventually came to embrace the very supraclass theories they had once rejected. Their newly adopted views found expression in a cluster of key terms that began to appear increasingly in their writing: "modulation," "variousness," "skeptical realism," "moral realism," "the imagination of disaster," "the end of ideology," and, in the arena of political polemic, "liberal anti-communism" and "anti-anti-communism." These coinages were an attempt to convince themselves and others that they had moved forward instead of backward. Yet most of their "new" views about the sociological character of the Soviet Union and the "straight-line thesis" that Leninism automatically leads to Stalinism had been stated decades earlier by the Mensheviks and other opponents of the October Revolution, and the political program they espoused for the reform of capitalism hardly went beyond the New Deal reforms they had criticized from the left.

The particular current of post-WW II social thought associated with many of the New York intellectuals' political and cultural ideas was correctly characterized by Robert Booth Fowler as that of "Believing Skeptics," proclaimers of a selective kind of skepticism that is nothing less than ideology *sui generis*. Not only was the notion of "end of ideology" an ideological stance itself, but the supra-class values of "realism" and "modulation" were equally deceptive. In truth, the program and perspectives of most of the group in the postwar era embodied support for capitalism, with a veneer of criticism to salve their consciences. In 1967, Philip Rahv, who was suddenly retransformed into a leftist, offered a trenchant critique of the role played by a sizable number of New York intellectuals in the American Committee for Cultural Freedom: "The people who accepted CIA subsidies without being clear in their minds as to what was involved are in many ways to be compared to the 'fellow-travelers' and 'stooges' of the 1930s, who supported Stalin's reading of Marxism and his murderous policies even as they spoke of the Russia he despotically ruled as a 'workers paradise' and a 'classless society.' But in contrast to the 'stooges' of yesterday, the 'stooges' of today are paid cash on the line for their various declarations."

*   *   *

THE MOVEMENT OF THE NEW YORK INTELLECTUALS from revolutionary anti-Stalinism to a self-proclaimed "liberal anti-communism," with the corresponding shift in class allegiance, has to be seen in a socio-historical light, not merely as an individual phenomenon. Once on the path of supporting US imperialism as the answer to Stalinism, it became increasingly easier for many of them to renege on support of progressive domestic legislation as well. In the 1960s, some of the New York intellectuals were more distressed by rebelling students, women, and blacks than they were by the slaughter of Vietnamese peasants and by US support to reactionary dictatorships around the world. In 1972, Hook, Kristol, Podhoretz, and a number of others voted for Richard Nixon as the "lesser evil" against George McGovern, although they were registered

177

Democrats. In 1980 they and many others supported Reagan.

What remained most consistent in their ideological outlook was their virulent hostility to Stalinism, increasingly equated with Leninism and ultimately any form of revolutionary Marxism. They seized on the fact that Leninism and Stalinism had a sequential relationship and certain superficial similarities, jettisoning their earlier belief that the latter was in essence a negation of the former.

In the 1960s it became popular for some New Leftists to excoriate the ex-radical New York intellectuals as sell-outs, opportunists, and phonies. While some individuals within the group may deserve these epithets, such ad hominem attacks do little to explain the evolution of an *entire generation*—for even though the New York intellectuals have their particular history, they are only a few dozen among thousands of intellectuals as well as workers, ex-Trotskyists as well as ex-Communists and ex-Socialists, who were deradicalized after the 1930s. What is required is an exploration of the social and historical factors that encouraged this unfortunate but not predestined transformation of revolutionary Marxists into an entirely different political species. Some of these factors can be summarized as follows.

• First, the ability of the anti-Stalinist New York intellectuals to sustain a revolutionary political outlook in the early and middle 1930s was partly dependent on events that inspired them with confidence in the working class as a force for radical social change. There were the heroic strikes of the 1930s—dock workers in San Francisco, truckers in Minneapolis, auto workers in Michigan—and the rise of the CIO. The courage and idealism of the rank-and-file of the labor movement seemed to portend the new socialist order, while capitalism appeared impotent in the face of the Depression.

• Second, during the Spanish Civil War the activity of the POUM, the anarchists, and the Trotskyists in the face of both Francoism and Stalinism was a further source of inspiration. It seemed possible that a revolutionary alternative to both the USSR and capitalism might develop in Europe. Also, Trotsky was still alive, an authentic revolutionary voice arguing for the compatibility of communism and democracy, and exposing Stalinism from a Marxist point of view.

• Third, the New York intellectuals led economically marginal lives. Only a few—Burnham, Hook, Schapiro and Trilling—had university positions. Several of the men were supported by their wives; a number had WPA jobs from time to time; those who were students came from poor families and lived at home. They did not anticipate financial success under existing social arrangements.

By the end of WW II, everything had changed, particularly those circumstances that had been largely responsible for turning these intellectuals into revolutionaries in the 1930s. Despite a postwar upsurge, the working class movement failed to become sufficiently re-energized and soon declined. American capitalism, on the other hand, appeared to be entering a period of unprecedented prosperity.

The international scene seemed bleaker than ever to them. There were no socialist revolutions in Europe and their anti-Stalinist perceptions were not shared by the left. The Soviet Union emerged from the war with enormous political power and enhanced prestige in the European left. In a short time, the Cold War began, followed by McCarthyism.

Finally, the New York intellectuals' political rethinking did not evolve in isolation from important changes in their social status. The new wealth of postwar America provided considerable opportunities for them to pursue careers in publishing and the universities, especially with their anti-Communist credentials highly publicized through their activity in the American Committee for Cultural Freedom. As Alfred Kazin recounts in *New York Jew*, these were heady times when, unlike in the 1930s, the New York intellectuals were all on the *inside*. In the absence of a militant working class pole, many of them gravitated toward the seats of power in bourgeois society where they were welcomed for the services they had to offer: "The cold war and McCarthy era needed them, raised them, publicized them. Sometimes. . . the government financed them. Those who had so long talked of alienation, who had proven the iron necessity of alienation, who had loved the theory of alienation and especially *their* alienation, were now with the government of the United States as advisers on Communism, 'experts on Communism.' "

By the time there was a resurgence of social and political

struggle in the 1960s, many of these intellectuals had hardened into apologists for American imperialism and could no longer be moved. But a few others—such as Dwight Macdonald, Mary McCarthy, F. W. Dupee, and Philip Rahv—broke free of their conservatism or political quiescence, moving sharply left. This suggests that, had the postwar labor upsurge sustained itself in the 1940s, at least some of the New York intellectuals would have continued on their leftwing path.

Today we stand on the verge of what may yet turn out to be the most significant economic crisis and explosion of class battles in American history. History is not circular, but certain problems must be resolved before there is the possibility of real progress. If the best hopes and aspirations of the New York intellectuals in their early and admirable phase are to be fulfilled, the development of a genuinely revolutionary anti-Stalinist socialist movement remains the next important step.

Bibliography

Selected List of Works on the New York Intellectuals
Aaron, Daniel, *Writers on the Left: Episodes in American Literary Communism* (New York: Avon, 1962).
"Edmund Wilson's Political Decade," in *Literature at the Barricades: The American Writer in the 1930s,* eds. Ralph F. Bogardus and Fred Hobson (Alabama: University of Alabama Press, 1982), pp. 174-86.
Atlas, James, *Delmore Schwartz: The Life of an American Poet* (New York: Farrar, Straus, and Giroux, 1977).
Bell, Daniel, "The 'Intelligentsia' in American Society," in *The Winding Passage: Essays and Sociological Journies, 1960-1980* (New York: Basic Books, 1980), pp. 119-137.
Burnham, James, and Max Shachtman, "Intellectuals in Retreat," *New International* 5, no. 1 (January 1939): 3-21.
Chace, William M., *Lionel Trilling: Criticism and Politics* (Stanford: Stanford University Press, 1980).
Cochran, Bert, "Intellectuals and the Cold War," in *Adlai Stevenson: Patrician Among Politicians* (New York: Funk and Wagnalls, 1969), pp. 343-98.
Cooney, Terry A., "Cosmopolitan Values and the Identification of Reaction: *Partisan Review* in the 1930s," *Journal of American History* 68, no. 3 (December 1981): 580-598.
Crews, Frederick, "The Partisan," *New York Review of Books,* 23 November 1978, pp. 3-9.
Diggins, John, *Up from Communism* (New York: Harper and Row, 1975).
Fiedler, Leslie, "*Partisan Review:* Phoenix or Dodo?" *Perspectives* 15 (spring

1956): 82-97.

Gilbert, James B., "James Burnham: Collectivism Triumphant," in *Designing the New Industrial State* (New York: Quadrangle, 1972), pp. 266-284.

Writers and Partisans (New York: Wiley, 1968).

Gold, Mike, *The Hollow Men* (New York: International, 1941).

Green, Philip, *The Pursuit of Inequality* (New York: Pantheon, 1981).

Hindus, Milton, "Philip Rahv," in *Images and Ideas in American Culture,* ed. Arthur Edelstein (Hanover: University Press of New England, 1979), pp. 197-203.

Hollinger, David, "Ethnic Diversity, Cosmopolitanism and the Emergence of the American Liberal Intelligentsia," *American Quarterly* 27 (May 1975): 133-51.

Kadushin, Charles, *The American Intellectual Elite* (Boston: Little, Brown and Company, 1974).

Kostelanetz, Richard, *The End of Intelligent Writing: Literacy Politics in America* (New York: Sheed and Ward, 1974).

Krupnick, Mark, "Lionel Trilling, Freud, and the Fifties," *Humanities in Society* 3, no. 3 (summer 1980): 265-282.

"The New York Intellectuals: Losing Touch with Tradition," *The Christian Century,* 3-10 June 1981, pp. 636-640.

Kuspit, Donald B., *Clement Greenberg: Art Critic* (Madison: University of Wisconsin Press, 1979).

Lasch, Christopher, "The Cultural Cold War: A Short History of the Congress of Cultural Freedom," in *The Agony of the American Left* (New York: Vintage, 1968), pp. 61-114.

"Modernism, Politics, and Philip Rahv," *Partisan Review,* 47, no. 2 (1980): 183-94.

The New Radicalism in America (New York: Vintage, 1967).

Longstaff, S. A., "The New York Family," *Queen's Quarterly* 83 (winter 1976): 108-29.

"Partisan Review and the Second World War," *Salmagundi* 43 (winter 1979): 108-29.

McAuliffe, Mary Sperling, *Crisis on the Left: Cold War Politics and American Liberals, 1947-1954* (Amherst: University of Massachusetts Press, 1978).

Nash, Michael, "Schism on the Left: The Anti-Communism of V. F. Calverton and his *Modern Quarterly," Science and Society* 45, no. 4 (winter 1981-82): 437-452.

Nobile, Philip, *Intellectual Skywriting: Literary Politics and the New York Review of Books* (New York: Charterhouse, 1974).

O'Neill, William L., *The Last Romantic: A Life of Max Eastman* (New York: Oxford, 1978).

Pells, Richard, "From Depression to War," in *Radical Visions and American Dreams* (New York: Harper and Row, 1973), pp. 330-364.

Shechner, Mark, "The Elusive Trilling, Part I," *The Nation,* 17 September 1977, pp. 247-250.

"The Elusive Trilling, Part II," *The Nation,* 24 September 1977, pp. 278-280.

"Lionel Trilling: Psychoanalysis and Liberalism," *Salmagundi* (spring 1978): 3-32.

Steinfels, Peter, *The Neo-Conservatives: The Men Who Are Changing America's Politics* (New York: Simon and Schuster, 1979).

Wald, Alan, "Herbert Solow: Portrait of a New York Intellectual," *Prospects: A Journal of American Cultural Studies* 3 (December 1977): 418-460.

James T. Farrell: The Revolutionary Socialist Years (New York: New York University Press, 1978).

"Memories of the John Dewey Commission: Forty Years Later," *Antioch Review* 35 (fall 1977): 438-51.

"The *Menorah* Group Moves Left," *Jewish Social Studies* 38 (summer-fall 1976): 289-320.

"Revolutionary Intellectuals: *Partisan Review* in the 1930s," in *Literature at the Barricades,* pp. 187-203.

Webster, Grant, *Republic of Letters* (Baltimore: Johns Hopkins University Press, 1978).

Whitfield, Stephen J., *Into the Dark: Hannah Arendt and Totalitarianism* (Philadelphia: Temple University Press, 1980).

Selected Autobiographies and Memoirs of the New York Intellectuals

Abel, Lionel, "New York City: A Remembrance," *Dissent* 8, no. 3 (summer 1961): 251-59.

"Sartre Remembered," *Salmagundi* 56 (spring 1982): 101-127.

"The Surrealists in New York," *Commentary* 72, no. 4 (October 1981): 44-54.

"Through a Glass Darkly," *Dissent* 28, no. 4 (fall 1981): 442-456.

Barzun, Jacques, "Remembering Lionel Trilling," *Encounter* 23, no. 3 (September 1976): 82-88.

Bazelon, David, "A Writer Between Generations," in *Nothing But a Fine Tooth Comb* (New York: Simon and Schuster, 1969), pp. 17-48.

Bell, Daniel, "First Love and Early Sorrows," *Partisan Review* 47, no. 4 (1981): 532-551.

Farrell, James T., "Dewey in Mexico," in *John Dewey: Philosopher of Science and Freedom,* ed. Sidney Hook (New York: Dial Press, 1950), pp. 351-377.

"A Memoir of Trotsky," *University of Kansas City Review* 23 (summer 1957): 293-298.

Fiedler, Leslie, "Bergen Street: 1933," in *Being Busted* (New York: Stein and Day, 1969), pp. 11-28.

Halper, Albert, *Good-Bye Union Square* (New York: Quadrangle, 1970).

Hook, Sidney, "Anti-Semitism in the Academy: Some Pages of the Past," *Midstream* 25, no. 1 (January 1979): 49-54.

"The *Modern Quarterly,* A Chapter from Radical History," *Labor History* 10 (spring 1974): 241-49.

"Remembering Max Eastman," *American Scholar* 45, no. 2 (summer 1979): 404-416.

"Remembering Whittaker Chambers," *Encounter* 46, no. 1 (January 1976): 78-89.

and Diana Trilling, "Remembering Whittaker Chambers: An Exchange Between Diana Trilling and Sidney Hook," *Encounter* 46, no. 6 (June 1976): 94-96.

"Some Memories of John Dewey," *Commentary* 14 (September 1952): 245-53.

Howe, Irving, "Mid-Century Turning Point: An Intellectual Memoir," *Mid-stream* 21, no. 6 (June-July 1975): 23-28.

"The New York Intellectuals," in *Decline of the New* (New York: Horizon, 1970), pp. 211-265.

"New York in the Thirties," *Dissent* 8, no. 3 (summer 1961): 241-250.

"Philip Rahv: A Memoir," *The American Scholar* 45, no. 3 (fall 1979): 487-498.

"The Thirties in Retrospect," in *Literature at the Barricades,* pp. 13-28.

Kazin, Alfred, *Starting Out in the Thirties* (Boston: Atlantic Monthly Press, 1965).

New York Jew (New York: Knopf, 1978).

Kristol, Irving, "Memoirs of a Trotskyist," *New York Times Magazine,* 23 January 1977, pp. 42-43, 50-51, 54-57.

Lelchuck, Alan, "Philip Rahv: The Last Years," in *Images and Ideas in American Culture,* pp. 204-219.

Macdonald, Dwight, *Memoirs of a Revolutionist* (New York: Meridian, 1963).

McCarthy, Mary, "Interview," *Paris Review* 27 (winter-spring 1962): 58-94.

"My Confession," in *On the Contrary* (New York: Noonday, 1962), pp. 75-106.

Novack, George, "How the Moscow Trials Were Exposed," *International Socialist Review,* May 1977, pp. 3, 4, 10-11.

"My Philosophical Itinerary: An Autobiographical Foreword," in *Polemics in Marxist Philosophy* (New York: Monad, 1978), pp. 11-37.

"Radical Intellectuals in the 1930s," *International Socialist Review* 29, no. 2 (March-April 1968): 311-333.

Phillips, William, "Another Congress, Another Time," *Partisan Review* 49, no. 1 (1982): 7-9.

"How *Partisan Review* Began," *Commentary* 62, no. 6 (December 1976): 42-46.

"What Happened in the 30s," in *A Sense of the Present* (New York: Chilimark, 1967), pp. 12-29.

Podhoretz, Norman, *Breaking Ranks: A Political Memoir* (New York: Harper and Row, 1979).

Making It (New York: Bantam, 1969).

Roskolenko, Harry, *When I Was Last on Cherry Street* (New York: Stein and Day, 1965).

Trilling, Diana, "Lionel Trilling: A Jew at Columbia," in *Speaking of Literature and Society,* ed. Lionel Trilling (New York: Harcourt, Brace, Jovanovich, 1980), pp. 411-429.

Trilling, Lionel, "Afterword," in *The Unpossessed,* ed. Tess Slesinger (New York: Avon, 1966), pp. 311-333.

"Some Notes for an Autobiographical Lecture," in *The Last Decade: Essays and Reviews* (New York: Harcourt, Brace, Jovanovich, 1977), pp. 226-241.

"Whittaker Chambers' Journey," in *The Last Decade,* pp. 185-203.

Wolfe, Bernard, *Memoirs of a Not Altogether Shy Pornographer* (New York: Doubleday, 1972).

Is America Modern?

ALAN WOLFE

MODERNIZATION, IN RETROSPECT, WAS THE ORGANIZING CONCEPT of postwar American political sociology. Rival candidates—the end of ideology, post-industrial society, pluralism, formal rationality, bureaucratization, and consensus, to name a few—can all be viewed as illustrations of the master hypothesis that the US, and by implication other advanced industrial democracies, was moving in a direction that could be judged more enlightened, more decidedly "modern," than the stage out of which it passed. Underlying the optimism of the Great American Celebration that was sociology were two widely shared notions: modernization was good, and America was rapidly becoming the most modernized society in the world.

In no other thinker is the centrality of modernization more closely recognized than in the writings of Daniel Bell. As early as his first essay for *The New American Right* (1955), Bell viewed the shenanigans of Joseph McCarthy and his followers as a "turbulance born not of depression, but of prosperity."[1] As America matured, Bell argued, it brought within the sphere of organized politics formerly exluded groups like poor farmers and the working class, stabilizing the political system. But not everyone accepted these trends, and especially among those whose status was threatened by them, there developed a poli-

---

ALAN WOLFE *is Professor of Sociology at Queens College and the Graduate Center, City University of New York. The author of* America's Impasse: The Rise and Fall of the Politics of Growth *and* The Limits of Legitimacy: Political Contradictions of Contemporary Capitalism, *he is also a frequent contributor to* The Nation *and a member of its editorial board.*

tics of *ressentiment*. Later on, in 1962, Bell added to this framework the notion that changes wrought by the New Deal turned the United States into more of a technocratic meritocracy, in which "political position rather than wealth, and technical skill rather than property, have become the bases from which power is wielded."[2] Such transformations left behind an old elite, bruised and angry at the modern world: the peculiar moral and status-oriented concerns of the right—what today we call the social issues—were a product of this social, but not economic, displacement.

The tragic flaw of the radical right, in Bell's view, was its refusal to accept change, for change was the *sine qua non* of the modern condition. Also in 1955, in a paper read at a conference of the Congress for Cultural Freedom and later published as the first chapter in *The End of Ideology,* Bell put the matter this way: "The most salient fact about modern life—capitalist and communist—is the ideological commitment to social change. And by change is meant the striving for material, economic betterment, greater opportunity for individuals to exercise their talents, and an appreciation of culture by wider masses of people. Can any society deny these aspirations?"[3] Implicit in the question, for America at any rate, is the answer: the US modernizes to the degree that it accepts growth, merit, and democracy. "The United States," Bell concluded, "is probably the first large society in history to have change and innovation 'built into' its culture."[4]

Bell's subtle and often engaging attempts to delineate the effects of a modernizing culture on American institutions constitutes the unifying theme of the essays written between 1955 and 1959 and collected in *The End of Ideology.* From the perspective of more than two decades later, the title of the book appears ill-chosen, for it called unending attention to one of the weaker essays in the collection. When he examined the empirical matrix of American life in these essays, Bell's emphasis on the tensions of modernization produced durable, even radical, insights. For example, Bell argued that New York's longshore industry, despite the efforts of (often Republican) reformers, would continue to be racket-ridden so long as no other appropriate method of rationalizing the conditions of work existed. The specific features of the port—its shape-up, its deteriorating conditions, its immigrant work force—made irrelevant the kinds of gentleman's agreement union tactics of the AFL. Given these features of the industry, "industrial racketeering ...performs the function—at a high price—which other agencies cannot do, of stabilizing a chaotic market and establishing an order and structure in the industry."[5] Like many New Left critics of a later period, Bell recognized that the result was a pattern of accommodation "which worked to the benefit of the shopowners and the union barons and against the interests of the men."[6] But he warned that in the absence of a thorough rationalization of the "technological environment,"[7] racketeering would inevitably persist.

The implication of Bell's analysis of the longshore industry was that such corrupt practices as racketeering were a legacy of pre-modern industrial relations; unstated was the notion that as modernization progressed, such aspects of social life would crumble. Indeed, modernization meant many such transformations. The mafia, for example, was a "myth," irrelevant to a modern society. Moreover, Bell asserted that "there is probably less crime today [1955] in the United States than existed a hundred, or fifty, or even twenty-five years ago, and. . . today the United States is a more lawful and safe country than popular opinion imagines."[8] As crime goes, so does socialism. Eugene Debs, with his aching yearning for a utopian community, is as irrelevant to the modernizing tendencies of American life as the mafia, with its rituals and traditional sense of honor. If socialism withers away, Bell argues, so does the ruling class, for the rationalization and meritocratization of American life undermines both those who try to revolutionize it and those who no longer benefit from it. Yes, there is an end of ideology, says Bell, but this is not the major point, for there is an end to so many familiar things. In *The End of Ideology*, Bell was the prophet of modernity, advising all those who resisted the trends—socialists, radical rightists, mafiosi, alienated intellectuals—to give up their futile dreams and join him in welcoming the inevitable.

DANIEL BELL WORKED FOR YEARS ON *The Coming of Post-Industrial Society*, publishing bits and pieces of it in preparation for its arrival and implying that this would be his major statement. The book is written in a different style than *The End of Ideology*, more inflated, more self-important, more declarative of its uniqueness. But Bell's most ambitious book never did catch on; *Post-Industrial Society* lacks the bite of *The End of Ideology*, and in fact it never gained the attention that this earlier book did. The reason may be that in the course of working on the essays that compose it, Bell's opinions about modernization began to shift, leaving him, and his readers, confused about the implications of his analysis.[9]

At one level, *Post-Industrial Society* fits into the mold of Bell's earlier ideas, extending his notions of the meritocratic and rationalizing change from the world of goods production to the world of service delivery. If capitalism extended the sphere of functional rationality far beyond feudalism, then post-industrial capitalism raises the rate of change exponentially. Change itself changes, Bell argues, for we are witnessing rates of change beyond the belief of even nineteenth century man. The most important of these changes, documented with a range of numbers and references to scientific literature of every sort, is the growth of knowledge and technology, now the defining features of the modern condition. "The central point about the last third of the twentieth century, call it the post-industrial society, the knowledgeable society, the technocratic age, or the active society, is that it will require more societal guidance, more expertise."[10] Inevitably, Bell concluded, planning will replace the market, the corporation will be "subdued" by politics, and, as Bell had suggested as early as 1962, skill and education will replace property and wealth as the social bases of rule. Post-industrial society is modernization projected into the future.

By the time that post-industrial society arrived toward the end of his volume, Bell began to articulate some second thoughts about the whole phenomenon. Science, Bell discovered, becomes so important in political and strategic terms that its neutrality can come under attack from vested interests. Post-industrial society is meritocratic, but not necessarily egalitarian. Sufficient production of goods does not mean an end to scarcity, for information and time are subject to scarcities as well. Efficiency and technology, finally, do not bring with them their own culture; if anything, they are accompanied by a wild hedonism—Bell calls it an antinomian dimension to culture—that asserts Dionysian protests against Apollonian results. No longer does the optimist speak: "a post-industrial society gives rise to a new Utopianism, both engineering and psychedelic. Men can be remade or released, their behavior conditioned or their consciousness altered. The constraints of the past vanish with the end of nature and things."[11]

Some of the confusion caused by the speculations at the end of *Post-Industrial Society* were clarified when Bell collected his various essays dealing with *The Cultural Contradictions of Capitalism.* Then it became clear that Bell, the liberal optimist welcoming modernization, had turned into Bell the conservative skeptic distraught at its arrival. By 1978, when Bell wrote his preface to *Cultural Contradictions,* the antinomian trends hinted at in his previous book had come to assume a major role in his thinking. Modernity to him now had a dual, and quite contradictory, character. On the one hand, capitalism broadened and deepened the rationality and calculability of modern society, but at the same time, modernist trends in culture emphasized the pre-rational, mythopoetic desires of individual need. Rousseau is as much a representative of modern thought as Locke. In the 1950s, modernity, to Bell, meant change; by the 1970s, he argued that "the fundamental assumption of modernity, the thread that has run through Western civilization since the sixteenth century, is that the social unit of society is not the group, the guild, the tribe, or the city, but the person."[12] The counterculture takes its place alongside the multinational corporation as a symbol of the modern condition.

Interestingly enough, both Bell the liberal and Bell the conservative exaggerated the permanence of what now seem to be transient trends. On the one hand, the rationalizing tendencies of modern life were not nearly as complete as Bell implied. Most conspicuously, Bell's notion that planning and politics would "subdue" the corporation seems a bit premature in the age of Reagan and Thatcher. Indeed, the success of politicians whose roots lie in the rightwing is difficult to square with the hypothesis that the American right represents a protest against modernity; as I have argued elsewhere, it makes far greater sense to view the right as advocating an alternative path to modernity to the one articulated by Cold War liberals.[13] More than at any period since the New Deal, the 1980s have seen bourgeois thought become explicitly anti-rational, extolling faith and chance, denigrating predictability and calculability, and speaking openly of mysticism and subjectivity.[14] Antinomianism there is, but in defense of capitalism, not in opposition. Bell was far too sanguine in expecting capitalism to behave according to its own classical justification.

But if Bell the liberal overemphasized the rationality of modern corporate life, Bell the conservative also exaggerated the permanence of radical cultural opposition to those practices. The psychedelic consciousness that so upset him, the nihilism of art, literature, and music, the emptiness of the modernist revolution, all seem passé at a time when Berkeley hippies open restaurants and seek out growth industries for Wall Street. In *Cultural Contradictions*, Bell interpreted the rise in cults as a response to the decline in the sacred, yet religion, including the most established, is on the upswing. Bell noted, as a response to cultural norms, a revolution of rising entitlements, yet cutbacks in entitlements by conservative administrations indicate how contingent this "revolution" was all along. Bell wrote that "the emphasis of modernism is on the present or the future, but never on the past,"[15] yet a wave of nostalgia seems characteristic of modern America. In short, rereading *Cultural Contradictions,* one feels that one is examining a book that not only failed to predict the future, but misinterpreted many of the events emerging when the book was written.

Daniel Bell traveled a long way in his intellectual development. In 1955 he wrote an essay, published in *The End of Ideology,* which claimed that America was not a mass society. In 1971, discussing "The Sensibility of the Sixties," Bell argued that, at least in the realm of culture, the theorists of mass society were correct. Yet despite changes of heart like these, Bell is a consistent thinker. Whether he praised modernism or denounced it, Bell made it the centerpiece of his analysis. The common thread that unites Bell the liberal with Bell the neoconservative is the idea that, for better or worse, America has been the leader in the experience of modernity. Yet has it been? Is America modern? If it is, what does modernity mean? These are the kinds of questions that need to be investigated. In the remainder of this essay, I will argue that America's experience with modernity was unique and extremely ambiguous, making its reaction to the political, social, and economic crises of the 1980s awkward and, occasionally, bizarre.

* * *

BEFORE 1893, EVERY CITY IN AMERICA had its own time. Since church bells struck the hour when the sun was directly overhead, noon in Boston took place twelve minutes—actually eleven minutes and forty-five seconds—before noon in New York. Work habits, transportation and everyday life were, as a result, impossible to plan and control. A "modern" society demanded the standardization of time. Time did become standardized in America, divided into four zones within which uniformity existed, but the process by which it happened tells us a great deal about the American experience with modernity. Congress did not pass a law, nor did state governments act. Instead, after strong endorsement from groups like the American Society of Civil Engineers, the railroads jointly placed their time-tables on a standardized basis. There was resistance; Chicago, for example, refused to go along for a brief spell. But eventually the system compelled obedience. And time in America was adjusted to become railroad time.[16]

While this was taking place, a system of rural free delivery was created in the American countryside. Before its creation, the collection of mail was a social experience in which people gathered in town to chat and exchange information. In 1891, the Postmaster General proposed that direct home delivery be established, so that farmers could order goods and have them shipped directly home. Despite the objections of local merchants, who would be sure to lose out to national retailers, Rural Free Delivery had too many powerful supporters behind it, and a significant degree of modernization came to rural America. That the Postmaster General responsible for creating this particular device was John Wanamaker, America's leading retailer, once again demonstrated the close relationship between the development of corporate capitalism and modernization American style.[17]

Examples like these suggest that in America modernization took on a unique style when compared to Europe. Especially

191

among late-blooming capitalist powers like Germany and Japan, modernization was a process directed by the state toward the specific objectives of industrialization, urbanization, and universalization. America, by contrast, pursued what can be called *modernization by default*, the creation of a national system of regulated capitalism led, not by the state, but by private corporations and created, not through planning and direct action, but by haphazard occurrence. America modernized in spite of itself, never completely aware of what it was doing. The result was that a concentrated, powerful, and integrated political economy was created in the United States while Americans were convinced that they lived in a rural, individualistic, and unorganized environment. America, in other words, was simultaneously modern in its political economy and pre-modern in its ideology. (I am not going as far as Jackson Lears, who has argued that an anti-modern ideology paved the way for modernist transformations, but I think there is much of value in what he claims.)[18]

The legacy of modernization by default exists everywhere in the US, but two examples may illustrate its persistence. In 1982, the failure to pass an equal rights amendment (ERA) to the US Constitution became manifest. By all the criteria of Weberian rationality, the specification of equal rights for women is part of the modernization process, so much so that, in theory, the issue should not even be controversial. But premodern ideology is so strong at the level of public consciousness that once the ERA was subject to open and public debate, its chances of passage appreciably diminished. For all those Americans convinced that modernity is evil, no matter how much their actual lives are subject to the dictates of consumer capitalism, the ERA became a convenient symbol of what they detested. Americans do not like modernity when it is proclaimed as modernity; they will accept all kinds of modernizing innovations in the way they buy goods, but not in the way they treat each other.

Even more revealing of the contradictory aspects of American modernity was the reaction in the United States to various proposals to adopt the metric system. As in the standardization of time, business interests were convinced that a global economy demanded the standardization of measurement. Losing out to foreign competition and unable to afford two sets of machinery, manufacturing industries sponsored the attempt to turn feet into meters. But it was a hopeless task, doomed to fail once the public was invited to participate. Unlike the situation in 1893, there was, evidently, more democracy in the United States, and since popular sentiment is so distinctively anti-modern, corporations were, in the 1980s, unable to impose their will on the rest of society. If the contrast between implementing standard time and the metric system means anything, America was more modern in 1890 than in 1980.

The problem with the analysis of Daniel Bell and other students of modernity was that they assumed the process to be of one piece. Rationalization in the area of science and technology would be accompanied by rationalization in politics and economics; only in the area of culture, according to Bell, was there autonomy, and this was only recognized late in his writings. But in America modernization was not of one piece; the United States experienced what can only be called combined and uneven modernization. A fabulous, indeed stunning, revolution in the arena of technology was accompanied by a retrogression in the arena of public consciousness. To borrow Marxist language again, the forces of production are modern, while the relations of production are antique.

A major consequence of the political crisis in the US—or perhaps it is a cause—is that modernizing elites have lost control over the modernization process. Since the last decade of the nineteenth century, self-consciously modernizing elites, operating from Hamiltonian premises, have attempted to transform the United States into an industrial and military power over the opposition of localist, often Jeffersonian, opposition. From the nationalism of Herbert Croly to the explicit neo-Hamiltonianism of Samuel P. Huntington, such action-oriented intellectuals have recognized the Sisyphean task of moving such an awkward and cumbersome polity as the United States toward what they believed to be its true destiny. Two world wars, a Great Depression, and a Cold War all made their contribution; by the middle of the 1960s, America seemed firmly ensconced along a path of greater economic planning, military power, and welfare provision—cardinal features of the modernist synthesis. Much self-congratulatory talk was heard about how America had come of age. An increasingly stable society at home guided an increasingly stable world order.

ONE SHOULD NEVER UNDERESTIMATE the force of anti-modern consciousness, as the best and the brightest, in their infinite hubris, did. No sooner had America adapted to its modernity than a counterrevolution against it began to pick up steam. Modernizing elites were attentive to everything but the popular will. Secure in their anti-democratic instincts, they assumed that once the obvious material benefits of rapid industrialization were passed down to ordinary people, the security of organized capitalism would be permanently achieved. It never occurred to these planners that ordinary people had moral principles and social priorities. Ironically, given its own anti-democratic creed, the New Right touched a deep popular need by raising issues of conscience, ones that no other powerful group in American society was willing to touch. As the economic and military synthesis of corporate liberalism began to crumble under the weight of its contradictions, anti-modernist tendencies, always latent, pushed themselves to the surface more than they were pushed by the New Right. In some ways, it is a wonder that it took as long as it did for a politician like Ronald Reagan to become president.

If the corporate liberals were guilty of excessive arrogance, the New Right is guilty of living a lie which, in my opinion, will ultimately be responsible for its undoing. For it is dynamite to preach anti-modernity in thought while presiding over an ever greater rationalization of economic and social practices. Unlike the older right, with its isolationist bent and respect for localism and competitive enterprise, the New Right under Reagan has borrowed from the corporate liberals an emphasis on economic growth, corporate concentration, technological fetishism, and military power. Whether its project can "work" is one question; whether it is compatible with values that emphasize traditional sex roles, hierarchy, and respect for order is another. The forces around Reagan are attempting to modernize America according to the dictates of a pre-modern consciousness. Only in America, with its radically underdeveloped political culture, could such an effort even be proposed; not even in America can it succeed.

Modernization, whether in the Third World or as part of the ongoing saga of advanced capitalism, is a wrenching, frightening process. Traditional social ties and values are destroyed, jobs are lost, stability threatened, and roles reversed. In the postwar period, America's reactions to these tendencies have taken two general forms. On the one hand there is the liberal optimism of someone like Daniel Bell, preaching the necessity of change as if it were antiseptic, and then turning in disgust at manifestations that it is not. On the other hand there is the New Right, willing to make an effort to lead change, all the while claiming to be conservative and respectful of traditional values. The American people have been offered a choice between two paths to modernization, one of which treats them with contempt and the other of which denies what it is doing.

The result of all this is that the United States faces a turning point in its history unsure that such a point exists and uncertain where to turn. America has modernized by default, but the point has been reached where modernization by default is no longer adequate. Not only do traditional American remedies no longer work, they exacerbate the situations they are supposed to relieve. Americans simultaneously are demanding further modernization while strongly resisting changes in behavior and attitude necessary to meet those demands. Some examples:

• Americans recognize that changes in productivity are necessary to make their country more competitive against Japan and Germany, but they are willing to allow conservative management, responsible for the lag in productivity in the first place, an unusual freedom to fail to modernize;
• Americans seem to desire increased national military protection, but they rebel against paying for it and are surely unwilling to live according to standards of military vigilance;
• It has become clear that the political structure of the United States is a rag-tag system of mutual vetoes and vested privileges, unable to pass legislation and unwilling to establish standards, yet there is little energy present to rationalize the system, and even when "reform" takes place, as in the 1981 tax law, it highlights and broadens the inequities of the system;
• A certain anxiety exists that America has lost its power and status in the world, yet when called upon to act in a mature way

in world affairs, the American state responds with dramatic and childlike tantrums unworthy of either the responsibilities or the rewards of power; Americans desire superpower status without engaging in superpower conduct.

America, in a word, is being victimized in the present by its luck in the past. Experiencing extraordinary economic growth, and avoiding a war fought at home for a century, Americans learned that modernization comes without substantial costs. That was an unfortunate lesson, for in fact the costs of modernization are enormous. Now that America can no longer grow or expand its military capacity without giving up something else, the popular response is to refuse to recognize the costs, to punish politicians who point out that such costs exist, to vote enthusiastically for other politicians who say that there are no costs, and then to turn in anger against the latter when costs are inevitably paid. So long as a desire to modernize technology and economic life coexists with a desire to preserve pre-modern political consciousness, America will be engaged in a futile search for a political happiness it cannot experience, bound to chew up its leaders, turn on its dissidents, enrage its allies, and startle the world with its irrationality.

* * *

NOW THAT AMERICAN SOCIOLOGY no longer plays the unanimously self-congratulatory role it did in the 1950s, the time has come to reevaluate the costs and benefits of modernity. Writers like Daniel Bell have already begun to do so, for implicit in the neo-conservative critique of society—always present in more explicit conservatives like Robert Nisbet[19]—is the feeling that modernist transformations cause more problems than they solve. Yet just as it was premature to celebrate modernity too casually, it may be equally incorrect to dismiss it too rapidly. Especially for those on the left, the lesson must be learned that modernity is a mixed process that compels careful and discriminating analysis. (One writer who expresses a healthy ambivalence toward modernization is Marshall Berman.)[20]

As with so much else in American society, the left has been of two minds concerning modernization. One tendency within socialist ideology is a more-modern-than-thou attitude, reflected in rural electrification, the transformation of farmers into workers, a more universalized and complex state, and economic concentration leading toward planning and rationalization. Urban, cosmopolitan, intellectual, the American left, if it had any power, could see itself stepping into the crisis of the bourgeois parties and leading the way through the impasse to an ever more rationalized society. Indeed, socialist concepts seem attractive to liberal economists like John Kenneth Galbraith and Lester Thurow precisely because the market no longer seems capable of allocating resources in anything like a modern way.

At the same time, from Ruskin and Morris to the environmentalists in the US, there has always been a significant degree of anti-modern sentiment in the socialist movement. Protesting against uniformity and mechanization, the left has also been rural rather than urban, romantic instead of intellectual, and organic as opposed to cosmopolitan. If this wing of the left had any power, it would call a halt to growth and economic rationalization, urging a preference for decentralized solutions and appropriate technology. The left has been as Janus-faced as Daniel Bell, welcoming modernization on the one hand but protesting its arrival on the other.

I expect a tension over the question of modernization to remain present on the left, and even to stimulate ideas, so my purpose will not be to call for a resolution of this tension. As one who is both attracted to the critique of industrial society offered by no-growth advocates, but who is also convinced that such a critique is invariably elitist, I can only urge that both tendencies be more open and self-scrutinizing about their attitudes toward modernity. If socialists are attracted to a Japan, Inc. model of industrial reorganization as a solution to the economic crisis, they have an obligation, political as well as moral, to discuss the social costs of the disruptions that will ensue and to develop plans for minimizing those costs according to principles of equity and social justice. There are no technological solutions to the present impasse, and those on the left who claim that there are, or who ignore the human problems that a technological fix would involve, are being as dishonest as the established powers. There is nothing wrong in urging modernity, since change is indeed inevitable. There is a good deal that is wrong in not being open about what one advocates.

At the same time, if the left moves toward a critique of growth, and in my opinion it should, it has an obligation to address the unpopular and thorny issues of how already existing benefits, the products of growth in the past, will be made available to those who do not have them, victims of no growth in the future. It is insufficient to call for environmental restrictions without talking of full employment or to urge an end to suburban sprawl without mentioning tax breaks for mortgage payments. It is not growth per sé that has caused the crisis, but the unequal distribution of the benefits of growth, a distinction which often gets lost in the environmentalist critique of contemporary capitalism.

It is somewhat unusual, and still somewhat uncomfortable, for the left to deal with issues involving modernization, for questions of class, the state, and political economy are so much more familiar. No doubt there will be resistance to addressing the issue of modernity at all, based on the notion that if we toppled the present ruling class and replaced it with another, issues of control, bureaucracy, rationality, and planning would somehow be resolved. This is why I began with Daniel Bell, because postwar American sociology, for all its ideological bias and complacency, was asking the right questions. The question of modernity *is* a question that compels an answer. America is neither as modern as the younger Daniel Bell believed nor as choked with reactions against modernity as the older Daniel Bell felt. America is remarkably modern in some ways, astonishingly anti-modern in others. To be relevant to its future, the American left faces the difficult task of sorting out the aspects of modernity it wants and the aspects it should rightly resist.

Footnotes

1. Daniel Bell, ed., *The Radical Right* (Garden City: Anchor Books, 1964), p. 47.
2. *Ibid*, p. 21.
3. Daniel Bell, *The End of Ideology* (Glencoe: Free Press, 1960), p. 29.
4. *Ibid*, p. 35-36.
5. *Ibid*, p. 160.
6. *Ibid*, p. 179.
7. *Ibid*, p. 161.
8. *Ibid*, p. 137.
9. This point is developed by Peter Steinfels in *The Neo-Conservatives* (New York: Simon and Schuster, 1979), p. 169.
10. Daniel Bell, *The Coming of Post-Industrial Society* (New York: Basic Books, 1973), p. 263.
11. *Ibid*, p. 488.
12. Daniel Bell, *The Cultural Contradictions of Capitalism* (New York: Basic Books, 1976), p. 16.
13. Alan Wolfe, "Sociology, Liberalism, and the Radical Right," *New Left Review* 128 (July-August 1981): 3-27.
14. The clearest example is George Gilder, *Wealth and Poverty* (New York: Basic Books, 1980).
15. *Cultural Contradictions*, p. 50.
16. Alan Trachtenberg, *The Incorporation of America* (New York: Hill and Wang, 1982), pp. 59-60. See also David Noble, *America By Design* (New York: Knopf, 1977).
17. Stuart and Elizabeth Ewen, *Channels of Desire* (New York: McGraw Hill, 1982), p. 67.
18. Jackson Lears, *No Place of Grace* (New York: Pantheon, 1981).
19. Robert Nisbet, *Social Change and History* (London: Oxford University Press, 1969).
20. Marshall Berman, *All That Is Solid Melts into Air* (New York: Simon and Schuster, 1981).

Socialist Freedom

RICHARD LICHTMAN

No FIELD OF INQUIRY BETTER ILLUSTRATES the dual function of ideology as false consciousness and legitimation of existing power than political philosophy. And in no instance is this more true than in regard to the subject of the freedom of the individual. Works which have dominated philosophic discussion in the present era—Popper's *The Open Society and its Enemies, Two Concepts of Liberty* by Isaiah Berlin, and Nozick's *Anarchy, State and Utopia*[1]—are of far less interest for their intrinsic merit than as ritual signifiers in the dramaturgy of the Cold War.

There is nothing in this situation which ought to surprise us, however. The deep hold that alienated labor and class power exercise over the nature of social consciousness, supported by control of the media, the domination of academic institutions and the instrumentality of the political system, all converge to produce the apologia for existing theories of bourgeois freedom that currently afflict us. What is of more concern is the lack of socialist theory to counter this massive "liberal" presence. And here again it is easy enough to list the justifications for socialist theoretical disarray: the absence of accredited positions of power; the fragility of constant minority opposition; the exhaustion of continued countermovements; the legal, political, academic and cultural harassment that is used by established power to weaken socialist movements. At some point, however, it is necessary to examine our own inadequacy and consider

RICHARD LICHTMAN *is on the faculty of the Wright Institute in Berkeley. A founding member of* Socialist Review, *he is the author of* The Production of Desire: The Integration of Psychoanalysis into Marxist Theory *(New York: Macmillan, 1982).*

whether we have exercised our own responsibility for the development of an alternative to the prevailing ideological hegemony of bourgeois views of freedom.

There are, of course, a number of important socialist works in political theory. They tend to be of several distinct sorts: exegesis of Marxist texts, analysis of attempts at socialist revolutions, and critiques of prevailing capitalist power. These are necessary and important works of theoretical praxes. Notably lacking, however, is a socialist critique of the philosophic foundations of the prevailing liberal view on individual freedom and the development of an appropriate countervailing socialist vision. In short, what is lacking is a credible socialist utopian perspective. Such attempts as have already been made have been regarded with deep suspicion by Marxists and often dismissed by them with the same contempt used to ridicule and expose bourgeois ideology and hypocrisy. A deep suspicion of philosophical idealism, of moralistic flight from practical strategy and tactics, and of a still persistent legacy of base and superstructure have thoroughly discouraged meaningful attempts to construct a socialist vision of individual freedom. In this essay I will outline a socialist alternative to liberalism. Such a brief account will obviously simplify very complex issues. There is nevertheless an advantage at times in the sacrifice of detailed elaboration to synopsis. I will first discuss the negative definition of freedom which has served as the cornerstone of liberal theory and the positive theory to which it is counterposed; I will then follow Marx through his unmasking of the bourgeois facade; and finally, I will indicate why only socialism can nurture genuine freedom of the individual.

The Negative Definition of Freedom

THE HISTORY OF PHILOSOPHICAL THOUGHT has produced a number of competing conceptions of freedom. But in the contemporary era the debate has unfortunately been narrowed to a conflict between negative and positive definitions. According to Isaiah Berlin, who stands in the long tradition of Hobbes, Hume, Mill, Bentham, Russell and Knight, negative freedom is "simply the area within which a man can do what he wants."[2]

What the negative notion emphasizes is that freedom requires the absence of impediments to the fulfillment of individual desire. So Hobbes insists: "A freeman is he that is not hindered to do what he has the will to do,"[3] and this theme is repeated with variations by all the adherents to negative freedom. Differences exist on whether it is "wish," "desire," "want," "will," or "act" that is the subject of freedom, and also on the definition of "restraint." But overall, the common thrust of the argument is clear.

The first thing to note about the negative theory of freedom is that it is a contradiction in terms. A system of purely negative freedoms is a logical absurdity.[4] Now it may be said in reply that negative theorists have certainly understood this point and have conceded that some restraints must be imposed upon individuals to make freedom either possible or valuable. Hobbes is an obvious case in point. All liberal theorists would prohibit acts of individual violence against fellow citizens and specific incursions by the state that exceed its rightful boundaries. This rejoinder is correct but does not go to the heart of the matter. The basic issue obscured by the negative theory of individual freedom is that without prevailing positive structures the individual would not exist at all, and under a reign of wholly negative freedoms there would consequently be no individuals to exercise the virtue of negative freedom itself. This point can be seen in a variety of ways.

First of all, if the individual infant were not immediately "interfered with" from birth it would never come to be. This point must be taken not merely in the crude sense of its biological existence, however, but in regard to the entire range of human capacities and sensibilities. If the child had not had "imposed" upon it the language, customs, symbolic structures and codes of its own culture, it would never move to the point of any form of individuality. For individual existence is a human achievement and is inseparable from the influence (incursion) of society. That is why liberal discussions of interference with the privacy of the individual are so often vacuous or idiotic. Is language a social imposition which destroys the infant's freedom to babble, or is it a necessary aspect of any being which could be said to exercise freedom? If the latter point is conceded, then it must also be acknowledged that we are social from our inception and the issue of freedom can no longer be viewed as a confrontation of the private individual with the state, but as a question about what sort of individual it is most appropriate for us to nurture. Socialism, like liberalism, is grounded in the claim to self-determination; its fundamental advantage over the negative counterfeit of this virtue is its recognition that both the self and the modes of its determination are of their essence social.

We can note the same point from the side of structure. A wholly negative structure is a contradiction in terms. All societies of necessity proscribe, prescribe and permit. But the forms of demand and denial must be coordinated to form a structure. If in some impossible fantasy, individuals could be imagined to arise in a completely unstructured society, they could not be conceived of as existing within it. There would be no channels for them to move along if the potentially infinite responses of their fellow members were not delimited and ordered around themes that served to unify common life.

In his excessively polite review of Berlin's *Two Concepts of Liberty*, C. B. MacPherson notes that "his negative liberty is ... too narrowly conceived, and that it is at bottom a mechanical, inertial concept of freedom which is fully appropriate only to a complete market society."[5] We need to return to the ideological significance of this observation. Note, however, that the notion of negative freedom is altogether inappropriate even for the marketplace. A market society incorporates the values of equality, mobility, inventiveness, progress, competition and quantification, and rejects the alternatives of traditional authority, cooperation or centrally planned production. In fact, the capacity to choose among alternative forms of occupation and consumption is itself a very specific structured decision whose value and consequences would certainly have been rejected by other social orders. In other words, the particular maximization of market choices associated with laissez-faire liberalism is *a system*, not the absence of one, and it is incompatible with values such as tradition, stability, integration, permanence and similar virtues that were of fundamental importance to other societies. In short, the maximization of market choices is a specific value inconsistent with other values and assumed at the sacrifice of competing structures.

This point may seem too trivial and obvious to bother noting, but it is so often neglected in bourgeois discussions that it is better to risk boredom than overlook the significance of its absence. For once the necessity of structure is noted, it is a short step to the realization that societies are essentially constituted by an ordering of values, a "determination" that creates a particular formation of empowerments, encouragements, opportunities, restrictions, and absolute prohibitions. But once again this shifts the entire theoretical discussion from the task of demarcating the protective boundaries of a supposedly natural, private individual to a discussion of the most appropriate determination of the particular social individual we wish to encourage.

The simple, constantly overlooked truth is that a "market society" is *a society*, not the absence of one. It will only operate on the basis of a specific ordering of valued preferences through the participation of individuals who thereby constitute this system. The participation of individuals in this system is not neutral, and it follows that the useless question of whether the absence of restraints insures negative freedom must be replaced by the meaningful inquiry into which particular activities and constraints are aspects of which particular forms of social individuality.

If the negative concept of freedom is logically impossible, it cannot be adequate for any social system, market or otherwise. If a writer as astute as MacPherson can mistake this point there must be something particularly seductive about the negative concept. What makes the account so compelling is that we have come to take for granted the positive activities which are the necessary counterpart to the supposedly sacrosanct protected liberties of marketplace participants. We are so accustomed to self-aggrandizement, competition, accumulation, private domination, and callous disregard of others that we tend to overlook these *"positive freedoms"* for which the negative freedoms of the marketplace are the prerequisite. The rhetoric of the marketplace tends to obscure the obvious fact that the state is prohibited from interfering with the very specific wishes of some individuals in the marketplace for the precise reason that it is mandated to interfere with the very specific freedoms of others. In the pure theory of the marketplace, for example, the state is prohibited from interfering with a *legitimate* contract as the counterpart of its obligation to interfere with those illegitimate associations of producers, consumers or laborers that would negate the fundamentally *private* aspect of the contract itself; that is, the state is prohibited from interfering with some freedoms because it is obligated to protect other freedoms. In short, the ideology of the negative, marketplace conception of freedom supports the illusion of freely choosing individuals confronting a neutral system of market laws—Smith's invisible hand. The laws themselves are viewed as impartial rather than the enforcement of atomistic competition and eventual class domination; or, if they are seen to have important social consequences, it is not in regard to an interference with freedom but rather with other values which human beings may deem important.

THE ABSENCE OF ANY SUCH SOCIAL REFLECTION marks the ideological character of such works as Berlin's *Two Concepts of Liberty*. Focused on what he considers to be the tyrannical implications of the positive concept of freedom, Berlin has little interest in capitalist domination. Class exploitation and the maldistribution of social benefits cannot be wholly ignored, but they receive an airy rebuttal. First, because interference with private liberty is only ascribed to the intended consequences of *particular* acts of infringement, the capitalist *system* is spared indictment for interfering with the freedom of its alienated and impoverished members to satisfy their wish for security, health, comfort, education and other manifestations of a humane life. The fact that these individuals cannot do or get what they want is not condemned as an interference with their freedom, however unfortunate it may be on other grounds. The maldistribution of private freedoms seems of little concern to the theory of liberty.

This position, as with much of contemporary liberal theory, represents a decline from the view of Mill, who a century ago noted that

> the generality of labourers in this and most other countries have as little choice of occupation or freedom of locomotion, are practically as dependent on fixed rules and on the will of others, as they could be in any system short of actual slavery. . . .[6]

Even if these conditions were not originally intended by the capitalist class, the fact that it has both a powerful interest in their maintenance and the power to change them renders it responsible for their continuation. But Berlin has another defense against the need to indict liberalism. He appears not to be convinced that the subordination of one class to another is the result of social arrangements at all, a view which once again puts him very far behind the considerations of Smith, Bentham and Mill, all of whom had few doubts on the subject. He is consequently relieved of any such social analysis, let alone a social critique, and can entertain his privatistic fantasy unencumbered by such practical distractions as capital and labor. So MacPherson notes:

> On these grounds I may conclude that the unequal access to the means of life and labor inherent in capitalism is, regardless of what particular social and economic theory is invoked, an impediment to the freedom of those with little access.
> We may conclude that a formulation of negative liberty which takes little or no account of class-imposed impediments, whether deliberate or unintentional, is not entirely adequate.[7]

Of course, Berlin is not wholly silent on this point, and acknowledges that to keep an entire class deprived through ignorance and poverty is to affect the status of their liberty. But this condition is seen not as a deprivation of their liberty itself but of the conditions of their liberty. So men may need "medical help or education before they can make use of an increase in their freedom."[8] But if these oppressed unfortunates want medical care and education, does it not follow, even from Berlin's argument, that they are deprived of the freedom to acquire the conditions of their freedom. Does it not remain clear that capitalism is still to be indicted for its infringement upon the equal access to human liberty.

The Positive Definition of Freedom

WE HAVE SEEN THAT THE NEGATIVE THEORY of freedom is a logical absurdity functioning as an ideological mask for capitalist power. The generic definition of freedom is the capacity of some human agent (or some aspect or collection of human

207

agents) to be free of given restraints for the sake of particular purposes. The philosophical ground of the fallacy of negative freedom is the simple fact that negation presupposes positive goals, so that the absence of restraints is logically related to the capacity to act for specific ends. Consequently, a positive conception of freedom is implicit in any account of freedom, negative or otherwise. What is actually at stake in the history of disputes regarding the nature of freedom is less the definition itself than a disagreement regarding: 1) the mode of possession of freedom—circumstantial, natural or acquired; and 2) that aspect of the self which is deemed the proper logical subject of freedom—want, limited want, desire, communal desire, choice of alternatives, or moral fulfillment.[9] That is, conflicts regarding the nature of freedom are ultimately conflicts regarding the ontological or moral nature of self and society.

On our account, then, the positive concept of freedom is implicit in the generic meaning of the term. According to Berlin, the positive concept of freedom is concerned to emphasize self-mastery: "I wish my life and decisions to depend on myself, not on external forces of whatever kind."[10] This seems hardly in opposition to the negative concept that Berlin has defended, but he goes on to argue that the two notions "developed in divergent directions not always by logically reputable steps until, in the end, they came into direct conflict with each other."[11] Self mastery in the hands of idealists came to be defined as the domination of the superior part of ourselves over our lower nature. And when our superior self was then identified with a social totality as articulated in the wisdom of a similarly superior elite, the stage was set for the radical redefinition of freedom as the domination of an elite faction—representing our superior nature—over the backward masses, still encumbered by their inferior selves. We are then made subject to theories which maintain that we can be compelled to be free and to tyrannies which decimate millions in the name of this inverted freedom. This is certainly a horrendous scenario but I will argue that there is no intrinsic logic to this purported totalitarian development of positive freedom and that Marx's theory offers the most trustworthy defense against the possibility of betrayal of liberty.

It is instructive to note that as the proponents of negative freedom have accused the adherents of positive freedom of gross perversions in redefining the term, the contrary charge has been made by the latter against the libertarians. Nor is this reciprocal indictment as odd as it may seem. Everything depends on how one defines "self" and "self-mastery." If the self is defined primarily in terms of its wants and inclinations, then anything which prevents their realization will stand as a barrier to freedom and "being forced to be free" will express a horrible perversion. But if the self is defined in terms of its capacity to act in accordance with the moral law or the superior aspect of its nature, then passion and ignorance may be seen as the primary impediments to the self's "genuine" freedom, and negative freedom will itself be viewed as an immoral perversion. That is why from the perspective of the positive concept of freedom the negative view has so often been viewed as license. So, Socrates speaks of the democratic man as possessing "neither law nor order; and this distracted existence he terms joy and bliss and freedom."[12] Or Aristotle: "In democracies of the more extreme type there has arisen a false idea of freedom which is contrary to the interests of the state."[13] And Calvin speaks of "fanatics, who are pleased with nothing but liberty, or rather licentiousness without any restraint."[14] And the position is echoed by a large number of philosophers from Spinoza, Rousseau and Kant to Hegel, Bradley and Green.

As I have observed, there is a general tendency for negative theories to define the self in terms of its wants and inclinations. Certainly from this perspective, the idea that one can be compelled to be free is a hideous turn of illogical power. For it amounts to saying that freedom consists in being compelled to want what another wants one to want, a doctrine difficult to credit with any sense except as a rationalization for the use of external domination. And since the positive doctrine has, in fact, often been used this way in practice there is good reason for vigilance. But the difficulty with this approach is that it obscures what is simultaneously defective in both the negative and positive approaches, and throws us back upon the negative conception, which we have already described as a subterfuge of corporate-capitalist power. In short, because we are dominated by the ideology of liberalism we are constantly presented with the argument that the positive conception of freedom perverts the *fundamental* definition of freedom and condemns us to totalitarian oppression. But the fact that the negative conception perverts a contrary positive notion of genuine freedom and throws us back on the ravages of capitalist domination is rarely asserted. For in capitalist "democracies" there also exists, in fact, precisely the enormous pressure to "want what one wants" which is the apparent implication of totalitarian theories. The two concepts of freedom and the societies proposed as their embodiments show more convergence than the antagonism which is so often insisted upon.

Let us return to the extreme negative view which defines freedom as the ability to do what one wants. We have already noted that this conception obviously involves the goal of positive gratification as well as the absence of interference. Such ends, we noted, involve positive structures for their development and realization. This is another way of saying that "want" in its purely animal sense cannot be the appropriate subject of *human* freedom; for what distinguishes the most rudimentary sense of human want from that of the most highly developed animal is precisely the human capacity to order inclinations in a hierarchy of comparative merit and social relevance. As Taylor observes, "the capacities relevant to [positive] freedom must involve some self-awareness, self-understanding, moral discrimination and self-control, otherwise their exercise couldn't amount to freedom in the sense of self-direction."[15] Once a theory of freedom recognizes this point, however, and begins to grade, order, and synthesize wants in some overarching conception of their comparative place in a system of wants, it has moved inexorably into the domain of positive freedom. And it has moved also from the realm of want to that of desire, social responsibility, and moral obligation. For the notion of positive freedom is intrinsically the contention that our selves are more fully recognized and nurtured through a particular moral hierarchy than through a random concatenation of isolated or competing impulses.

If we do not define ourselves as subjects of momentary inclinations but as the enduring and deepening center of progressively enriched and socially integrated concern we will readily understand how the "freedom" of a momentary inclination may inhibit or destroy the freedom of our more fully realized selves. This point has always had its philosophic merit, but it is particularly pertinent in an age of indoctrinated consumer demand, institutionalized false consciousness and manipulated inclination. If it is clear enough to common sense that a subject under post-hypnotic suggestion, while *free* to carry out the experimenter's pre-established demand, is not free in any sense that accrues to the dignity of a human being, it should also be quite clear that the massive intrusion of carefully constructed manipulation has rendered the negative notion of freedom no more appropriate than the notion of freedom prevailing in *Brave New World*.

HAVING ARGUED THAT ANY MEANINGFUL THEORY of human freedom must contain a positive aspect we can turn once again to the charge of libertarians that anything more than absence of restraint must lead to the perversion which identifies freedom with the forced obedience to the will of another.

Since many libertarians find little to terrify them in the positive definition of freedom as self-mastery, what is the logic by which they claim that this apparently benign notion is fated to turn malevolent? Let us cite something more of Berlin's statement:

> The "positive" sense of the word "liberty" derives from the wish on the part of the individual to be his own master.... I wish to be the instrument of my own, not of other men's acts of will. I wish to be a subject, not an object; to be moved by reasons, by conscious purposes which are my own, not by causes which affect me, as it were, from outside.... I wish, above all, to be conscious of myself as a thinking, willing, active being, bearing responsibility for his choices and able to explain them by reference to his own ideas and purposes. I feel free to the degree that I believe this to be true, and enslaved to the degree that I am made to realize that it is not.[16]

I believe the tyrannical implications of the positive doctrine develop from the following considerations:

1. Since the positive conception moves from alleged sheer absence of constraint to self-determination, it introduces a

normative consideration. For now some aspect of the self—its self-realization or self-mastery, for example—is regarded as superior to its other elements. Even Berlin's reference to being "moved by reasons, by conscious purposes which are my own...I wish...to be...a thinking, willing, active being, bearing responsibility for his choices," indicates this fact and furthermore implies that we can be mistaken about ourselves. Certainly we may not be moved by reasons when we believe we are, or not be moved by those reasons which we credit as our motives.

But if it be true that we can be mistaken, then Taylor is certainly correct in asserting that "the subject himself can't be the final authority on the question of whether he is free; for he cannot be the final authority on the question whether his desires are authentic, whether they do or do not frustrate his purposes."[17] But once it is established that the subject is not the final authority, the question naturally arises of whether some other person or persons can more accurately make this determination.

2. The issue of human self-deception is merely an abstract, philosophical consideration, however. The anguishing question is whether in the world as we know it, the contention is both true and relevant. It is a difficult question to approach because to answer in the affirmative is immediately to brand oneself as anti-democrat and an apostle of tyranny. The mere hint of such a suggestion is enough to turn the great mass of theorizing on the subject into rancid hypocrisy. Writers who have no hesitation in asserting that in the whole range of human endeavors most individuals are backward, underdeveloped, and ignorant, suddenly become enraged when their common view is applied to politics and particularly the nature of freedom. Even libertarians, who certainly claim that the negative view of freedom is correct and the positive view mistaken and intolerable, present themselves in the guise of relativism when the issue of superior authority arises. It is therefore a welcome relief to be forced to struggle with such works as Marcuse's *Critique of Pure Tolerance*[18] or the following reflection of MacPherson on the transformation of self-mastery into tyranny:

There is no doubt that the concept of positive liberty *has* been ...
perverted, *has* been used to deny the very freedom for human
self development that it began by invoking. Nor is it to be
doubted that the transformation has generally proceeded by
the way of the postulate that most men have been so stunted or
debased by the social institutions in which they have had to
live that they are themselves incapable of changing them, and
that such change must therefore be primarily the work of a
select group, whether it be an intelligentsia advising a benevolent monarch...or a politically aware vanguard party.... The
terrible thing about this is that *the postulate is often correct.*[19]

However, it does not at all follow that even if some individuals
can claim superior insight into the fulfillment of others, they
have a right to impose their convictions. This is a crucial fallacy in the "logic of tyranny" and I will have more to say about
it presently.

3. If we recognize that the particular distribution of negative
freedoms depends on the structure of political and economic
power—that our ability to satisfy desires *without the interference* of a recalcitrant social system depends on our control of
that system—then we must also recognize that participation in
the determination of social power is a necessary condition for
the exercise of even negative freedom.

As MacPherson notes: "unequal access to the means of life
and labor inherent in capitalism is, regardless of what particular social and economic theory is invoked, an impediment to the
freedom of those with little or no access."[20] But then MacPherson cannot argue as he does that "the desire of the individual to
be his own master, to be self-directed, to be moved by his own
conscious purposes...is surely different from participation in
the controlling authority."[21] Self-determination and participation in the power of that commonwealth which determines the
nature and distribution of my freedoms are, if not identical,
clearly inseparable. As a social being, to be self-mastered is
finally to master the process by which I am constituted. The
fact that participation in the social process—in a democracy,
for example—does not insure the protection of one's freedoms,
is not an argument against the need for such participation, but
against its corruption.

The familiar rebuttal designed to show that negative liberty and participation in sovereignty are distinct usually notes that a benign despot may monopolize political power for the purpose of defending negative freedoms. Several difficulties afflict this rejoinder:

a. Even if it were true that participation in sovereignty and freedom from interference were distinct, this could not affect the admittedly positive freedom of self-mastery.

b. Furthermore, we have already argued that no such distinction between the right to be left alone and self-mastery can be defended; therefore, the right to sovereignty and the right to be left alone to do as one wishes, cannot be separated.

c. If negative freedom is only the space from which one carries out positive acts, then the most benign tyrant must of logic severely restrict the most significant negative freedom—the freedom to determine the nature and meaning of privacy and self-determination.

4. We have reached the point at which personal freedom is seen to be inseparable from democratic freedom—the freedom of all to participate equally in the "rightful"[22] determination of sovereignty. Since most discussants accept the judgment that the freedoms of individuals may and generally do conflict, it follows that the restriction of some freedoms is necessary for the realization of others. In this socially distributive sense, then, interference with lower, that is, lesser freedoms, may be necessary for the protection of superior freedoms. In our own country, the overwhelming majority of individuals would immediately experience a manifest increase in their freedoms to occupation, health, education, security, creativity, and general welfare if those currently exercising inordinate power were denied the exercise of this abuse.

5. Beyond the point at which some individuals may be coerced to expand the freedom of others, there exists a realm in which individuals may rightly be said to be coerced to increase their own freedom. There are two legitimate instances of this right, and one particular corruption in which lies latent the identification of positive freedom and tyranny.

a. It is sometimes appropriate to compel individuals to engage in activities which they would only agree to after the fact. The traditional example is the education of children. It is so easy to abuse the point of this principle in justifying colonial domination, class oppression, and other social injustices that it becomes an easy target for adherents of negative freedom. Yet, putting aside all the relevant issues of time, place, and manner, the point in its limited context seems to me valid. Children are freer for being intelligently educated than for being ignorant, whether they initially agree or not.

b. A second traditional principle takes us from the sphere of children to adults. As Rousseau argued, "It is in order that we may not fall victims to an assassin that we consent to die if we ourselves turn assassins."[23] The key term here is "consent." For after committing such a crime, an individual who originally agreed to his own rightful punishment might certainly struggle to avoid the personal consequences of his previous commitment. His freedom of security, however, depended on the obedience of all, which includes his own. His momentary violation stands opposed to his primary contract, and he may be held against his momentary will to the implications of his more permanent social being: or as Rousseau put the point, to enjoy the rights conferred by society, one has to participate in its obligations.

6. This takes us to the crucial step in the argument that positive freedom leads inexorably to the tyranny of forcing individuals to be free. Having accepted the previous series of arguments up to this point, is it possible now to halt one's fall into totalitarian domination? It is not only possible but necessary, if we consider the line of development carefully. What must be underscored is that our previous argument justified the curtailment of negative freedom and the converse imposition of positive freedom in only three situations: a) in dealing with those not sufficiently mature to understand the imposition in question; b) when the freedom of some interferes with the freedom of others; and c) when individuals break the commitment of their own consent. Nothing in these arguments can justify a wholly different contention—that society, or some social agent, can enforce a

system of freedoms upon those who reject on principle the freedoms being imposed upon them. Human beings in their reasonable maturity cannot be forced to be free.

FOR ALL THE PASSION AROUSED ON THIS POINT, by defenders of negative freedom, their arguments against "forced freedom" are often extremely weak, however. Such contentions as the well-known laissez-faire claim that no expert can know us better than ourselves, or that individuals are too varied for such expertise even to be conceptualized, or that human beings are happier without interference seem unable to bear the weight imposed on them.

The fundamental and sufficient reason for denying "the imposition of freedom" is that it violates human autonomy. For our dignity as human beings consists in our ability to be our own lawmakers. Autonomous human beings are members of a society which self-consciously, reflectively and critically constructs the domain of its own existence; its community, its institutions and the very form of its own transcendence. Such practices as are imposed on individuals without their informed consent, or which they impose on themselves without comprehension, engage them at a level beneath their humanity and thereby degrade them. The authenticity of human life lies in its self-determination. And while it may sometimes be necessary to interfere with given individuals for the sake of expanding the freedom of the community, the argument cannot be imposed on society by anything like a dominant person or party without damaging or obliterating the ground of human dignity.

For individuals to be true to themselves, they must act in the light of reason, which is *understood* to be a compelling basis for action. Dignity itself is directly related to this ability to determine the appropriateness of beliefs and the legitimacy of commitment. Neither habit, force, fear, passion nor brute inclination can justify the claims of freedom. Mill eloquently expressed this core conviction:

> There is a class of persons . . . who think it enough if a person assent undoubtedly to what they think true, though he has no knowledge whatever of the grounds of the opinion, and could not make a tenable defense of it against the most superficial

objections . . . assuming that the true opinion abides in the mind, but abides as a prejudice, a belief independent of, and proof against, argument—this is not the way in which truth ought to be held by a rational being. This is not the training of truth. Truth thus held, is but one superstition the accidentally clinging to the words which enunciate a truth. . . .[24] Customs are made for customary circumstances . . . though the customs be both good as customs, and suitable to him, yet to conform to custom, merely *as* custom, does not educate or develop in him any of the qualities which are the distinctive endowment of a human being. The human faculties of perception, judgment, discriminative feeling, mental activity, and even moral preference, are exercised only in the making of a choice.[25]

Freedom cannot be imposed because choice and rational persuasion cannot be imposed. And there can be no committed practice without free choice.

When the "rational state" acts as a surrogate for "the common will," "the rational good," "imputed class consciousness," or other conditions of ideal potentiality, those persons for whom it claims to speak continue in their actual ignorance, partiality and self-delusion. They remain subservient, passive, and powerless. To escape this condition, they must exercise their own powers of choice and judgment, transform their own nature, and learn from their own weaknesses and growing strengths. In countries weighted by massive poverty, ignorance, superstition, and authoritarian servility, the mode of emancipation will have to allow for such realities. To think that the long and violent history of bourgeois civil liberties could be peacefully introduced all at once is certainly simplistic, at the very least. But if the "leadership" that makes an emancipatory break with the past cannot distinguish education from indoctrination and dissent from disloyalty, no genuine movement toward human emancipation will ever occur.

We can sum up this aspect of the discussion in the following way:

Thesis—The pure negative freedom of unrestrained self-gratification is impossible because the formation of an individual requires a positive structure. It is morally reprehensible because it reduces individuals to the level of homogeneous, quantitative desire and does not grant what is unique to the human condition—the capacity to order one's life through the evaluative discrimination of what is most fully human in ourselves.

Antithesis—The pure positive theory of freedom is impossible because the imposition of ends requires a free, protected place where individuals must make their own decisions and define their being. It is morally reprehensible because it reduces the highest capacity of human beings—our ability to act as autonomous agents of self-determination—to mechanical habit, customary obedience or terror.

Synthesis—Socialism is the provision of equal access to the social power, permitting individuals a meaningful voice in the declaration of their being.

The fact that socialism is so generally equated with tyranny tends to obscure the clear democratic commitment in the Marxian origins of this movement. It is to this issue that we now turn.[26]

Socialism and the Individual

THE IDENTIFICATION OF SOCIALISM IN GENERAL, and Marxism in particular, with various ostensible "communist" regimes has a variety of causes. Primary, of course, is liberalism's ideological interest in discrediting Marxism. The long standing American tendency to quarantine communism as a dangerous, foreign, anti-American doctrine was particularly inflamed at two specific moments in American history: first, with the cataclysm of the Russian Revolution, and once again with the construction of the Cold War. To malign Marxism through association with the Soviet Union obviously required the denigration of that regime, but this task was appreciably easier than dealing conscientiously with Marxism itself.

However, the socialist left has engaged in its own sins of commission and omission. First, it has fallen into so profound a tendency to ridicule and revile bourgeois freedom that reasonable observers see it as lacking any appreciation for the substance, let alone the form of traditional civil rights and liberties. The ease with which numerous Marxist critics of liberalism move from the valid rejection of the hypocrisy and atomistic limitations of bourgeois freedom to an absolute rejection of its contribution to any civilized conception of social existence leads to reasonable anxiety about their own intentions. When writers like Lukacs provide a metaphysical defense of Stalin on the basis of the Party's claim to stewardship of genuine class consciousness, the cause of Marxist democracy is seriously weakened.

But beyond the often reckless disregard of the bourgeois contribution, fundamentally flawed as it is, there is the emptiness of what so many on the left propose as socialist alternatives. Either the mythology of the base-superstructure is taken to imply that the political realm will automatically settle the issue of democratic participation, or a naive populist anarchism, such as that displayed by Lenin in *State and Revolution*, seems to obviate the need of careful foresight. Neither of these positions aids the development of a serious Marxist alternative.

In the remaining pages of this essay I will suggest the direction of a Marxist socialist account of freedom. Marx provides a fruitful clue in his analysis of the stages of justice, which can be found in various of his writings,[27] particularly in "Critique of the Gotha Program," where he analyzes the transition from capitalism through socialism to communism along the following lines:

1. In the early stage of transition the rights of individuals as producers and consumers are based on market exchange, moving toward cooperation.

2. From the total social product, before distribution of the proceeds of production, various social costs of production are deducted.

3. From the means of consumption, various deductions "intended for *the common satisfaction of needs*, such as schools, health services, etc."[28] and for social relief are carried out.

4. The new society which emerges from capitalism is still "economically, morally and intellectually stamped with the birth marks of the old society."[29]

5. After social considerations, individuals get back exactly what they contribute.

6. The same principle prevails as regulates market exchange

—the exchange of equal values. "Hence, *equal right* here is still in principle—bourgeois right."[30]

7. There is no longer a contradiction between bourgeois principle and practice, and this requires that a parasitic, leisure class be eliminated. This transformation marks an advance.

8. But the principle employed is still defective. Though a principle of equality is applied—"the right of producers to the labor they supply"—this principle is applied to unequals because human beings differ in their physical and intellectual capacity to produce. "This *equal* right is an unequal right for unequal labor."[31] The principle thus fails to recognize the effect of previous class differences and treats unequal individual endowments as "natural privileges."

Individuals are brought under an equal standard. But unequal individuals—"and they would not be different individuals if they were not unequal"[32]—can be so measured "from one *definite* side only . . . only as *workers* and nothing more is seen in them."

9. "Right can never be higher than the economic structure of society and its *cultural development* conditioned thereby."[33] (emphasis added).

10. "In a higher phase of communist society, after the enslaving subordination of the individual to the division of labour, and therewith also the antithesis between mental and physical labour has vanished; after labour has become not only a means of life but life's prime want; after the productive forces have also increased with the all-round development of the individual, and all the springs of co-operative wealth flow more abundantly—only then can the narrow horizon of bourgeois right be crossed in its entirety and society inscribe on its banners: From each according to his ability to each according to his needs!"[34] In short, the applicable standard has now shifted from the *abstract* and *dehumanizing* criterion of the capacity to work measured in quantities of labor time, to the human capacity to reproduce one's self as a full human being in the rich realization of one's potentialities. The new principle of justice is the equal respect for the self-realization of differently endowed individuals. Whereas the previous principle of equality forced men and women under equal constriction, they are now equal in the power and encouragement given to their expansive self-realization.

It would be a mechanical exercise to replicate for freedom the stages in the development of justice. But the two notions are too thoroughly intertwined for their realization to diverge fundamentally. Freedom in its bourgeois stage is also prominently marked by the fierce contradiction of its theory and practice. The right of negative freedom—to be let alone to pursue one's desires—is clearly marked by class domination. Some have more power than others to be uninhibited in the realization of their inclinations, as they conversely possess much greater power than others to be left alone. So Marx notes that "the right of property originally appeared to be based on one's own labor. Property now appears as the right to alien labor, the impossibility of labor appropriating its own product."[35]

Since both what individuals want to be free to do and their power to carry out these wants are largely determined by social class power, the negative notion of freedom can be seen as a masquerade for domination. The incursion of capitalism into previous communal solidarity leads to a vortex in society and the individual, a vacuum whose emptiness is made and filled by the violent inflowing of capitalist power. Even Constant, whom Berlin cites as the most eloquent defender of freedom, notes: "Nearly all the enjoyments of the moderns are in their private lives: the immense majority, *forever excluded from power*, necessarily take only a passing interest in their public lives"[36] (emphasis added).

The right to be left alone can be seen here for what it is—pure ideology or the desperate rationalization of those excluded from the power of owning "private" capital.

And yet, as Marx insists, capital produces not only the preconditions of human technological mastery, but of human self-fulfillment as well:

> The great civilizing influence of capital . . . the development, hence, of the natural sciences to their highest point; likewise the discovery, creation and satisfaction of new needs arising from society itself; the cultivation of all the qualities of the social human being, production of the same in a form as rich as possible in needs, because rich in qualities and solutions—production of this being as the most total and universal possible social product, for, in order to take gratification in a many-sided way, he must be capable of many pleasures, hence

> cultivated to a high degree—is likewise a condition of production founded on capital.[37]

However, for reasons which are well understood and need not be reviewed here, individuals cannot fulfill their potentialities under capitalism. To realize themselves they must transcend themselves. Their own communal relations, rather than a source of reified dependence and despair, must be subject to their own communal control. The first stages of freedom will be concerned with replacing capitalist property institutions in the world and in one's self. The elimination of exploitative power based on property will render individuals less and less subject to class oppression. But their desires, hopes, relations and their very selves—possessive, autarchic, and combative—are likely to persist. The great moving transition to a new stage of freedom comes not from collectivizing public property, but in the struggle for communal equality and shared responsibility—which require, of course, control over property—and in the creation of a new selfhood in which the universal need for self-realization absorbs the centrifugal fragments of possessive individualism.

Since human nature is intrinsically social, it can only fulfill itself through control of its social world. In stages of human development, the highest stage, Marx maintained, is "free individuality, based on universal development of individuals and on their subordination of their communal, social productivity as their social wealth...."[38] The primary achievement of their "social productivity" is their own social nature, however. So for the first time human beings can posit and realize their own purposes, make the world transparent to their own intentions, recognize and enhance each other in reciprocal labor, and identify themselves as the purpose of their agency.

In this process will they have destroyed the enclaves of bourgeois individuality? Have they made themselves over into wholly social beings who have lost the stature of truly individual beings? But "private interest is itself already a socially determined interest."[39] However, their bourgeois privacy was in reality the powerless insularity of their social alienation. Through communal participation their social-individuality now becomes available to them. Whereas previously their cherished freedom of speech, press and association served largely as the ideological mask of dominant corporate monopolization of the means of development, communication, dissemination, and of the very formation of ideas, they will now have equal access to the creation and consumption of the public mind. Whereas previously their democratic commonwealth was constantly subverted by the egoism of private aggrandizement, they will now find encouragement and recognition in the cooperative pursuit of their reciprocal fulfillment. Their control over the means of their objectification will structure their opportunity to manifest and appropriate themselves as their own creation.

This is visionary utopianism, and so it should be. There is no necessity to the present degradation of human nature. Only human arrangements stand between mankind and its highest freedom, the choice of its own enhancement, the realization in a form yet unimaginable of future developments. When the social realm is made available what will human beings make of their right to choose? Why do we wish to be free of state or collective intrusion if not *for* the pursuit of peace, justice, culture, love, aesthetic perfection and exploration of our world and of ourselves? What do we truly long for if not the opportunity to develop ourselves in a society of our choosing, one that manifests our own self-reflective transformation and speaks in our voice. The world of capital has made us so stupid, so constricted and curtailed, that we tend to believe individuality is the opposite of what it is—the enemy of the social realm.

But individuality has always in the generic sense been social. Isolation, hostility and powerlessness are as much social constructions as love and recognition. The question that plagues the bourgeois critique of socialist freedom is how individuals can simultaneously be socially constituted and autonomous. The crucial insight of Marxian socialism is the understanding that *autonomy is itself a socially constituted relationship*. The liberal ideals of autonomous self-determination, freedom of critique, and public dialogue, the multiplicity and independence of mediating communities are possible for the first time under socialism.

Nevertheless, it is true that the individuality so prized by the bourgeoisie will likely pass away, as have all previously constituted forms of individual human nature. For while it is undeniably true that the individual is the locus of social existence, its "individual" character over social time has clearly changed. In no case has its nature been "natural," "given," or "original." In its bourgeois form, individuality is marked by an enlarged repertoire of diverse skills, sensitivities, and capacities which cannot be utilized for human fulfillment. As in the case of technological mastery, the latent and burgeoning forces of self-transformation are stifled and repressed by the irrational, atomistic, hostile, and alienated structure of social power. So the ideal continues to beckon, and the void is filled with the festering of desire and hope.

Just as the ideal of equality that played so crucial a role in the ideology of capitalism was not destroyed in Marx's conception of socialist justice but rather was transcended—restructured in a human manner—so freedom too will be transformed. The old sense of individual freedom, "morally and intellectually stamped" with the pathology of the old society as "the liberty of man regarded as an isolated nomad, withdrawn into himself,"[40] can be expected to be replaced only with slow, painful difficulty. The social bonds of capitalist individuality—indifference, antagonism, and despair—will recede only as the realization of co-operative democratic participation in social life develops. The spirit of the change is the release and enhancement of the desire for self-mastery, which arises under capitalism but cannot be completed there.

IN CONCLUSION LET US TURN TO THE PREMIER instance of bourgeois freedom to illustrate the meaning of socialist transcendence. What will come of freedom of speech and association in a socialist commonwealth? On the one hand, something of their ideal contribution will persist—critical self-consciousness and public dialogue, the diversity of people's lived experience, the multitude of mediating association, the right to move wholly within the unique discourse of one's self. Yet at the same time everything will change in a new communal life. For the old liberties will forfeit that lethal quality which derives from the combat of bourgeois competition and class antagonism. The right and need to speak remain, but the ends for which one speaks, the purpose and intention, the telos of speech, are transformed.

The most astute critic of bourgeois free speech, Alexander Meiklejohn, has clearly and simply driven home this point. In his critique of the traditional social Darwinian defense of free speech through the competition of ideas in the marketplace he notes:

> We think, not as members of the body politic of "We, the people of the United States," but as farmers, as trade-union workers, as employers, as investors. . . . And our aim, as we debate in those capacities, is not that of finding the truth. . . . Our aim is to "make a case," to win a fight, to make our plea plausible, to keep the pressure on. And the intellectual degradation which that interpretation of truth-testing has brought upon the minds of the people is almost unbelievable. . . . It has made intellectual freedom indistinguishable from intellectual license.[41]

Under socialism the individual mind in its various modes will persist, deepen, and expand. But the manner of differentiation, the diversity of perspectives, these will be transformed. Combat and distraction will recede as the primary motives of discourse, and the public mind grows through its equal availability to all. A people will be able to voice and hear the possibilities of their reciprocal fulfillment, their place and meaning in the commonwealth, their contribution to the public welfare. The pathology of bourgeois culture leads to the conviction that differentiation is always the staking out of territories, the exclusion and defeat of others. At its higher plane differentiation is rather the embrace of others in a love of humankind. It is the mutual recognition of common diversity, the contribution of each to the condition from which each draws in freedom the prospect of a fully human life. Socialist freedom is the transcendence and completion of the liberal ideal. The dignity, autonomy, self-realization, and individualism which capitalism of necessity evoked as its ideological self-legitimation becomes under socialism the concrete conditions of its own existence, "an association, in which the free development of each is the condition for the free development of all."[42]

Footnotes

1. Karl R. Popper, *The Open Society and its Enemies* (London: Routledge & Kegan Paul, Ltd., 1949); Isaiah Berlin, *Two Concepts of Liberty* (London: Oxford University Press, 1958); Isaiah Berlin, *Four Essays on Liberty* (London: Oxford University Press, 1969); Robert Nozick, *Anarchy, State and Utopia* (New York: Basic Books, Inc., 1974).
2. Berlin, *Two Concepts of Liberty*, p. 7.
3. Thomas Hobbes, *Leviathan* (Oxford: Clarendon Press, 1929), p. 161.
4. See F.H. Bradley, *Ethical Studies* (Oxford: Clarendon Press, 1927), "To be free from everything is to be—nothing," p. 56.
5. C.B. MacPherson, *Democratic Theory* (Oxford: Clarendon Press, 1973), p. 95.
6. Cited in MacPherson, p. 99. MacPherson provides an excellent discussion of the issue.
7. *Ibid.*, p. 101.
8. Berlin, *Two Concepts of Liberty*, p. 9, footnote.
9. I follow here the basic schema provided by Mortimer Adler in *The Idea of Freedom*, two volumes (Garden City: Doubleday and Company, 1958). Adler's work seems to me still an invaluable aid to discussions of freedom, though it is seldom cited.
10. Berlin, *Two Concepts of Liberty*, p. 16.
11. *Ibid.*
12. Plato, *The Dialogues of Plato*, translated by B. Jowett, two volumes, Republic 561 D.
13. Aristotle, *Politics*, trans. by B. Jowett, Book V, Chapter 9, 1310, 25-35.
14. John Calvin, *Institutes of the Christian Religion*, Vol. II (Grand Rapids: Wm. B. Eerdmans Publishing Co., 1949), p. 771.
15. Charles Taylor, "What's Wrong with Negative Liberty?" in *The Idea of Freedom*, ed. Alan Ryan (Oxford: Oxford University Press, 1979), p. 179.
16. Berlin, *Two Concepts of Liberty*, p. 16.
17. Taylor, "What's Wrong with Negative Liberty?" p. 180.
18. Robert Paul Wolff, Barrington Moore Jr., and Herbert Marcuse, *A Critique of Pure Tolerance* (Boston: Beacon Press, 1969). Marcuse's essay is entitled "Repressive Tolerance."
19. MacPherson, *Democratic Theory*, p. 106.
20. *Ibid.*, p. 101
21. *Ibid.*, p. 108. MacPherson (p. 109, footnote) makes participation in sovereignty a "prerequisite" for self-mastery. Since self-mastery can also be seen as a prerequisite for participation in sovereignty the relationship is dialectical and the two notions inseparable.
22. By "rightful,'" I mean not only "correct" or appropriate" but refer also to a sovereignty which protects specific rights beyond the quantitative measure of a democratic majority. Two of the most important of these rights are the right to free speech (participation in the public dialogue and freedom of association) and the equal right to participation in the construction of the law.
23. Rousseau, *Social Contract*, Book I, Chapter 5.

24. John Stuart Mill, "On Liberty," in *The Philosophy of John Stuart Mill*, ed. Marshall Cohen (New York: The Modern Library, 1961), pp. 225-226.

25. *Ibid.*, p. 252.

26. That Marx's position is radically democratic seems clear to any reasonable reading of his works. For a particularly persuasive presentation, see Hal Draper, *Karl Marx's Theory of Revolution* (New York: Monthly Review Press, 1977).

27. Besides "Critique of the Gotha Program," see the *Economic-Philosophic Manuscripts*, particularly the manuscript, "Private Property and Communism."

28. Karl Marx, "Critique of the Gotha Program," in *Selected Works in Two Volumes* (Moscow: Foreign Languages Publishing House, 1962), Vol. II, p. 22.

29. *Ibid.*, p. 23.

30. Note the incorporation and transcendence of Hegel's concept of justice in *The Philosophy of Right* N49, N209. The fundamental thrust of Marx's argument is against the dead equality essential to the capitalist constitution of abstract labor.

31. Marx, "Critique of the Gotha Program," p. 24.

32. *Ibid.*

33. *Ibid.*

34. *Ibid.*

35. Karl Marx, *Grundisse* (Baltimore: Penguin Books, 1973), p. 458.

36. Cited in Steven Lukes, *Individualism* (Oxford: Basil Blackwell, 1973), p. 65.

37. Marx, *Grundisse,* p. 409.

38. *Ibid.*, p. 158.

39. *Ibid.*, p. 156.

40. Karl Marx, *Early Writings,* ed. T.B. Bottomore (New York: McGraw Hill, 1964), p. 24.

41. Alexander Meiklejohn, *Political Freedom* (New York: Oxford University Press, 1965), pp. 73-74.

42. Karl Marx, *Selected Works,* Vol. I, p. 54.

Poland in Perspective

DANIEL SINGER

> *The revolution is the only kind of "war"... in which final victory can only be prepared by a number of "defeats."*
>
> Rosa Luxemburg

T HE PURPOSE OF THIS ESSAY is not to bury Solidarity with faint or fulsome praise. The Polish labor movement is not dead. It has suffered a terrible defeat and has been driven underground once again, but it is potentially much stronger today than it was in the spring of 1980, on the eve of its momentous breakthrough in Gdansk. The sixteen months that followed cannot be uprooted from the minds of the Polish people, and it is, therefore, absurd to draw the conclusion from the Polish events that all is quiet and immutable on the Eastern front.

It suits our establishments to present a picture of the Soviet bloc as a mighty and unchangeable monster. If socialism can be identified with Jaruzelski's military dictatorship and Marxism with the regime prevailing in Moscow the very idea of a radically different alternative would be discredited and, if this hell could then be described as permanent, as a system from which there is no return, it would render the propaganda of our defenders of the *status quo* that much easier. They have, inci-

---

DANIEL SINGER *fits perfectly into the Stalinist definition of a "rootless cosmopolitan," except that he has a British passport. Born in Warsaw, he was brought up in Paris, Geneva and London. Formerly on the editorial staff of* The Economist *as the expert on the Soviet bloc, he is now a freelance writer and broadcaster. He is the author of* Prelude to Revolution *(New York: Hill and Wang) about the 1968 events in France, and more recently,* The Road to Gdansk *(New York: Monthly Review Press). He is also the European correspondent for* The Nation.

dentally, been helped in their task by all sorts of ex-radicals who require this vision of gloom to justify their disengagement or their conversion.

Yet one cannot seriously use what happened in Poland as proof of the success or the stability of the prevailing regimes in Eastern Europe. Quite the contrary. Seen in historical perspective, these events confirm what only a few argued beforehand, namely that the neo-Stalinist system, if one looks below the surface, is torn by social contradictions and faced with a major economic crisis. They also confirm that, although dismissed as a spent force by pundits everywhere, the proletariat is most likely to play a crucial role in the transformation of the bloc.

Admittedly, the hope for a peaceful transition raised by the victory of the labor movement in Gdansk has been dashed. More generally, the prospect of change raised certain questions and problems: namely, that liberalization in any East European country can only develop in the long run if it spreads, ultimately, to Russia itself, which is naturally anathema to the men in the Kremlin. Thus the movement both cannot be and yet must be contagious. But if there is a Rubicon that cannot be crossed, can this frontier be shifted? Moreover, given the evident fact that *power from below* represented by the working class is, in the long run, incompatible with power *from above,* that is the dictatorship of the Party whether in civilian or in military clothing, can one imagine a conflicting co-existence, a transitional compromise, imposed by the imperatives of geography? Or are these countries condemned either to some form of "creeping revolution" or a bloody confrontation?

These questions are more pertinent now than ever because the military coup merely drove the class struggle underground. General Jaruzelski must still find a way to make the workers work, while the leaders of Solidarity are still bound to ponder what would happen if, say, a general strike were successful. The shadow of Soviet intervention has not vanished. Indeed, the assessment of the risks of a popular explosion lies at the heart of a debate dividing the underground leadership of Solidarity today. Nor is the discussion of only local interest. What is at stake is crucial for the whole of Eastern Europe and, by the same token, for socialists all over the world. Interest, however, should not be confused with cherishing illusions.

Having just argued that our opponents are telling the Polish tale in terms of gloom and despair in order to discourage any radical action here, I must add at once that triumphant optimism is also out of place while Solidarity is banned and thousands of its supporters are still in jail. The Polish story simply suggests that there is scope for action and room for reasoned hope.

Lessons of Gdansk

SEEN AS A WHOLE, over a period of time, the Polish experience shows both the fundamental political weakness of the authorities and an astonishing development of the movement itself. The wave of strikes culminating in the historical Gdansk victory in summer 1980 was qualitatively different from its predecessors, namely the spontaneous rising against higher prices in the winter of 1970-71 and the brief riots of 1976, through which the workers confirmed their *veto* power; in other words, their capacity to question the will of the Party.

Quite consciously, the movement tried to avoid past mistakes and thus avoid a bloody confrontation. The workers remained in their factories refusing to come out into the streets. The strike committees gave orders banning the sale of alcohol in their respective regions. No anti-Soviet scribblings were to be seen or speeches to be heard at that time despite the passionate dislike for the mighty neighbor. The labor movement thus surprised everybody by its newly-found discipline and maturity.

The second and, for me, an even more striking ripening occurred during the crisis itself. On August 14, when the strike at the Lenin Shipyards began, the demand for a genuine, independent union did not even figure in the workers' platform (which was limited to the reinstatement of Mrs. Walentynowicz, a wage increase, and the building of a monument for the victims of 1970). Only a handful of the strikers, members of the illegal Committee for the Free Trade Unions of the Maritime Coast (Walesa and Walentynowicz, Borusewicz, the Gwiazdas, Lis and Pienkowska being the best known among them) spoke in favor of such an organization. Within days the idea of a few became the conviction of thousands and then of millions. This

231

has been confirmed by the so-called "experts," i.e., the intellectuals who came from Warsaw to offer their services to the workers. In the shipyards, they got the same message from everybody: on this we shall not budge—if we don't get free trade unions there will be no agreement; if we do everything is negotiable.

This is not meant as an apology for the sect or a suggestion that history is really made by "active minorities." But the Polish example is a reminder, most significant for us all, of how dramatically political consciousness alters in a revolutionary situation. It is also a reply to moderate leaders who always conceal their own timidity (and sometimes unavowed interests) with the seemingly wise warning: "the masses are not ripe."

Be that as it may, within a couple of weeks the idea captured the imagination of the working class in Poland and of a whole people. It compelled the government, the ruling Party and even the Russians to yield. They were forced to accept, however reluctantly and provisionally, something that only days earlier seemed totally unthinkable—the birth of a genuinely independent union within the neo-Stalinist system. This not only destroyed forever the sacrosanct myth of the CP as the magically authorized incarnation of the working class, it also immediately raised the question of how such a system can function with a counterpower, with a real and not merely formal labor movement.

Collision Course

THE NEW ORGANIZATION REALLY REPRESENTING the working people of Poland was thus faced with the old one, claiming to be the representative of the proletariat by birthright. Were they doomed to fight almost at once or was a period of collective coexistence possible? Before even attempting to answer this question, we must glance at the protagonists and at the economic situation, whose rapid deterioration precipitated the *denouement*.

The Biggest Union in the World

Proportionately this is what Solidarnosc was and still potentially remains. Elections to its first Congress in 1981 confirmed that total membership amounted to 9.6 million or roughly three-quarters of the total working population outside farming (which need not be taken into account since there was a separate Rural Solidarity). The ratio of union members to urban labor force is thus more than three times higher than in the United States, and it considerably surpasses the proportion in countries where labor unions are considered mighty, like Britain or Germany. Nor will anyone argue that people were bullied by the state to join Solidarnosc. Hence, it deserves its claim as the biggest free trade union, and this is a factor to keep in mind now that the Polish authorities have "revived" an allegedly independent union while bypassing the elected members of Solidarity.

The huge membership also provides an answer to the official accusation that Solidarity had within its ranks reactionary nationalists and "extremists." Actually the union was full of everything. Representing the bulk of the working population, it reflected its various moods, including the confusion resulting from 35 years of rule by oppressors and exploiters disguised as socialists. The political spectrum within Solidarity stretched from nationalists belonging to the KPN,[1] fairly influential, say, in Upper Silesia, to Edmund Baluka and his comrades in Szczecin, who considered themselves revolutionary communists. These divergencies did not become more readily apparent partly because the experiment did not last long enough, partly because Solidarnosc never had a real debate on the future shape of society, and largely because the ruling Party, by defying rather than wooing the union, usually managed to unite all factions against it.

The third interesting feature of Solidarity, which may be gathered from the table below, is its essentially regional structure. True, Solidarnosc had its craft or professional organizations, its unions of miners or teachers. These, however, were subordinated to territorial bodies. The delegates to the Congress were chosen on this basis and so were the leading national organs.[2] Jaruzelski and his military commanders are determined to prevent the resurrection of the labor movement on territorial lines on the grounds that it would be too "political."

Fundamentally, they are right. This method of organization lays the emphasis on the interests of the class as a whole, the class-for-itself, and not on the narrower, "trade unionist," to use Lenin's terminology, interests of its various sections. It must be remembered that Solidarity stumbled into this structure almost incidentally and that its leaders orginally hoped to "stay out of politics," sticking to union matters and "leaving the governing to the government." Obviously, the very idea was rather absurd. In a country where the Party has a monopoly of power, the creation of a genuine labor union was an openly political act and so was the exercise of newly won prerogatives. Nevertheless, the confrontation was precipitated by the economic crisis and by the performance of the Communist Party. As shortages became more acute, the rank-and-file wanted their union to become involved in management, indeed to take it over. As to the CP, its reluctance to relinquish any power whatsoever was driving Solidarity into requesting an increasing share of that power.

SOLIDARITY MEMBERSHIP BY REGIONS

Upper Silesia (Katowice)	1,400,000
Mazowsze (Warsaw)	911,000
Lower Silesia (Wroclaw)	916,000
Krakow Region	645,000
Gdansk Region	532,000
Lodz region	463,000
Poznan region	429,000
Szczecin region	353,000
Lublin region	332,000
Bydgoszcz region	276,000
Total (including 27 other regions and 4 voting areas)	9,600,000

The Party and its Apparatus

Which Party really? When the crisis started the CP or rather the PUWP (Polish United Workers Party) officially had about 3.1 million members.[3] Admittedly, the CP was the ruling Party and it did not require great courage or abnegation to join its ranks. After ten years of Gierek's pragmatic reign, the already small number of people who were in the Party out of conviction must have dwindled to ridiculous proportions. Nevertheless, a mass party with an important working class membership was bound to be affected by an upheaval shaking society to its very foundations. According to rough estimates, one out of three CP members joined Solidarity. The Party's typical system of command from above was temporarily threatened by the attempt to set up "horizontal structures" regrouping mainly disconnected members of a town, a region, and then trying to forge links across the country.

Many Solidarity advisers made the mistake of confusing the Party rank-and-file with the leadership, the mass membership with the apparatus. As ordinary card holders were visibly bewildered and cells in factories which had been Party strongholds collapsed, Solidarity advisers more or less assumed that the army, the police, and all other organs of repression were somehow vanishing in similar fashion. From the right premises that the power of the PUWP rested, in the last instance, on Soviet support, they drew the wrong conclusion that the Party had almost no life of its own. Solidarity thought so much in terms of a direct Soviet invasion that it neglected the risk of intervention by proxy and, when the coup came from within Polish frontiers, it was taken by surprise.

It may be argued that this was also the reason why Solidarity did not use the weight represented by its members to influence the policy of the PUWP both from within and from below. Let me make it quite clear at once that I do not swallow stories describing the struggle within the leadership of a CP as a battle between villains and the seekers of socialist democracy. The latest of such versions tried, in the summer of 1982, to present General Jaruzelski as a "liberal" because he had gotten rid of the "hard-head" Stefan Olszowski from the Party secretariat. Actually, Olszowski, though down, is not out: he was appointed foreign minister and is still a full member of the Party politburo. Besides, if the ambitious Olszowski—who, formerly in favor of economic reform, opted for a tough line toward Solidarity—has been downgraded, many of those who remain at the top—Milewski the policeman, Albin Siwak the Solidarityhater, or Jaruzelski and his fellow generals themselves for that matter—are no better.

The men who took over from Gierek after their defeat in Gdansk did not want to hand power over to the proletariat. The victory of the workers had compelled them to retreat and they wanted to reconquer most of the lost territory. All of them agreed on Party rule from above. They merely differed on the manner, the tactics, the concessions that could be tolerated. These differences were, under the circumstances, as politically important as the need to intervene directly and not by proxy would have been for the Russians. It is possible to venture that, had it thrown its full weight into this battle, Solidarity might have exercised a certain influence on the Party's inner struggle.

If this chance existed, it did not last very long. Paradoxically, the Ninth Congress of the PUWP, in July 1981, which at the time was hailed abroad as the beginning of liberalization, probably marked the beginning of its end. The Congress looked so hopeful from the outside because it witnessed the most dramatic purge of the top leadership any CP had ever known.[4] But, on closer scrutiny, those who were eliminated had not been exceptionally conservative, nor those who replaced them particularly liberal. They were middle rank *apparatchiki* along with a good sprinkling of men in uniform. Having survived the electoral test, they wanted to assert their power and, since Solidarity refused to yield, they quickly picked the military solution. On October 18, General Jaruzelski replaced Kania as boss of the Party. After the meeting on November 4, between Jaruzelski and Walesa in the presence of Archbishop Glemp, mighty Solidarity was offered a junior role (one seat out of seven) in a Council of National Reconciliation. Time was now visibly running out. On December 2, special squads stormed the Warsaw barracks of firemen cadets and, ten days later, all hell broke loose. On the night of Saturday December 12, General Jaruzelski carried out his efficient and militarily successful coup.

Yet to understand why things moved so fast, we must stop for the moment to look at the economy.

The Economic Accelerator

We now know that the drop in production in 1981 was not quite as steep as had been forecast at the time. Domestic output fell by "only" 13 percent. If one adds to it the 7 percent drop in the two previous years, you get a level more than one-fifth lower than in 1978. And production fell by another 8 percent in the first half of 1982.[5] All of these figures, unprecedented in postwar Europe, East or West, are official and they speak for themselves.

In view of subsequent attempts to put the blame for everything on Solidarity, it is useful to recall that the downward turn in the production curve began well before the events of Gdansk and that an official report published five months before the coup admitted honestly that most ingredients of the crisis had accumulated, or rather had been aggravated, during the Gierek era. Wrongly directed investments, distorted prices, inflationary pressures, a debt to the capitalist world approaching $23 billion at the close of 1980, plus a great deal of general mismanagement—all this is enough to explain what happened later.[6] This is why I would tend to dismiss the opposite charge that the government cultivated the crisis for political reasons. Throughout, it had two irons in the fire—hesitating between a deal and a confrontation with Solidarity—and was therefore ready to make political capital out of economic "chaos." I don't think it was consciously courting disaster.

In any case, the fast deteriorating situation was rendering key decisions urgent and was completely changing the political climate. When standing in lines is just a nuisance, you may leave the management to the appointed managers. But when shortages become acute, when the shelves are empty and every member of the family has to spend several hours a day standing in line, the mood changes. The rank-and-file of Solidarity now wanted the labor movement to take over the running of the economy. Any socialist who traveled to Poland at the end of 1980 will tell you about the contempt expressed at any mention of *autogestion* (after all, they had had their experience with phony workers' councils); the following year, *samorzad*, self-government (clearly referring to factories and offices) gained currency as a more acceptable term.

The fashion spread together with the crisis. In the spring of 1981, the so-called Network of Leading Enterprises, inaugu-

1981, the so-called Network of Leading Enterprises, inaugurated by graduates of Gdansk, began to spread the idea of self-management. By summer, the Lodz and Lublin regions were groping toward a less technocratic conception. There was never a proper debate about how the whole scheme would be applied on a national scale, how much it would rely on the market and how much on planning. The absence of a serious, thorough debate was due to lack of time, to a reluctance to bring conflicts within Solidarity into the open and, above all once again, to the Party's knack for uniting its opponents.

No doubt the rulers were faced with a dilemma. Three times they tried to cut living standards by dramatically raising prices—in 1970, 1976, and 1980—and thrice they had to give in, threatened by the counter-offensive of the workers. Now they had to cope with an organized labor movement. They either had to smash Solidarity or pay a price for its blessing, because without its collaboration no project of reform stood a chance. The regime tried to have it both ways. It wanted both the union's help and the monopoly of power. Solidarnosc was faced with the other side of the same dilemma. With the economic situation growing more catastrophic every day, it could no longer stay aloof. It therefore asked for guarantees and compensations. It is significant that its key demands involved powers for the working people, power to manage the factory and to run the "self-governing republic."

Inevitably, the whole question soon centered around power as such. Self-management meant that the Party was no longer to be the master in the factory. The vote for managers would deprive it of the vital *nomenklatura*, the right to appoint its chosen people to key jobs. Finally, economic policy could not be determined in the new system without the approval of Solidarity and, hence, without some institutions for sharing decisions. Very rapidly, the CP was forced to make a choice between some kind of institutionalization of dual power and the crushing of Solidarnosc. We know that it opted for military dictatorship rather than for sharing power with the workers. But did that alternative really exist?

Was a Historical
Compromise Possible?

IF ONE ACCEPTS A FATALISTIC INTERPRETATION of history, in which anything that has happened had to happen, the question does not even arise. Jaruzelski ended the debate by providing the answer. On the other hand, the problem itself remains relevant for Eastern Europe as a whole and, having argued earlier that a compromise between the social forces existing in Poland and the imperatives of geography was a possibility, I would like to restate the case so that it can be perceived clearly, within its context and within its limits.

The Case Defined

In the best of cases, this chance was always presented as a hope or even the glimmer of a hope. It had to be studied because it probably offers the only opportunity of peaceful transition. Fundamentally, Lenin's assertion that "two powers cannot exist in a state" and that "the dual power expresses but a transitional stage in the development of a revolution" holds true.[7] In the case of Poland, this transitional stage was determined by geography, by the risks of Soviet intervention. This indeed was taken into account from the very start. A mass movement like the Polish wave of strikes in the summer of 1980 would logically have led to a seizure of power but for this factor. Indeed, this consideration was written into the Gdansk Agreements. The passages in Article One admitting the leading role of the Party in the state and recognizing the permanence of existing alliances are a tribute to geography. Thereafter, though no clear line was ever drawn, everybody was aware of a Rubicon, of a frontier not to be crossed if one wanted to avoid direct Soviet intervention.

A second limitation springs from the first. The revolution must be a creeping one, the sudden seizure of power must be replaced by a gradual conquest of powers because of Russia's shadow. For the same reason, dual power cannot be a period of stability, but one of permanent trial of strength, a sort of Cold War with its own rules and regulations. For the labor movement it must mean, through a series of advances and retreats, a progressive consolidation of successive positions until the

239

ultimate transfer of power, which will have to coincide with a similar shift in Moscow.

But why should the Polish chieftains and their Russian masters accept a process designed to lead to their doom? They have shown that they do not have to. They could also have assumed that the historical trial of strength would turn to their advantage. The Polish party leaders, or at least some among them, had their own grounds for venturing in that direction. First, we saw that if they genuinely wanted to reform the ailing economy and not just smash the opposition, their only chance to do so was in conjunction with Solidarity. Second, if worse came to worst, they too would have been swept aside, the Russians carrying along even more obedient servants in their luggage.

As for the Russians themselves, they were likely to intervene to prevent the contagion, knowing that they could always count on finding some Polish Bilaks (Vasil Bilak was a key Czech political figure during the Prague Spring who collaborated with the Soviets). However, if the Kremlin had to reckon with the government and the Party, backed for once by the organized working class and the nation at large, it might have hesitated and also looked for a compromise. Jaruzelski, whom many are now trying to whitewash, spared the Russians this difficult choice.

Actually, before the coup, Poland had outlined an institutional framework for the transition with two chambers potentially representing the protagonists of dual power. The first chamber was to be the old Polish Parliament or *Sejm*, in which the "leading role of the Party" would continue to be insured by some kind of electoral device. The second, whether called Economic and Social Council or whatever, was to be the spokesman on the national scale of local workers' councils, the practical expression of self-management. There was no agreement even within Solidarity on whether this Council should be separate, with consultative and veto powers, or whether it should share in the management of the economy. Nor was it clear what its prerogatives would be. But a body that included genuinely elected delegates from factories and offices across the land would inevitably have acquired authority. It might have contributed to a resurrection of planning and to the invention of forms of workers' democracy. This proved too much for the rulers who finally offered Solidarity one out of seven seats on some Council of National Reconciliation. The mighty new labor movement had to be contented with the role of stooge.

Everything stated above makes it clear that a peaceful solution throughout Eastern Europe—not a frictionless one but one without major bloodshed—would have been, and will be in the best of cases, a most perilous exercise. This does not in any way diminish the guilt of the culprits. Jaruzelski and his henchmen may well one day have to take the blame for an explosion and bloodbath to come.

It still remains to examine critically the arguments of some people on the far left in the Western world who believe that Solidarity is paying a price for its timidity, that it should have made an open bid for power.

Objecting to Objections

In the famous Bolshevik controversy over Brest Litovsk, you may side with Bukharin, with Lenin or with Trotsky in the middle; you may even, like in the old joke about the conciliatory rabbi, say that all three of them are right; you can't, however, take the German army out of the story. Similarly, one can't take the Soviet army out of the Polish equation, as some of the leftist critics of Solidarity seem to do. After all, the whole idea of a historical compromise in the East European context, of institutionalization of dual power, etc., was not born out of theoretical predilections or ignorance of the repressive nature of the state. It is a response to concrete circumstances and to the threat of Soviet troops. Admittedly, obsession with the threat would have led to inaction, would have prevented such conquests as those of Gdansk. Though the frontier is not rigid, however, it has always been assumed that an open bid for power would precipitate a Soviet invasion.

In terms of formal logic, the critics have a case for seeing the Vietnamese as a good example for the Poles of a people taking on a superior enemy. The snag is that everything—the terrain, the circumstances, the geography, the possibility of getting arms, etc.—was different. The odds are that the Polish movement would have been crushed like the Paris Commune or the Hungarian insurrection, and would have taken decades to recover, whereas now, though having suffered a temporary defeat, it is potentially intact.

In practical terms, the advocates of a bid for power should also say more concretely how and when during the brief sixteen months of Solidarity it should have been attempted. Everybody knows the one obvious date: the end of March, at the time of the so-called Bydgoszcz affair, when the labor movement showed its strength in a warning strike and Walesa reached a compromise with the government on the eve of a general, unlimited strike. Yet even then, had the strike toppled Party rule, the broad assumption is that the Russians would have come to its rescue, which takes us back to square one. Besides, whereas Walesa and his advisers had been attacked for making their decision undemocratically, without proper consultation, nobody criticized them publicly for not launching the offensive. (Even in private, the most one can report is a glimmer in the eyes of some of the actors when recalling that exhilarating moment when "everything seemed possible.") Only afterwards, and mainly in the nationalist circles of the KPN, was the line developed that Solidarity should just forge ahead with its own policies and damn the consequences. Later still, when the confrontation began to look inevitable, the strange suggestion was floated about reaching an agreement with the Russians above the head of the Polish CP. (Moscow was supposed to give up its Communist partners for the sake of guarantees about troop movements, alliances, etc., granted by Poland's new leaders.)

Western advocates of a bid for power should not be dismissed because they were writing from the safety of their offices. In that case, outsiders would never be allowed to criticize a policy. The trouble is that their comments seem to confuse various phases in the short story of Solidarnosc and to treat its members as the direct descendants of October, led by the Bolsheviks, but rather unsuccessful because they have no Lenins in their ranks. Now, for better or for worse, Solidarity was a very different kettle of fish. A vast movement of the working class, it was no party, had no clear program, not even a concrete vision of the future. The economic debate at the first Congress of Solidarity was confused, allowing for all sorts of strange alliances between radicals and liberals. And it cannot be said that the social and political content of the concept of a "self-governing Republic" emerged crystal-clear from the proceedings.

As a socialist, I remain convinced that if Solidarity had a project and a vision, if it had started earlier and proceeded further with the idea of workers' councils on the national scale, it would have been able not so much to get the support of more people, since popular backing was in any case enormous, but to mobilize them better, to combine open agreements at the top with a simultaneous consolidation at the bottom, in the factories and in the regions; it might have been in a better position to carry the movement through intervals between storms. As it was, when the government showed its bad faith too crudely, Solidarity was driven to produce its ultimate threat—the demand for free elections. This was no longer a question of "dual power." It was a plain bid for the transfer of power, since nobody in Poland had doubts about the overwhelming victory of Solidarity (a point to keep in mind now that efforts are being made once again by Jaruzelski's stooges and his foreign defenders to present the banned union as just one of many Polish factions).

The other snag concerning Western references to the "active strike" as a weapon for the conquest of power[8] is not so much that they are made with hindsight, but that they refer to slogans, ideas and events of the late autumn of 1981. By then the collision was imminent and the concept of dual power overtaken by events. It was much too late to stage an offensive active strike. It was more than high time to get ready for a general strike as a defensive weapon and to prepare structures for future activity underground. Even its best friends must admit that Solidarnosc reacted at first as if caught by surprise. It is not unfair to add that Lodz, the textile town with working class traditions, presented as a place almost on the verge of an active strike, did not show as much resistance as Gdansk, Wroclaw or the industrial region of upper Silesia.

Let there be no mistake about who is to blame for the Polish tragedy and no illusion about what could have been achieved by cleverer tactics. Let us repeat that, in the best of cases and with the best of possible leaderships, the task lying ahead of the growing opposition movement in East Europe is formidable. Everywhere outside of Russia, the movement can only rely for its final survival on contagion, knowing full well that any step in that direction—like Solidarity's appeal to the working people of Eastern Europe—is taken by Moscow as a challenge. Everywhere they must both venture into uncharted territory and be aware of the fact that beyond a certain point they will provoke foreign as well as domestic intervention.

The crucial factor is that the banks of the Rubicon are not fixed forever. Who would have guessed at the beginning of August 1980 that at the end of that month the workers of Gdansk would win the right to set up free trade unions in Poland? Yet this flexibility of frontiers does not mean that they have vanished altogether. Opposition throughout Eastern Europe will have to guess, like Walesa and his comrades did in the Lenin Shipyards, how far they can go. The labor movement, acting as a spearhead, will have to define more clearly its means and its objectives so as to sustain a long march, because this painful and perilous advance will last until an assembly of real workers' councils is held in Moscow, the capital of a country which still dares to call itself the land of the soviets.

Finally, this debate over the risks of confrontation and those of compromise is not a debate over spilt milk. It is carried on today in the Polish underground and will be echoed in the other countries of the Soviet bloc as, spurred by the economic crisis, Eastern Europe gets on the move.

And What About the Catholic Church?

I WILL NOT ANSWER, LIKE PETER SELLERS impersonating a Tory electoral candidate: "And what about the Catholic Church indeed!" I have never tried to conceal the importance of the Church in Polish politics. Simply, in this essay, concentrating on the new and crucial, I have attempted to stress the class struggle and its vagaries, to emphasize the revival of the labor movement and the decisive impact it will have on the final outcome.

Yet the fellow-travelers who put this question rhetorically, hoping to damn Solidarity through guilt by association, would do well to ponder why, after more than 35 years of allegedly Communist rule, the Church is much stronger in Poland than it was before the war? The disappearance of national and religious minorities—of Jews and Germans, White Russians and Ukrainians—provides only a partial explanation. The main reason is to be found in that very rule of the so-called Communist regime, which has, if one may put it this way, bestowed a new virginity on the Catholic Church.

It has done so in two ways. Positively, by eliminating compromising allies—the capitalists and the big landowners—thus making it easier for the clergy to switch from the defense of the rights of property to that of the rights of man. Negatively, by its own performance. As the PUWP, the allegedly Communist Party, became the symbol of oppression and injustice, the Catholic Church, the main organ of resistance to the regime, became the symbol of resistance to injustice and oppression. Hence, its enhanced prestige and its almost universal acceptance.

Undoubtedly great, the influence of the Church should not, however, be exaggerated. Its limitations were perfectly illustrated in August 1980, when Cardinal Wyszynski's call for the workers to end the strike found no echo. The Church, in other words, cannot go far with concessions without running serious risks. Its dilemma has been particularly acute since the military coup. On one hand, the Church wants to avoid bloodshed and has a great deal to lose in an open conflict (while the *junta* is quite willing to make further concessions in religious matters in exchange for a degree of political support). On the other hand, if in its search for a compromise it gave the impression of betraying Solidarity, the Church, within months, would lose much of the capital accumulated in the years of resistance. Hence, the twists and hesitations of its policy "since the war," to use the fashionable Polish description for the period following the putsch of General Jaruzelski.

Voices from the Underground

IN ONE SENSE, THE POLITICAL LANDSCAPE and the moral climate of Poland have been altered totally by the military coup. The exhilirating experiment in freedom is over. The Party is parading openly in uniform. In the ninth month after the putsch, as these lines are written, all the main leaders of Solidarity are still interned, while thousands of militants are in jail, sentenced under the summary jurisdiction of a martial law known in Polish as the "state of war." The contrast with the past is striking, a Season in Hell coming immediately after the Season of Hope.

But the problems did not vanish with the advent of the generals, and they reassert themselves in the grim new context. True, the jackbooted masters outdid their predecessors. According to their own estimates, at the beginning of 1982 they managed to double the nominal cost of living and to cut real incomes by about a quarter, on average. Yet, according to the same official calculations, production is still going down and is not expected to reach its previous levels for years. You can bully people into obedience. You cannot achieve with bayonets what even Solidarity would have found difficult to accomplish at a time when the workers felt they were gaining mastery over their fate. Today in Poland there is a yawning gap between the rulers and the people, and the regime is treated more than ever as an occupying power in its own country. Martial law goes on as if to illustrate the political bankruptcy of a militarily successful coup.

Solidarity, too, is discovering some of its old dilemmas in the entirely new surroundings of the underground. Originally stunned by the unexpected blow, it rapidly recovered and began to rebuild its structures, with a provisional leadership, an impressive network of publications and even occasional broadcasts carried out despite the ruthless repression of martial law. But at the same time, it has been finding out that to organize passive resistance of an army of labor is a much harder task than to direct the armed resistance of small disciplined units. It is not easy to keep tempers under control, particularly among the young. The leadership of Solidarity has thus revived in the underground the old debate about whether the risks of explosion are contained in a policy of cautious compromise or in one of bold offensive.

The discussion started almost at once with an article by Jacek Kuron, smuggled out of the internment camp of Bialoleka in February 1982. The former leader of KOR, known previously for his awareness of the line not to be crossed, was now pleading that the union must get ready for a general strike and even for a popular rising. Was it a conversion to violence? Not quite, since he was still arguing in terms of *si vis pacem, para bellum:* this was possibly the only way to force the rulers to negotiate and thus avoid a tragic confrontation.

Amid the articles in reply, the most significant was one by Zbigniew Bujak. Though only 28 years old, Bujak has quite a past behind him. Drawn into the action by his friends from KOR, this former electrician from the Ursus tractor factory was elected president of Solidarity for Mazowsze (the greater Warsaw region) and is today one of the four members of Solidarity's leadership underground.[9] In his piece, this tough ex-paratrooper argued for moderation and against the centralization of the movement with its risk of head-on collision. He was thinking in terms of a long march and, like the other participants in this debate, leaned heavily on Kuron's former thesis about civil society gradually gaining terrain from the state.

Naturally aware of this borrowing, Jacek Kuron replied in his second article[10] that the situation had changed. You can only gradually conquer space if there is room for it and if the other side is ready to concede some ground. The imperative now is to force the rulers to the negotiating table before it is too late. Thus the divergence between the two sides is over tactics, springing from different assessments of the temper of the people and of the readiness of the authorities to soften their line without a major threat. Kuron's case was probably strengthened by subsequent events. In May 1982, defying the forces of repression, thousands of Poles went into the streets in Warsaw and Gdansk, in Krakow, Wroclaw, Sczecin. And in July, the miserable concessions proposed by Jaruzelski must have come as a disappointment to those who had expected some form of compromise as a result of restraint advocated by the Catholic Church. On the other hand, Solidarity has managed so far to keep the movement in check. Looking to the future, the outcome of this trial of strength will ultimately depend, as it did in the past, on the capacity for resistance of the Polish working class, and that is why, judging by precedents and by the experience of the first months of military rule, Jaruzelski and his henchmen are, historically, on the losing side.

WRITING EXACTLY TWO YEARS AFTER the extraordinary strikes in the Gdansk region, but also after the temporary defeat of the movement, what lessons can we draw from Poland if we don't need, like all sorts of *nouveaux philosophes,* a message of gloom to justify inaction but if we don't either, like some of the activists, see a Bolshevik revolutionary around every corner?

Earlier this year, traveling across the United States to speak under the auspices of American Workers and Artists for Solidarity, I had time to glance through all sorts of publications. In one, I found a familiar face with a strange caption. The picture was of Janek Rulewski, the rather exuberant leader of Solidarity from Bydgoszcz. The caption said, "I have the feeling that I am participating in a rally in Moscow or St. Petersburg in 1917 when Lenin exhorted the workers' councils to take power." The surprise came from the fact that Janek Rulewski was known as one of the leaders of Solidarity who was most anti-communist in every sense of the word. Recalling the occasion, I grasped the misunderstanding. Rulewski did say something of the kind at a July meeting of the National Commission, adding that 64 years had elapsed since and what may have been good for them then was not good for Solidarity now.

Sticking to the context and being literally correct, I could have made the same point as the publication. After all, at that interesting session, attended by most leaders and key advisers of Solidarity, only Rulewski spoke against self-management and workers' councils.[11] If I left it at that, I would give the impression that all the others were revolutionary socialists. But it would have been the wrong impression. No revolutionary socialist group made much headway as such during the 16 months of the great upheaval. Actually, the very word socialist was relegated to an appendix in the program adopted by the Solidarity Congress.[12] It will be answered that the KOR veteran, Professor Edward Lipinski, did proclaim at the Congress, amid tremendous applause: "In my opinion, it is their so-called socialism that is anti-revolutionary and anti-socialist"[13] and, with even greater relevance still, that socialism is not just a question of words. The fact remains that the mood by then was moving in a nationalist direction and that no important faction emerged within Solidarity which, dissociating itself categorically from the oppressors in Marxist disguise, offered openly socialist solutions. And the military coup, however tragically absurd it may seem, will be put on the debit side of Marxism. There as well as here.

Now I, in turn, am giving a one-sided version, because the Polish events have also shown the topicality of socialist problems. In a country shaken by an egalitarian working class movement, in a land where the means of production have been nationalized and nobody suggests that "the Lenin Shipyards should be handed back to the Lenin family,"[14] the question of power at all levels, from the factory to the central state, is placed rapidly and nakedly on the historical agenda and gets embryonic answers suggesting that this power should be handed over to the working people. As a socialist, I draw two very encouraging conclusions from Poland. The first is confirmation that the working class can play a historical part "presenting its own interests as the superior interests of society as a whole." The second is the way in which, despite the prejudices against Marxism, socialist problems are thrust upon the movement in Eastern Europe. It is in their interest and ours that they should also find socialist answers.

Just over two years ago, on the eve of the strike in Gdansk, I thought I was finishing a book on Eastern Europe forecasting the revival of a labor movement in the Soviet bloc, arguing that the mole did not stop digging on reaching the Elbe, and also that in our socialist quest we can count on potential partners in Eastern Europe:

> This is not a triumphant message [I then ended]. It promises no certain victory. It does not even ensure that when things begin moving they will necessarily and at once move in a progressive direction. On the other hand, after a period when history had terrible hiccups and then gave the impression of standing hopelessly still, it is quite encouraging to be able to assert this inevitability of change, to proclaim *E pur si muove*, adding with the modesty imposed by our past failures and current disarray, that we have a part to play in this common movement.[15]

Today I would say the same only more so.

Moulin Persas, August 19, 1982

Postscript

Provisional Stalemate

It took Jaruzelski and his henchmen nearly a year to partly consolidate their position. On October 8, 1982 they finally dared to outlaw Solidarity. The underground leadership of the union, after much hesitation, opted for a series of reactions, beginning with a six-hour strike on November 10. By then, a deal must have been struck between the regime and the Catholic Church since, two days before the proposed stoppage, Archbishop Glemp preached in favor of regular work and Lech Walesa wrote to General Jaruzelski. The strike was a flop and the junta then felt strong enough to assume a liberal posture, freeing Walesa, suspending martial law and releasing those interned under its provisions.

Few were foolish enough to believe that everything was now for the best in the best of possible satellites. Finally freed, Walesa was taken for a ride by plainclothes policemen as soon as he proposed to speak in public. Martial law suspended, its worst provisions—including the tying of workers, like serfs, to their factories—were simply written into common law. Most internees released, there are still 1,500 political prisoners in Poland officially, and double that number according to unofficial accounts. The government has also singled out seven regional leaders of Solidarity for a second "Moscow Trial," five members of KOR having probably opened the sinister serial by the time these lines are published. The military dictatorship does not feel strong enough to relax.

The relative failure of the strike was not due primarily to the waverings of the underground leadership or the betrayal of the Catholic hierarchy: it resulted from the circumstances, from the natural weariness of the Polish proletariat. To go on strike in Poland today means to face the likelihood of jail and almost the certainty of being fired (there are tens of thousands jobless for political reasons). People are ready to take such risks for one crucial confrontation, not for a series of symbolic stoppages and demonstrations. The trial of strength last November showed that, at this stage, Solidarity is unable to paralyze the country. But the Party is utterly incapable of mobilizing the proletariat as was revealed by its inability to recruit members for the new labor unions. Provisionally, it's a stalemate. To tilt the balance in their favor, the military commanders must break the workers' passive resistance, while the labor movement must invent new forms of action, possibly including the use of the new puppet unions.

While accurately emphasizing Walesa's cross and the strikers' nationalism, most commentators seem to have missed the essential lesson of the Polish events—the rediscovery of the political weight of the labor movement. When the workers scored victories—in 1970, 1976, 1980—the whole society moved forward. When they suffered setbacks—in December 1981 or last November—the rulers were in a position to cut living standards, restrict the frontiers of freedom, set the stage for political trials. But the labor movement, though it has lost battles, remains fundamentally undefeated. Sooner rather than later, it is bound to resume its struggle in Poland. It is also likely to shape the future throughout Eastern Europe.

What should we do to help? The immediate task is to mobilize against the impending political trials. The Western left must take the lead in this protest in order to restore its own reputation and, by the same token, to contribute to what Eastern Europe probably needs most at this point: the emergence of a socialist opposition, confident, inventive, capable of spurring the reborn labor movement to sustained action leading to the radical transformation of the entire Soviet bloc.

Paris, January 10, 1983

Footnotes

1. *Kofederacja Polski Niezaleznej* (Confederation of Independent Poland).
2. The 107-strong National Commision had 38 members who were automatically included as presidents of their regions, and of the 18-strong presidium 6 were included as presidents of the largest regions.
3. According to a report to the Ninth Party Congress, by July 1, 1980, 197,300 members had returned their cards, representing 6.3 percent of the membership.
4. Out of the 200 members of the new Central Committee only 17 had belonged to its predecessor.
5. See *Trybuna Ludu,* 27 July 1982.

6. See *Rzadowy Raport o Stanie Gospodarki,* (Governmental Report on the State of the Economy), Warsaw, June 1981.

7. In *The Tasks of the Proletariat in Our Revolution.*

8. Many commentators draw for this purpose on the articles of Z. Kowalewski, now in Paris, who was a member of the presidium of Solidarity in Lodz and a delegate to the national Congress. His articles, published first in *Le Monde, Le Matin,* and a Swedish publication, have been translated into English.

9. Called Provisional Commission of Coordination. The other three members are Wladyslaw Frasyniuk (Wroclaw), Wladyslaw Hradek (Krakow), and Bogdan Lis (Gdansk).

10. Kuron's first piece was called "Theses for a Solution for a Situation Without Solution," and was republished by *Le Monde,* 31 March 1982. Bujak's article, "War of Position," was, like many others in this controversy, published in the underground *Tygodnik Mazowsze.* Kuron's second piece was entitled "You Now Have the Golden Horn," *ibid.,* no. 13, 12 May 1982.

11. On July 25, 1981. The text of the debate was published in *Solidarnosc,* no. 19, 7 August 1981.

12. "We want to stress that we are not against the socialist principles of the regime, but against those elements in the system which are the very contradiction of socialism." One of the variants of the economic motion, signed, among others, by Ryszard Bugaj, Zbigniew Janas and Bogdan Lis.

13. See report on the Congress in *Solidarnosc Press Agency AS,* no. 40, 26-28 September 1981.

14. I have often quoted this expression. I heard it first from Vlady Kibalchich, a painter living in Mexico who is the son of Victor Serge, the famous French revolutionary of Russian origin. I actually heard it in July 1981 in Warsaw, acting as an improvised interpreter between Kibalchich and Kuron in the latter's apartment in Zoliborz.

15. *The Road to Gdansk* (New York: Monthly Review Press, 1982).

Can "Real Socialism" Be Reformed?

JIRI PELIKAN

CAN THE SYSTEM OF SO-CALLED "real socialism"* in the Soviet bloc be reformed? Can it return, or at least come close, to the ideals of socialism, as a system that gives the working people *more* freedom, *greater* equality and social justice, a *greater* share in the control of the economy and political affairs, in brief, that combines the advantages of collective ownership of the means of production with political democracy? This ques-

---

* In a choice example of Orwellian Newspeak, the Soviet Union has dubbed its own regime and those of its satellites, "real socialism."

JIRI PELIKAN, *born in Czechoslovakia in 1923, joined the underground Communist Party in 1939, becoming an active participant in the resistance movement. Arrested by the Gestapo, he managed to escape and remained underground until the end of the war. (His parents were arrested by the Gestapo as hostages and his mother was killed.) After the war, he was active in the Communist student movement, and in 1956 was elected president of the International Union of Students. At the time of the Prague Spring in which he participated actively, he was Director of Czechoslovak Television, a member of Parliament, and a member of the Central Committee of the Party. After the Russian invasion, he was expelled from the Party and the Parliament and deprived of his nationality. Since 1969, he has lived in Italy working as a journalist and editor of* Listy, *the organ of the Czechoslovak socialist opposition. He became an Italian citizen in 1977, and in 1979 was elected on the Italian Socialist Party (PSP) ticket as a Deputy to the European Parliament. He is the author of a number of books, among them his autobiography,* S'ils me tuent, *published by Grasset, Paris.*

tion is posed with greater urgency than ever as a result of the December 13, 1981 military coup which has halted the renewal process in Poland for a long time to come.

After the defeat of the Prague Spring in 1968 a considerable section of the left believed that the period of reforms "from above," started by Khrushchev in the USSR and culminating in "socialism with a human face," advocated by Alexander Dubcek, had been exhausted and that the only realistic path was a movement "from below," outside the framework of the ruling Party and state apparatus. Disappointment with the Cultural Revolution in China and developments in Cuba led to even greater hope for Poland, given the 1981 events, in which the protagonists were the masses—above all, the working class which had succeeded in organizing independent trade unions to counterbalance the ruling bureaucracy. The question now is: does the temporary defeat of that movement mean the end of hopes for change in Poland and the other East European countries—as the right claims—or is this merely part of an overall process of emancipation in the Soviet bloc which will continue in a different form?

To answer this question we will analyze two of the "models" of democratization in the Soviet bloc, the Prague Spring and the Polish Summer, and find out how they differ and what they have in common.

First, let us clarify what we mean by "reform." Basically, it is a transformation of institutions, practices, laws, etc., which results not in a change of the system but in its "improvement" or "development" in the direction of greater democracy. We are concerned with reform of so-called "real socialism" or the Soviet model of socialism as it developed in the USSR under Stalin and was later exported to or imposed on the other Soviet bloc countries. (At this point I do not intend to touch on the theoretical question of whether these regimes or systems are truly socialist or whether they are state capitalist or simply bureaucratic dictatorships or possibly countries in a state of transition from capitalism to socialism, etc.) These countries reveal the following major features:

1. an absolute monopoly of power of the Communist Party (though its name may vary);

2. state ownership of all major means of production (which is

not the same as collective ownership or ownership by the producers as conceived by the founders of socialism);

3. the functioning of trade unions and other mass organizations as "transmission levers" of the Communist Party, which
makes all the decisions;

4. the existence of a state ideology excluding all differing
views, which are suppressed by censorship, and the repression
of all those "who think differently" or "dissidents" as they are
generally called;

5. the hegemony of the USSR vis-à-vis all other countries of
so-called "real socialism" and the notion that loyalty to the
USSR is the touchstone of so-called "proletarian internationalism" (the latter meant as contrast to patriotism and national
independence, which are rejected as "nationalism").

Some Soviet bloc countries display certain special features
(for example, in Poland, private ownership of land and a considerable measure of autonomy of the Roman Catholic Church;
in Hungary, a certain type of economic reform; in Rumania, a
degree of autonomy in foreign policy, etc.) but since the *essence*
of these regimes remains the same, their major contradictions
and problems are identical. So *reform* in these countries means
changes in the way they function and some marginal adjustments which, however, never affect the essential features of the
system. If the changes were to transform the core of the system
it would be possible to speak of a *revolution*, a violent or
political one, in which a different social group or class would
take power. However, reforms can be so far-reaching that at a
certain stage they turn into a revolution since they create a new
system differing basically from the previous one. (That would
be true, for example, if the ruling Communist Party were
replaced by a plurality of political parties.)

HAVING DEFINED THE MEANING OF "REFORM" we can analyze
the substance of the reforms attempted during the 1968 Prague
Spring and the 1980-81 Polish Summer. I shall not deal with the
two processes separately against the background of their
historical development but jointly, to emphasize all they had in
common and where they differed. I want to make it clear from
the start that the *essence* of the two processes was the same, as
it is likely to be for similar movements which already have

made or will make their appearance in other countries under Soviet hegemony. I stress this because there is a tendency in the West to highlight the peculiarities of the Polish situation, pointing to those aspects in which Poland differs from Czechoslovakia and the other Soviet bloc countries. These aspects are certainly not negligible: almost 80 percent of the land in private ownership, the considerable role of the Roman Catholic Church, traditional Polish nationalism, the militant tradition of the workers' movement in the past decade, etc. But if we compare the 21 points of the Lenin shipyard agreement in Gdansk, which became the program of the Polish Summer and of the Solidarnosc independent trade union organization, with the major points of the Czechoslovak Communist Party's Action Program in 1968, it is clear that the basic demands are identical or very similar (and they link these two movements with the Hungarian revolution in 1956 and the East German popular revolt in 1953; we even discern common roots with the famous Kronstadt uprising of 1921).

The crucial question is the monopolistic position of the ruling Communist Party, established at the end of the 1950s based on the Soviet model. The renewal movements in Czechoslovakia in 1968 and in Poland in 1980-81 never aimed at overthrowing the regime and replacing it with another party or political force. The leading role of the Communist Party was accepted as a necessity: in the case of Czechoslovakia the CPCz began to win the trust of the majority of the population by supporting the renewal process, while in Poland the leading role of the Party was an acknowledged imperative which had to be respected to prevent the collapse of the regime and in order not to provide a pretext for Soviet intervention. In each case the proposals and demands for reform submitted to the Communist Party were confined to "mitigating" the power monopoly of the Party and also striving toward a "partnership" with other sections of the social and political spectrum.

According to the Czechoslovakian Action Program, the Communist Party is meant to rule not by virtue of a leading role established for all time by law (in the Constitution), but through striving to regain the confidence of all citizens by its policies and activities. In practice, this means that the Party must abandon bureaucratic and police methods of government and should, instead, always explain its program to the public, confront it with the views of the other partners and test its correctness in elections with a choice of more than one candidate.

Such a social partnership can include other political parties which, as distinct from the existing state of affairs, have a certain autonomy. But reform of the Party's role is not tantamount to a development toward democratic parliamentary political pluralism since it rules out a change of regime, as well as the existence of legal opposition. It is a development toward a different type of political pluralism, in which the ruling Party seeks solutions to all major problems by negotiations and a dialogue with the other partners—in Poland, for example, with the independent Solidarnosc trade union and the Roman Catholic Church, as well as the organizations of farmers, students, journalists, scientific workers, etc.

Another significant reform is the acceptance of the principle that working class interests need not always be identical with the interests of the socialist state and its leadership, and that the workers may have *their own trade unions* which are not simply a Party transmission belt but an autonomous partner of the government and Party, i.e., the regime. In Poland, pressure from below led to the creation of the independent trade union Solidarnosc, whereas in Czechoslovakia in 1968 the united trade union organization won independence from the Party and became the genuine defender of the interests of the working people. After the imposition of martial law in Poland, Solidarnosc was suspended and later, in 1982, outlawed. The authorities have returned the "trade unions" to their former role of executors of the will of the Party (a transmission belt).

A most important part of the reform of so-called "real socialism" is a set of measures in the *economic* sphere. Here, too, reform does not affect the essence of the system, i.e., the state ownership of the means of production; nor does it imply their return to former owners, even though it provides for the possibility of a limited private sector (in the service sector and agriculture) within the framework of a collectivized economy. But the main demand is the transformation of the role of the state economic plan, which should be worked out not merely by the planning center, but through consultation with the workers' organizations, especially the trade unions. It should be confined to setting out the overall orientation of the major branches of the economy, allowing sufficient elbow-room for the initiative of individual enterprises and for the impact of market forces, reflecting the pressure and needs of consumers.

*   *   *

IT IS COMMON KNOWLEDGE THAT THE ECONOMIES of the countries of "real socialism" do not function well. This is admitted even by leading representatives of the Party; the press talks about it, and improvement is sought. Various changes in the system of planning and management are tried but in most cases they fail to accomplish the expected results. The core of the problem is political, as demonstrated once again by the example of Poland. The economy cannot be improved unless confidence is restored and a dialogue resumed between the populace and the leadership. Neither huge dollar loans nor imports of the latest technology can do the job. But if confidence is restored between rulers and subjects "miracles can be achieved," as the leader of the Polish trade unions, Walesa, once said.

Further demands that appear in all the Prague Spring and Polish Summer documents are: to have access to information, to know the *truth* about the state of the country and its economy, and to have freedom of expression and criticism; hence, the necessity for lifting or at least easing censorship.

After all, how can a citizen know that he must work harder and not press for higher wages because the state is in debt, when he does not know how much his state owes and, therefore, how long it will take to pay off the debt? Nor does he know how much his state produces, what can be made available on the domestic market and what must be exported to obtain the currency for paying interest and purchasing new technology? Lenin once said that every cook ought to be able to understand the state budget as well as the household budget. But in the countries of "real socialism" only a very restricted circle of leaders, members of the Party Politburo, have this information. The actual expenditures earmarked for the army, police, the Party and state apparatus, various privileges, and foreign policy are a "state secret." They may not be discussed in the press, on radio or television. Censorship keeps a strict eye on this since it checks not only the press but also literature and scientific publications, including magazines for chess players and animal lovers, right down to wedding and funeral announcements. Nothing may be printed without the censor's rubber stamp, nothing may be broadcast without the prior consent of the censor stationed in all editorial offices.

That is why the demand for lifting censorship is common to all East European democratization movements. It is one of the fundamental conditions for democratizing political and public life. But such a reform is unacceptable to the Soviet leadership which regards censorship as a guarantee against the dissemination of "anti-socialist ideas." In Czechoslovakia, censorship was lifted in the course of the Prague Spring, while in Poland it continued. The renewal movement merely demanded its limitation on the basis of a new law. The 1968 reform movement in Czechoslovakia placed stronger emphasis on freedom of expression since writers, journalists and scientists were its moving force, whereas in Poland greater significance was attached to religious freedom in view of the importance of the Roman Catholic Church. That is why the demand for live relays of Sunday Mass by Polish Radio was one of the 21 points submitted by the Gdansk workers, while that demand was absent in Czechoslovakia in 1968, though there, too, the restoration of the functioning of all churches and religious freedom was seen as a fundamental part of the democratization process.

Certain Soviet bloc countries are made up of several ethnic groups but the centralized structure of the ruling Communist Party contradicts the promise of each ethnic group's autonomous development, causing tension and conflicts. A just solution of the national question has, therefore, been a part of the democratization process in countries such as Czechoslovakia, Yugoslavia, and, above all, the USSR, the largest multinational state of the world. The Soviet leadership is fairly tolerant on this matter and allows various alternatives in dealing with relations between different ethnic groups. In Czechoslovakia the reform of the relationship between the two major ethnic groups, the Czechs and Slovaks, on the basis of federation is the only reform that has survived the Prague Spring. Yet this limited degree of administrative and cultural autonomy is tolerated only within the framework of accepting the central authority of the Communist Party, depriving any ethnic group of the right of secession which Lenin promised the various Soviet Republics and which was guaranteed by the original Soviet Constitution. Nowadays, any voice in favor of independence for an ethnic group in the USSR or any other Soviet bloc country is branded "nationalist" or "separatist" and, according to the law, is a criminal act.

RELATIONS BETWEEN THE EAST EUROPEAN COUNTRIES and the USSR constitute the most delicate problem facing the reform movement. Since the Soviet Union dominates most of these countries and has imposed its own system on them, their citizens hold the USSR responsible for all shortcomings, from the lack of independence to a potato shortage. The subject of relations with the USSR is officially taboo and nothing may be written about it, yet it crops up the moment censorship is relaxed and greater freedom of expression is allowed. There can be no doubt that if the citizens of the East European countries could hold a referendum and freely choose the status of their country, the majority would vote for neutrality, for relations with the USSR similar to Austria's or Finland's, or at least the status of a non-aligned country like Yugoslavia. It is no accident that Jacek Kuron, one of the leaders of the Polish democratic opposition, wrote even before the events in 1980 that "Finlandization" would be immense progress for the East European countries. It would, he argued, mean that the USSR would acknowledge that these countries could claim a specific road to socialism in accordance with the traditions and mentality of their populations; it would allow them to carry out the necessary reforms and select statesmen vested with the moral authority and confidence of the majority of the population. In return, these countries would guarantee to respect Soviet strategic and economic interests.

But such a solution is impossible until a change takes place in Moscow and the Soviet leadership understands that it is more advantageous to rely on independent but loyal governments in Eastern Europe than on appointed governers, mistrusted by their citizens and therefore only able to govern through police repression and the presence of the Soviet army. Until this happens, subjugation to the USSR and all commitments arising from the country's membership in the Warsaw Pact and Comecon (Council for Mutual Economic Cooperation) must be respected. That was understood by the reformers who drafted the Czechoslovakian Action Program in 1968 and by the Polish renewal movement, with the exception of certain radical nationalist groups.

That is why the reform movement in Eastern Europe, while stressing the observance of military, economic and political agreements with the USSR also emphasizes the principle of "equality and mutual advantage," enshrined in these agreements but violated in practice. Moreover, there is a demand for greater autonomy in relations with Western countries, something the USSR tolerates at times, as in the case of Rumania, or even in Poland under Gierek. But the USSR cannot tolerate the consistent application of independence and equality: witness the excommunication of Yugoslavia from the "socialist" camp in 1948 and military intervention in Hungary in 1956 and in Czechoslovakia in 1968, even though in the case of the Prague Spring, its reform program did not demand even the degree of foreign policy autonomy enjoyed by Rumania.

SUCH WERE THE DEMANDS of the reform movement in Czechoslovakia in 1968, and in Poland in 1980-81. Even though the *programs* of the movements were similar, the *direction* and *methods* chosen to attain them differed. One can talk of *two* models or roads for the reform movement.

In Czechoslovakia, the impulse for reforms came from the ruling Communist Party or its reform-minded wing, aware of the necessity to seek new ways out of the crisis through a dialogue with the population. This was in large part in response to mass discontent with Party policy and an economic, political and moral crisis of so-called "real socialism."

Often described as a movement that originated exclusively "from above," the Prague Spring is now contrasted with developments in Poland, characterized by pressure "from below." This is not quite accurate. As I have pointed out, the 1968

Prague Spring was the culmination of a long process in which pressure "from below," i.e., popular discontent with Party policy, played a major role. Even though the Communist Party headed the 1968 reform movement, its subsequent progress throughout the first eight months of that year was marked by the mutual impact of both pressures. The initiative of the Party "from above" provided scope for the intitiative of the citizens "from below" and that pressure in turn forced the Party leadership to advance on the road to reform, constantly widening the participation of broad sections of the population in the country's political and economic life. I believe that this link between the two components of the reform movement was ideal because the Communist Party opened the way to reforms without ever losing control of the process, thus guaranteeing a gradual development free from spontaneous explosions and conflicts, always a grave threat to the stability of a state in a period of transition (as happened in Hungary in 1956).

But this brings us to a seemingly paradoxical conclusion: the fact that the Communist Party of Czechoslovakia headed the reform movement motivated the Soviet military intervention; similarly, the fact that in Hungary the Communist Party had lost control of the 1956 events served as a pretext for Soviet intervention. This allows us to draw the significant conclusion that the Soviet leadership decides in favor of direct military intervention in Eastern Europe and in the countries of "real socialism" in either of two situations: when the Communist Party itself becomes the initiator of reforms and a democratization process; or when the Communist Party is divided and loses control of the situation.

IN POLAND WE SAW QUITE A DIFFERENT MODEL of development in August 1980: the reform movement emerged entirely "from below," outside the Party and official institutions, inside the factories. Hence, its first demand was the establishment of independent trade unions which did not want an alliance with the Party but equal partnership. This difference was the logical outcome of earlier developments in Eastern Europe and in Poland itself. The reform movement, which had been supported by the Communist Party and had brought Gomulka to power in 1956, with a far-reaching reform program, was eventually stifled by repression. The defeat of the Prague Spring (and Khrushchev's fall in the USSR before that) brought to an end a period when proposals for change were submitted at the initiative of the Communist Party. "Reformist elements" were driven out of the Communist parties in a series of purges and campaigns of repression, forcing them into a "democratic opposition" as "dissidents," condemned to working underground.

That explains why, initially, the Polish movement declared that it was not interested in who ruled the Party and acted merely as a loyal opponent of the Party and government, i.e., the regime. Its aim was to extract the maximum number of practical concessions, including political and economic reforms, but with no desire for a share of power. In this sense, the Polish movment "from below" is altogether different from the Prague Spring. The moment the independent trade unions won official recognition, the movement "from below"—whether it wanted to or not—was instrumental in causing divisions in Polish society and the ruling Party. The Party divided into two tendencies. One faction regarded the Gdansk Agreement as a temporary concession that had to be made but would have to be liquidated the moment the Party recovered from its crisis; it wanted to suppress the movement with its own Polish forces and, if necessary, with the help of Soviet armor. The opposing faction saw the Agreement as a healthy step to further progress, based on a dialogue between the Party, the independent trade unions and other sections of Polish society. It believed in sweeping reforms to overcome the profound crisis. This latter tendency was also a response to internal pressure "from below," i.e., from the grassroots Party members who were in daily contact with the rest of the population and who identified with the struggle of the independent trade unions. There were one million Party members who belonged to Solidarnosc and insisted that the Party accept the union's just demands and carry out essential reforms.

One of the mistakes made by Solidarity's leaders was that they ignored this division within the Party and failed to support the position of these so-called "revisionist" forces, which facilitated martial law and domination of the Party by the dogmatists. (It cannot be denied, however, that even some of the revisionists, such as Rakowski, supported General Jaruzelski's coup as a "necessary evil.")

Though the situation in Poland is far from "normalized" despite harsh repression and the continuing state of emergency, we can draw certain conclusions about the possibility of reforming the so-called "real socialism" regimes.

LAUNCHING AND DEVELOPING A PROCESS of democratization in Soviet bloc countries is extremely difficult and complex. On the one hand, the Soviet leadership—at least the existing one—is always prepared to thwart it by armed intervention and, on the other hand, these Soviet-installed systems lack the mechanisms to make such changes possible. It would be naive of both the left and the right in the West to assume that the authoritarian regimes in Eastern Europe can be swept away by classical revolution and replaced overnight by a system of pluralist democracy or self-management. These systems can be reformed in the direction of greater democracy only by easing the Communist Party's monopoly of power and introducing certain democratic mechanisms to control it. The power monopoly cannot be destroyed since this would not be tolerated by Moscow or by the domestic Party and state bureaucracy. The champions of the renewal process in Poland saw the Communist Party's weakness and its inability to run the state as the instability of the regime and underestimated the Party's capacity to defend its prerogatives and strike a counterblow. They especially underestimated the extent to which professional soldiers and police are part of the Party *nomenklatura* and among the most privileged sections of society.

That such a powerful popular movement as the 10-million strong Solidarnosc organization, along with movements of farmers, students, young people, women, etc., could be defeated by domestic Polish military and police forces contradicts the theory that a strong movement "from below" is sufficient to force the ruling powers to surrender. A movement "from below" like the one in Poland is naturally a prerequisite for reforms leading to democratization. But if concessions won from the ruling bureaucracy are not to be merely illusory or temporary but genuine and lasting reforms of the system, there must be both pressure "from below" and cooperation with that section of the ruling Party prepared to accept certain, albeit limited, changes and, along with the working people, defend these changes against the USSR and conservative domestic forces. Some Solidarnosc leaders and a number of the rank-and-file failed to grasp this, rejecting any dialogue with the Party, even with the reform-minded forces within it. This intransigence only weakened the anti-conservative forces in the Party, some of whom left the Party prematurely, while others abandoned all hope of a compromise and went over to the opponents of Solidarnosc. It goes without saying, however, that the conservative forces in the Polish Party and in the Soviet leadership are the ones primarily culpable for the collapse of "national reconciliation," i.e., the search for a real compromise.

THE DEFEAT OF THE POLISH MOVEMENT bears out earlier lessons of the 1956 Hungarian Revolution and the 1968 Prague Spring, that attempts at democratization in the Soviet bloc countries are all but doomed if they remain confined to one country, no matter how favorable the conditions there. Only a renewal movement taking place simultaneously in at least two or three Soviet bloc countries stands the chance of thwarting any plan by conservative domestic forces to stifle such a movement by police or military action and of compelling the Soviet leadership to adjust its relations with these countries in a way analagous to existing relations with Yugoslavia. It is internationalism, a form of solidarity among the oppressed of different nations, that is called for to replace nationalism in the struggle against the common enemy.

But even a strong multi-national renewal movement in the East will constantly be exposed to the threat of Soviet intervention and to sabotage by conservative domestic forces. It therefore needs, in addition, international solidarity from the workers' movement and all progressive forces in the West. Such solidarity can save a renewal movement from the danger of ideological exploitation by international reactionary circles, seen by Moscow as a welcome pretext for a counterattack. This solidarity is also essential for the left in the West, since the success of the renewal movement can vest socialism with a new appeal and provide a fresh impetus to the workers' movement.

Furthermore, as the Polish experience makes clear, democratic movements in the East would be in a far stronger position if they were free of the iron logic of military blocs in Europe, which follows from the superpower conflict and allows the USSR to sustain its military, political and economic hegemony over the East European countries. That is why we should defend and encourage the policy of detente, although not in its Soviet version, which approves the existing division of Europe into two antagonistic blocs, each under the control of "its own" superpower. The Soviet version is also shared by certain Western leaders and, more particularly, business circles. They regard "Yalta" as the symbol of the division and adherence to "Yalta" as a means of stabilizing capitalism in the West, offering it the advantages of massive trade with the USSR, while simultaneously permitting politicians to underscore the ineffectiveness of the Soviet system as a warning for working people in the West.

The Western left would do well to support a different concept of detente, one that links detente to the gradual and nonviolent change of the political status quo, allowing the people of Eastern and Western Europe to choose their own roads freely, without the risk of military intervention or economic blackmail by this or that superpower. Solidarity with the peoples of Poland, Czechoslovakia, and the other East European countries striving to reform the Soviet system and achieve national independence is part of such a concept of detente. Silence in the face of persecution in the Soviet bloc, in exchange for more trade or concessions in the sphere of disarmament, is damaging to the struggle for democratization and the cause of detente and peace.

The Polish example, moreover, provides striking proof that those who believe that more trade with the Soviet bloc countries automatically leads to some kind of liberalization of these regimes are under an illusion. But the argument that complete isolation, or economic boycott of the USSR and the countries under its domination, is an effective instrument for change or might even topple these regimes is equally harmful. The totalitarian states have sufficient strength and reserves to remain in power and, when they feel the need, to intensify the oppression of their subject peoples. What is decisive is to promote new international relations that permit smaller nations to decide their own destinies, a right denied in a world polarized by the two superpowers.

FOR THE MOMENT, WE CANNOT PROVIDE an unequivocal answer to the question of the "reformability" of the systems of "real socialism." Even though attempts in the past have been defeated, the crisis of the Soviet regime is deepening and will produce new reform movements and changes. It is the duty of the left in the West to offer active solidarity to the Polish working people and their Solidarnosc union, to press for the release of all those still imprisoned and for an end to repression and the return to a dialogue between the regime, the trade unions and the church to bring about an acceptable compromise. The workers' struggle to democratize the system in Poland and other East European countries is part of the common struggle of all progressive forces in the world.

Translated from the Czech by Ruth Tosek

Currents within Soviet Dissidence

PYOTR ADOVIN-EGIDES

THE TERM "DISSIDENT," applied to those in the Soviet Union who refuse to conform to the pattern demanded by official-dom, tends to obscure substantial, even cardinal, differences among the dissenters. To understand the multi-faceted nature of the dissident movement, it would be helpful to begin with a brief review of the basic factors in Russian society generating opposition.

The Genesis of Dissidence

WHY IN RUSSIA where, we have been told, socialism exists (in full and final form no less), where there are no class differences,

---

PYOTR ADOVIN-EGIDES *was born in Kiev in 1917 and raised in an orphanage after his father was murdered by the Cheka (tsarist secret police). He received his Ph.D. from Moscow University. When the war broke out, he volunteered. Because he was taken captive by the Germans, he was imprisoned by the Russians from 1942 to 1949. He taught briefly, but after Stalin's death, convinced that Khrush-chev would set a new course, he volunteered as chairman of a kol-khoz. Stymied by bureaucratic restrictions, he left to work as a lec-turer at an institute and a university from 1960 to 1970. It was during this period that he started to demonstrate openly for demo-cratization and wrote* The Sole Solution, *in which he argued that there can be no socialism without democracy. He was arrested once more and confined to a psychiatric hospital for three years. In 1978, he and some dissident friends started* Poiksi (Searches), *a pluralistic journal with a strong socialist slant. Threatened with arrest for the third time, he left Russia in 1980. He lives in Paris, where* Poiski *is now published.*

no exploitation of others' labor, no social inequality, no national repression, no religious discrimination, where presumably the highest form of democracy reigns—not formal as in the West but real—has a protest movement developed? What is there to oppose if all social problems have been solved?

What happened was that during the period of the terrible purges of the thirties, reality could no longer be denied: not a single serious problem had been solved, nor had a single objective of the Revolution been realized. Among the basic ideals of the October Revolution was "factories to the workers, land to the peasants, all power to the Soviets." Yet, the workers did not get the factories, either directly or indirectly, since in a totally undemocratic country workers decide nothing. The land, given originally to the peasants, was taken away as they were forcibly driven into "collective" farms which are not collectively run. Power belongs not to the Soviets, not to the Supreme Soviet, not to the Council of Ministers, but rather to the Politburo of a single party which even Party members do not elect and which dominates the Soviets.

Thus, the country called the Union of Soviet Socialist Republics is, in fact, neither a union, nor made up of soviets, nor socialist, nor a republic. A union is a voluntary association, while our people are bound to the empire by force, without referendums or plebescites on the question of whether they want to be part of the "Union." The truth is that in our country whole nationalities have been expelled from their homeland. The Crimean Tatars to this day have not been allowed to resettle in the Crimea. National languages are overshadowed by Russian. National cultures are decaying. The national Republics are essentially without rights, powerless.

Nor is it a "Republic," since its public organs decide nothing and all power rests in the hands of usurpers. It is certainly not "Socialist," because socialism presupposes a society where the means of production belong to the producers, where the producers themselves distribute their product. In the "Soviet Union" the means of production are in the hands of a Party-state mafia beyond control of the workers.

Thus, history has once again—this time on a colossal scale—laughed Homerically at humanity. The October Revolution, which defined itself as "Great," which was to open the road to socialism, to achieve all the Paris Commune failed to, which was to liberate workers from alienation, from the inversion of subject-object relations, that revolution has been transformed into anti-socialism, a kingdom of the mafia elite where workers are enslaved with new forms of alienation and self-alienation and with a government that strangles thought and speech. The original socialist ideology has been replaced by the de facto imperial ideology of the "Third Rome." When Solzhenitsyn in his famous "Letter to the Authorities" "recommends" that they give away their Marxist ideology to the Chinese, it has a comical ring since they cannot donate what they neither have nor understand. They gave up Marxism and socialist ideology years ago, leaving it a verbal husk for the pacification of the masses.

BUT ISN'T IT TRUE THAT IN THESE 65 YEARS the country has made enormous gains? Yes, of course: many factories have been built, apartment buildings constructed, there are impressive skyscrapers and one of the best subways in the world, etc. But for these achievements the masses have been forced to pay an incredible price. The Kremlin mafia has sacrificed millions of slaves imprisoned in the Gulag, has brought the peasantry to utter ruin, in essence liquidating it, and has shed a sea of the people's blood.

Those who rationalize all this suffering argue that at least those who have survived the terror now receive their socio-economic rights: the right to work, to a free education, to medical care. They also claim that anti-Semitism, sexism and hunger have been eliminated.*

What is the reality?

• The right to work, in the form of eliminating unemployment, could be claimed by Hitler, as well, but that hardly made the Third Reich a workers' or socialist state. Actually the "right to

---

*Many Western leftists swallow this bait. For example, I participated in a symposium in Barcelona at which Manuel Azcarate, then in the leadership of the Spanish Communist Party, also spoke. While critical of the Kremlin, he nevertheless praised its "achievements." When I exposed the absence of social rights, his reply was a helpless gesture.

work," like other socio-economic rights in the Soviet Union, is a fraud. Hidden and open unemployment exists, something about which the Central Statistics Board is silent. In essence, the "right to work" has been turned into serfdom since the workers cannot bargain with their employers through unions and have no right to strike, while the peasants have no right to leave the kolkhoz. When a person has not worked at a government institution for over four months, he or she can be sent to prison for "parisitism," a sanction used against unemployed artists, poets, dissidents.

• "Free" medical care is of poor quality and requires expensive medication which workers must pay for themselves. Workers have no access to the luxurious specialized hospitals treating only the elite; instead they overflow into the corridors of inferior hospitals.

• Education is in fact not equal at all. In village schools it is poor, so poor that villagers, especially girls, very rarely get into institutions of higher education. The children of the Party elite and black marketeers, whose parents can afford to hire tutors, get into the universities in significantly higher numbers than the children of peasants and workers. In this connection there is the problem of "surplus" education: young people who have completed 10 years of schooling but have not been admitted into universities and do not know what to do with their "superfluous" education. As a psychological release, many become hooligans, even sadists since, while school gives them a certain amount of knowledge, it does not teach them to think or reflect. They have nothing to live by, nor can they take up a nonconformist lifestyle since that is banned in our country.

• During Lenin's lifetime anti-Semitism was condemned officially. Today it has become an integral part of the social order, taking such forms as restricting the number of Jews in universities, science, government. There is blatant use of racial slurs and appeals to the most vulgar, reactionary prejudices.

• Also in Lenin's lifetime, the emancipation of women and their equality to men was proclaimed. Women were offered equal education, equal right to work and equal pay. Today, these rights are largely a formality. In actual fact, women who work eight hours a day (often at hard physical labor and under the supervision of men) have to stand in grocery lines after work and then go home to do the most tedious housework (which has hardly been mechanized in our country). The lot of women in the kolkhozes is especially difficult.

• Then there is the stagnation of agriculture, the inability of the regime to feed its people, a prime cause of which is its inability to provide workers with an incentive to produce.

• Finally, and perhaps most important, socio-economic privileges are "given" at the expense of civil, political and individual rights and freedoms—freedom of speech, thought, elections, protest, assembly and press.

But didn't the USSR inspire liberation movements in the Third World, undercutting Western colonialism and demolishing the British, French and Portuguese empires? That, too, is true. But the great paradox of our age is that the USSR, so militant in its denunciation of the imperialism of all other countries, has itself emerged as the only power with a vast empire. It is the case of a thief running ahead of the crowd shouting, "Catch that thief!"

Characteristics of Dissent

THE HYPOCRISY AND REPRESSIVE NATURE of Soviet life have led a majority of people into opposition, some into open protest. What the majority of people sense, feel and know is expressed aloud by only a few. They are the dissidents. Their opinions can be expressed only in underground, samizdat publications, an act which exposes the individual to the danger of imprisonment.* The most significant are *Chronicle of Current Events,*

---

* After the appearance of the fourth issue of *Searches*, a journal initiated by my friends and me (we had prepared material for four issues and published them rapidly one after another before the KGB could prepare a "strategy" for destroying the journal), the KGB mounted a pogrom against our editorial board, confiscating the fifth issue and arresting three editors. Having already been in prison twice for a total of 11 years, I now found myself faced with the KGB's ultimatum of exile or prison. The editorial board decided that I should go abroad to facilitate the continued publication of *Searches*. After my departure, the KGB arrested three more of the journal's writers, followed by the arrest of

The Documents of the Helsinki Group, and our journal, *Searches (Poiski).*

Totalitarianism destroys a person's individuality, turning him into a slave of the state. It is domination by spiritual entropy and appears almost invincible. Nevertheless, there are individuals who, ignoring officialdom, much like partisans, have begun to act as if they were free, using their courage as a weapon to shatter the armor of entropy.

These modern day partisans have the courage to demand that the government act in accordance with its own laws, those in the Constitution, the Criminal Code and the regulations of the Communist Party. (Everyone else in the country has long been accustomed to the fact that the government enacts laws only in order to ignore them; they despise this deceitfulness but have learned to tolerate it.) They also have the courage to scorn all repression, to be unintimidated by demotions, firings, even by the threat of prison, the camps or psychiatric hospitals. In the West, these Soviet people are called dissidents. They call themselves the democratic movement or the human rights movement.

Some trace this enlightenment of a segment of our society to the "trial" of Sinyavsky and Daniel in 1965, an event that evoked a wave of petition signing. Almost a thousand people signed protests against this monstrous trial. Actually, dissidence predated this trial. It was evidenced soon after Stalin's death in 1953 (there were even distant glimmerings of it during his lifetime), especially after the Twentieth Congress of the Communist Party (1956) at which the Politburo, fearing the outbreak of a movement from below, decided on the disclosure of the "cult of personality" from above. The Party hoped that, through promises and a few reforms, the totalitarian system would be left intact. But the dissident movement gathered force when it became clear, after the October 1964 "palace coup," that the power elite which had overthrown Khrushchev was

---

Gleb Pavlovsky, the youngest member of our editorial board. More recently, they arrested yet another board member, Vladimir Gershuni, a veteran of the dissident movement. And still, *Searches* continues.

anxious only to consolidate its privileges and stabilize the regime, and would no longer consider reforms.

As the modern dissent movement took the path of open opposition to the totalitarian regime, it unequivocally renounced not only revolutionary violence but also underground struggle. This is a major difference between modern Russian dissidents and the Russian revolutionaries of the nineteenth and early twentieth centuries. However, experience has shown that the renunciation of all underground methods is a mistake and an increasing number of dissidents today are growing receptive to the idea of combining the methods of open and underground activism.

Finally, the dissidents within Russia and the political emigres, aware of what they are fighting *against,* find it somewhat more difficult to decide what it is they are fighting *for.* This too marks a difference between the contemporary oppositionists and the generation represented by Plekhanov and Lenin. It is difficult for dissident circles to define clearly their political objectives not because they lack the talent to do so but because all roads traveled in the past seem to have led to dead ends. Actually, it is all of humanity and not just Russian dissidents which finds itself in the position of Buridan's ass,* not knowing where to go, what to choose, what is best. Capitalism? But everyone in our country knows from childhood on that capitalism is an exploitative society, greedy, cynical and hypocritical. Socialism? "But," many tormented dissidents ask, "where is it? If socialism is what we have here then socialism be damned. We've never seen any other kind. Is a good kind even possible?"

The Spectrum of Dissident Opinion

ALL OF THESE AND OTHER PROBLEMS have given rise to a series of movements which the authorities repress, even smash, but which continue to live despite frightful persecution. These movements were interconnected and interdependent.

---

* A mythological animal who could not decide between two stacks of hay and, consequently, starved to death.—*Translator's note*

The human rights movement, for example, is made up of the Initiative Committee, the Helsinki Commiteee, the Psychiatric Commission and sections of Amnesty International. Originally, its focus was on such civil rights questions as freedom of speech, thought, and press, but it has broadened its concerns to include national and cultural issues and even the problems of free trade unions (which at first it did not understand) and the disabled.

The national, religious, cultural, and women's movements are interwoven. The workers' movement began by taking up economic questions. The first free trade union was organized by Klebanov with people who traveled to Moscow to complain about arbitrary rule by the authorities (there are many such complaints). Its goal was the reinstatement of people who had been laid off, i.e., the unemployed. Later, it established contact with the human rights, women's, and disabled movements.

An extremely significant movement about which the West has no knowledge yet is one made up of the young intelligentsia who have stopped working as historians, teachers, literary critics, medical technicians, geologists and physicists for a number of reasons. Some cannot bear to lie any more, others do not want to strengthen the armaments industry. Instead, they seek employment as stokers, loggers, security guards. Some become construction supervisors, hired on kolkhozes to build livestock enclosures and grain silos. They are disparaged as "hut builders" and "dowry seekers." But, in fact, their crews are the prototypes of self-sufficient construction collectives. Many of these young people become dissidents. Several members of the editorial board, as well as co-workers and authors, on the samizdat journal *Searches* have come out of this group of young people.

Then, of course, there is the samizdat movement, a network of underground publications including *Chronicle of Current Events, Searches* and other journals, monographs, articles and leaflets.

IDEOLOGICALLY, THE DISSIDENT MOVEMENT IS FAR FROM homogeneous. There are differences within it covering a wide political spectrum. In broadest terms, there is a division between the democratic and autocratic currents and, within each of these categories, there are important subdivisions. The democratic current includes such advocates of democratic capitalism as K. Lubarsky, B. Shragin, V. Chalidze, and T. Velikanova. Others are for democratic socialism, including R. Lert, L. Plyushch, P. Adovin-Egides, P. Podrabinek, E. Etkind, A. Levitan-Krasnov, V. Belotserkovsky, L. Kvachevsky, T. Mamonova. Two special cases in this category are Roy and Zhores Medvedev, about whom more later. And finally, the advocates of convergence of capitalism and socialism, for which A. Sakharov has spoken and which also includes A. Sokirko and his colleagues who advocate a new form of NEP. In 1981, representatives of these three tendencies met in Paris and formed the Democratic Union. A Coordinating Committee was elected including N. Dragosh, P. Adovin-Egides, V. Feinberg, V. Malinkovich, A. Shtromas and Yu. Voznesenskaya.

I list several names for each group to make clear that there are actual individuals involved in every current. For obvious reasons, I have not mentioned those who continue to live in the Soviet Union. Also, not all dissidents living in emigration have sufficiently defined views to be categorized precisely. This is true particularly for those who, in the most general sense, would be considered democrats. So, for example, Andrei Sinyavsky, who declares himself a proponent of democracy, has not further developed his views. The same is true for L. Kopelev; it is unlear whether he remains a socialist. As for V. Voinovich and V. Aksyonov, their precise political views are not known. In the category of those who are still undecided are V. Malinkovich, who is against both capitalism and state socialism but apparently increasingly favors a form of self-managing socialism. A special case is V. Turchin, who defends "ethical cybernetic" socialissm, a phrase whose political implications are not altogether clear. While the commitment of these dissidents to democracy is basic, it is necessary to go beyond that toward the formulation of a positive program which will answer the needs of the Russian people.

As for the autocrats, some believe in chauvinist theocracy (Shomanov), others are autocrat-imperialists upholding the preservation of the "single and indivisible" empire (Vagin); still others support either constitutional monarchy or some other form of autocracy as a transitional period that leads, one presumes, to democracy. Included in this last group are Solzhenit-syn, Bukovsky, Ginzburg, N. Gorbanevskaya, V. Maksimov.*

Interestingly enough, antagonistic cross currents participate in the same movements. In the most prominent, the human rights movement, there are not only democrats but autocrats, not only advocates of capitalism in one form or another, but also advocates of socialism and of convergence of the two. Unfortunately, this does not happen in all sections of the human rights movement. In the Moscow branch of Amnesty International there are both democratic nonsocialists like the excellent writer G. Vladimov, and democratic socialists like my friend and co-author P. Podrabinek, the father of two arrested dissident sons. But members of the Moscow Helsinki Commit-tee have not accepted advocates of democratic socialism since the arrest of Yuri Orlov, even though Orlov, the founder of the Committee, is essentially a socialist and though we socialists are in favor of an alliance of all the democratic currents.

In the national movement there are not only advocates of both democratic capitalism and democratic socialism, but also proponents of chauvinistic autocracy. In the Ukrainian nation-alist movement, for example, L. Plyushch, B. Kravchenko and others are advocates of democratic socialism; P. Grigorenko, who was once essentially a democratic communist, has since chosen a conservative path, and V. Moroz, whom we considered a democrat while he was in prison, now advocates autocracy and Russian nationalism.

The majority in the religious movement are in favor of demo-cracy. There are a certain number who favor monarchy and theocracy but there are also those who are for democratic socialism like Levitan-Krasnov, a Christian socialist and, more-over, a socialist revolutionary, since he believes that Russian totalitarianism can only be overthrown by a revolution which will clear the way for democracy and open the possibility of creating true democratic socialism.

A majority of the leaders of the women's movement—T. Gori-cheva, Yu. Voznesenskaya, N. Malakhovskaya—has taken on

---

* I wrote a critical analysis of this tendency called "To Carry Or Not to Carry an Umbrella," *Searches*, no. 2.

a religious and unsocialist coloration, a certain weakness for symbolic monarchy as a "symbol of national unity" within the framework of democracy. This is the attitude of those around the journal *Maria.* On the other hand, there is a socialist wing around the publication *Women and Russia,* of which T. Mamonova is the editor.

*   *   *

IT IS IMPOSSIBLE TO DETERMINE the program of the autocrats. What are they for? Solzhenitsyn, for example, yearns for the past, for pre-Petrine times. He believes that those who are responsible for the events leading to the October Revolution, totalitarianism and the Gulag are not only the prerevolutionary liberal Cadets, but the eighteenth century French materialists and the Renaissance humanists. If we follow that logic, we can go back to the early Christians since they spoke against social inequality. The forerunners of Hitler, then, are not only Nietzsche but also Hegel and Plato.

When Solzhenitsyn's supporters speak in defense of profaned Russian national culture, of memorials to the past, we can understand that. When they speak out as Slavophiles for Russian orthodoxy, that's their business. They can preach and practice whatever they like. But when voices among them begin to demand the canonization of Nicholas II, arguing that the Duma under him was a form of democracy, we are categorically opposed.* Even the name "Duma" [from the Russian word *dumat,* meaning to think—*Trans.*] signifies that in that body they only "thought" and "deliberated" but it was the tsar who decided. It follows that the Duma was not a parliament, i.e., not in essence a lawmaking body. If Solzhenitsyn's supporters want to go back to that kind of "democracy," I tend to doubt

---

* If one demands that Nicholas II be canonized because his innocent children were executed, why not demand the canonization of the workers who were killed on January 9, 1905? (Children were killed as well!) How can one canonize a tsar whose hands were stained with the blood of the people? Our autocrats assert that the monarch is a symbol of national unity, but France does perfectly well without such a symbol, and that nation is well unified. Isn't that so? Even royalists would hardly demand the canonization of Ludovic XV or Karl I.

that the Russian people will rally around them. The assertion made by the "transitionalists" (Bukovsky and Ginzburg) that the masses are not yet ready for democracy is insulting. Why such snobbish, arrogant condescension to one's own people?

No more acceptable are Solzhenitsyn's longings somehow to limit democracy and freedom of the press or his desire that Russia have a single Orthodox ideology, with the church sharing political power, which could lead to a Khomeini-type dictatorship.

In contrast to Solzhenitsyn, A. Zinoviev is an advocate of democracy. He does not accept Slavophilism and retrogradism. Where he does coincide with Solzhenitsyn is in his extreme anti-socialism, since he believes that socialism is what exists right now in our country. He asserts that there can be no other socialism than the type we have. That, so far as he is concerned, is "classic socialism." If that were not bad enough, he goes even further, delivering a series of sophist theses so pessimistic that they might well undercut the appeal of the dissident movement. His thesis is as follows: Under Stalin the country achieved classic popular sovereignty; therefore the masses are integrated into the regime today; hence the regime is stable.

But if the regime is stable and the people are integrated into it, why is there any struggle against it?

One cannot consider such a regime stable. If it were stable, it would not fear freedom of speech, would not destroy samizdat, would not imprison the editors of *Searches* who are demanding rights provided by the Constitution. Instilling fear by means of guns and tanks and force feeding the people with a diet of false propaganda are symptomatic of social insecurity, not inner strength. Repression is the trademark of instability. Such a state cannot be long-lived; 65 years, after all, is only one, two, three generations.

It is not difficult to disprove these Zinovievan "paradoxes," since they contradict reality and are essentially the usual kind of sophistry. By popular sovereignty, Zinoviev means the base prejudices Stalin aroused in the people. But even school children know that the term "popular sovereignty" is an exact translation of the Greek term "democracy," which Zinoviev himself says is absent. How can one claim as present something that is absent. It is a clear *contradictio in adjecto*.

As far as the presumed popular acceptance of the regime goes, there is a good deal of indirect evidence that the opposite is the case. (Indirect since, unfortunately, in our country there is no such thing as a Gallup Institute and representative surveys of the population are forbidden.) From my own personal experience as chairman of a kolkhoz, I can attest to the profound resentment of the regime among the kolkhozniks who say: "With Communists, you can't build Communism. The kolkhozes belong not to us but to them. They have taken the power away from the people." It is a sentiment shared by the urban working class as well. The tragedy is that through the use of repression the regime atomizes society, preventing contact between workers and those who might provide an answer to their question: "What should be done?"

THE RUSSIAN REGIME IS NOT GOING to wither away. Struggle is required, over many years, demanding personal sacrifices. The question is what form this struggle will take. The dissidents have opted for a course of nonviolence. That is why in my article in *Russkaya Mysl* (published in Paris on the occasion of Sakharov's 60th birthday), I referred to our era as the "age of Sakharov." In his name, the dissidents have proclaimed the principle of nonviolent struggle against social evils, a principle corresponding to the moral essence of the human being.

I fully agree with this principle but I define it more precisely as follows: the use of force against violence is not violence in a moral sense; on the contrary, the absolute repudiation of force in such a case can facilitate violence by the oppressor. Force is not to be equated with terror and the shedding of blood but can be viewed as the militant application of such techniques as strikes and civil disobedience. If that is how Levitin-Krasnov, a Christian socialist, understands revolution, I am in complete agreement with him.

The Polish tragedy indicates the necessity for a nonviolent struggle to win the army over to the people's side. That happened during the Portuguese revolution; a popular victory without bloodshed. It did not happen in Poland because at Poland's back stands the Executioner—the Soviet Politburo—whose guillotine cuts off the heads of whole peoples. The conclusion to be drawn is indisputable. The key to solving the present global

problems is not Poland, as we hoped all through 1981, or Czechoslovakia, as we had hoped in 1968, but Russia and the struggle
for democratization there. That is why we call on the progressive, especially leftist, forces in the West to aid the struggle of
Soviet dissidents, particularly socialist dissidents.

The Point of View of
Socialist Dissidents

SOCIALIST DISSIDENTS CLAIM THAT without democratization it
is impossible to achieve socialism in Russia. The world is,
however, still in thrall to the Great Myth of the existence of
socialism in the USSR, a myth that permeates the thinking not
only of conservatives but, alas, of many on the left as well. The
myth takes the following form for leftists: "But still ... still, it *is*
the Soviet Union, it is a *workers'* government, even if it is
deformed, as Trotsky himself said. At least, it isn't a capitalist
society. Therefore it is a socialist society."*

No, it isn't therefore—not at all therefore. The fact that capitalism does not exist in Russia does not mean that socialism
does. This century's greatest alogical construct is used by the
right as well as the pseudo-left; used by Reagan as well as
Andropov, A. Zinoviev as well as Marchais, Solzhenitsyn as
well as Gus Hall. All of them, alas, think that socialism exists
in Russia, with but this "slight" difference: the former believe it
to be evil while the latter believe it to be good. Most distressing
is that even a supporter of democratic socialism like the dissident Roy Medvedev views Russian society as socialist, albeit
primitive socialism, deformed, bad, because democracy is not
in very good shape in Russia.

All these people derive their beliefs from a false understand-

---

* I heard this ill-starred "at least" from Michael Foot and Tony Benn, with
whom I spoke at a Labor Party Congress to which I was invited. When I told
them that inviting socialist dissidents to their Congress was a step forward
and that inviting them along with a delegation from Moscow was two steps
backward, they pulled out this very same "at least" as a counter-argument. At a
recent Congress of the French Socialist Party I came up against this ritual "at
least" as well.

ing of socialism. What is socialism? Although there are many definitions, all should agree with the following negative formulation: socialism does not exist if the producers are alienated from the means of production, if they do not own and control them. It is precisely the denial of these decision-making powers in the productive process that characterizes Russian society. But, says Medvedev, and also Carrillo and Berlinguer, at least in the Soviet Union property is state property, not private property.

That is true but state property existed in ancient Egypt under the Pharaohs and that was Pharaoism, not socialism. Nationalized property becomes socialist only under fully democratic conditions, accompanied by self-determination. (It follows that the term "democratic socialism" is a tautology: undemocratic socialism is not socialism at all. We use the term to make our position more emphatic.)

What then is the social character of Russian society? This is truly a difficult question. Our society is a kind of sphinx. It turned out to be not at all like the society we had planned, primarily because of the one party regime. Our society can be characterized first and foremost negatively.

There is neither democracy, nor Soviet power, nor socialism. Nor are there collective farms, for a collective farm by definition is a cooperative and, one would think, should have a meaningful role in deciding what and how much to produce, to whom and at what price to sell its produce, and how to distribute its income. But none of this exists in Russia; the government decides everything. Thus, the collective farm does not correspond to its own definition, it ceases to be itself.

Nor are there any unions in Russia, for a union is an association independent of the government, which exists to defend hired laborers from their employers, even to the point of calling a strike. (Our "unions" do not have the right to do this.) Therefore, there is no working class since a worker is a person who is hired by the owner of the means of production and who, it follows, has the right to bargain over the conditions of the sale of his labor, either by himself or through a union. Nothing of the sort exists in our society; the government dictates everything to the worker.

A true peasantry does not exist. It was destroyed during the forced "collectivization." There are only state serfs, the helotization of the rural population. Not only does socialist property not exist, *there is no property* in the means of production; for property is accompanied by responsibility for it, and in Russia no one assumes responsibility for anything, neither to himself nor to the people.

We have no elections, as is well known. If only one name is listed on the ballot then there is no choice at all. There is not even a party, for one party is not a party, just as one class is not a class. And the Party in effect decides nothing, the Central Committee decides nothing, it only rubber stamps the decisions of the Politburo, which the Party does not elect. Because of this, our regime is like the Roman Council of Ten. In essence, there is no people but only a population, for a people is a population that takes part in deciding its own fate, which is not the case in Russia where, once again, the Politburo decides everything.

Individuality does not exist in Russia. An individual is not just any person, but an autonomous person who has the right to decide, and in Russia people can make no decisions in the political, spiritual or economic spheres. In the West, a hired worker does not possess a decisive voice in the workplace, but he has some voice in political life and so is a partial individual. Only under true socialism can a person be an individual in every sense of the word, i.e., genuine socialism is panpersonalism.

In essence, no such thing as society exists in Russia because the government has completely suppressed it, creating alienated and atomized people. And I would even go so far as to say that, in general, there is no government in Russia. Having suppressed society and become absolute the government annihilated itself as a government, that is, as an organ called upon by definition to serve society. (What else is a government?) Having suppressed its subject (society), the government turns into a mafia, into the executioner of those who gave birth to it.

In that case, what *does* exist in Russia? There is a *nomenklatura:* a sector of people who appoint themselves, verifying each other through the KGB, and who hold all leadership positions (along with attendant privileges), from shop steward, head of an academic department or director of a school, to the General Secretary of the Central Committee, head of the Presidium of the Supreme Soviet, and the head of the Soviet of Ministers.

A matrix system exists. If a class, an estate, or a caste is defined by its membership, in a matrix the opposite holds: the membership is defined by whether or not a person's qualities correspond to the demands of the matrix's nucleus. If they do not correspond, the matrix rejects that person, spits him out. Thus, only people who are capable of not thinking, of remaining silent, of submitting to their superiors and of extorting the fulfillment of commands from inferiors can become part of the ruling nucleus of the matrix. The slightest independent step leads to rejection by the matrix and then the person is nothing, nobody. When, for example, the Politburo expelled Shelest, Shelepin, Voronov, and even Podgorny (the head of government) they were reduced to living corpses and could no longer participate in political life, for they had been declared non-existent.

Statism exists. The state-party mafia permeates everything, all spheres of social life; it reigns over everything—the economy, culture and even everyday life. People's creative potential is suppressed, and the social entity is fraught with spiritual entropy and becomes *parasitic*. This becomes particularly clear when a "Soviet" person travels to the West. Everything we have turns out to be parasitically appropriated from the West: the asphalt and white lines on the roads, the traffic signals, the flashing lights on police cars, toilets and toilet paper, television, automatic cranes, fountain pens, typewriters, literally everything. It turns out that nothing either fundamental or from the technology of everyday life has been invented by us, to our shame, except for insignificant details. And it is not because we are less intelligent or lazier, not at all, but simply because under totalitarianism there is no creative freedom or stimulus to create.

And so our society is not state capitalism, as it is often called, nor state socialism, nor cooperativism. It may be called state totalitarianism or total statism, state mafiaism or mafia statism, a *nomenklatura*-matrix system or a matrix-like *nomenklatura*, etc., but the name is unimportant. What is important is that it is a dead-end system under which people *cannot breathe,* which is not capable of giving them either material or spiritual sustenance and which, for that very reason, feels compelled to expand beyond its borders.

Our Tasks

THERE ARE PEOPLE IN THE WEST who smile spitefully and say: "Well, the Soviet people want it that way . . . " When Jean and Nina Kekhayan and I participated in a round table discussion in a working class suburb of Lyon and I spoke on repression in the Soviet Union, in particular how I, a socialist, had been imprisoned twice and spent many years in confinement for my *socialist* beliefs, the Communist, Meunier, head of the Lyon section of the Franco-Soviet Friendship Committee said: "We have no business interfering in the domestic affairs of the Soviet people: they themselves chose their regime." I replied: "It isn't true. Our people never chose either their regime or the mafia which usurped power. The regime was imposed on the people at the point of a bayonet. In our entire history, there has never been a referendum on a single question. As for the farcical elections, there has never been any *choice*. If there is only one candidate on a ballot it is like god bringing Eve to Adam and saying, 'Choose your wife.' As for so-called 'interference in internal affairs,' we do not propose military interference (as Moscow does in Afghanistan and as it did in Czechoslovakia), but we believe that sharp criticism and a denial of economic aid are morally justified." The workers warmly supported the Kekhayans and me, not Meunier.

There are other people who ask with a wise look, "Well, but who supports you dissidents? Whom do you represent in the country?" We, the *socialist* dissidents can answer definitively: almost the entire population supports us because the suppressed majority of the workers do not want either capitalism or what now exists, nor do they want a return to the sixteenth century, not a Little Father Tsar, nor a Russian Orthodox Khomeini. Instead, they want genuine socialism and democracy, well-being and the opportunity to breathe freely. For the moment, the people are silent for we do not have even the minimal rights briefly won by the Polish workers in 1981, rights which are absolutely necessary for contact with the working class. But in order to awaken our people, in order to inspire them with hope, to arouse potential participants in the struggle, it is of paramount importance that they know that socialist dissidence is supported by socialist groups in the West.

This support can be expressed in several ways: by direct contact between the leadership of Socialist parties and socialist dissidents in emigration; by starting a socialist press (newspaper or magazine) in Russian (in contrast to such rightwing emigre publications as *Russkaya Mysl* or *Kontinent*, published in Paris); by aiding in publishing the Moscow samizdat journal *Searches*, which has strong socialist leanings, in the West; by publishing a series on problems of socialism in Russian to propagate the ideas of democratic socialism, something that Radio Liberty, the Voice of America and the BBC cannot do.

Such assistance can only come from socialists in the West and would not only contribute to strengthening the morale of socialist dissidents in emigration and help consolidate them, but do the same for socialist dissidents in Russia and help to activate others there.

Translated from the Russian by
Elizabeth Hesse and Tania Tchistiakov

Index

Abel, Lionel, 155, 156, 168
Abernathy, Ralph David, 88, 89
Abolitionist movement, 99
Abortion rights, 108, 109, 112, 116
Addams, Janes, 68
Affirmative action, 83
AFL, 68-69, 187
AFL-CIO, 23, 24, 25, 26, 36, 37, 73
African Blood Brotherhood, 69
AFSCME. *See* American Federation of State, County, and Municipal Employees (AFSCME)
Agee, James, 157, 159
Agents provocateurs, 5
Agrarian radicals, 150
Agrarian reforms, 78, 270
Agriculture, 273
Air controllers strike, 26-27
Aksyonov, V., 277
Allen, Robert L., 77
Alpert, Jane, 104-105
American Comittee for Cultural Freedom, 177, 179
American Disarmament movement, 4. *See also* Nuclear disarmament
American Federation of State, County, and Municipal Employees (AFSCME), 28, 36
American Federation of Teachers, 28
American Negro Academy, 80
American Plan, 34
American Railway Union, 27
American Society of Civil Engineers, 191
American Workers and Artists for Solidarity, 248
American Workers Party, 171
Amnesty International, 276, 278
Anarchism, 72
Andropov, Yuri, 145, 282
Anthony, Susan B., 106
Anti-communism, 163
Antinomianism, 189, 190

Anti-nuclear movement. *See* Nuclear disarmament
Anti-semitism, 64n, 272
Anti-war movement, v, 99, 105
Arendt, Hannah, 156, 159
Aristotle, 209
Arms spending. *See* Military spending
Art, 133
Atheism, 79
Atkinson, Ti-Grace, 100, 102, 105
Atlantic Monthly, 58
Atlas, James, 158
Atomic bomb, 70. *See also* Nuclear disarmament
Australia, 4
Austria, 260
Automation. *See* Technology
Automobile industry, 43

Baluka, Edmund, 233
Banner, Lois, 107, 108, 116
Barber, J. Max, 73
Barnard College, 97, 98, 104, 109
Barrett, Michele, 113
Barrett, William, 155, 157, 158, 159-164, 165, 166, 167
Barry, Marion, 88
BBC, 287
Beard, Charles, 67
Bell, Daniel, 156, 185-190, 193, 195, 196, 197, 198
Bellow, Saul, 155, 156, 157, 158
Belotserkovsky, V., 277
Benn, Tony, 282n
Bentham, Jeremy, 202, 207
Berg, Louis, 171
Berger, Victor, 68
Berlin, Isaiah, 201, 202, 204, 206, 207, 208, 211, 212, 221
Berlinguer, Enrico, 283
Berman, Marshall, 196
Big business. *See* Concentration of business

Bilak, Vasil, 240
Birth control movement, 66
Black, Joe, 89, 90
Black capitalism, 78, 80, 83, 84-85, 86, 87, 88
Black Congressional Caucus, 81
Black Enterprise, 85
Black nationalism, 64n, 69, 74, 82
Black Power movement, 70, 83
Black Reconstruction, 78, 80
Blacks. *See* Race and racism
Bober, M.M., 65n
Boddy, R., 48
Bond, Julian, 77
B-1 bomber, vi
Borusewicz, 231
Bowles, S., 48
Boyce, William, 69
Bradley, Tom, 88, 209
Brandeis University, 164
Brenner, Anita, 171
Brezhnev, Leonid, 128
Briggs, Cyril, 69
Brody, David, 35
Brotherhood of Sleeping Car Porters, 73
Brown, H. Rap, 70
Brownson, Orestes A., 66
Bruce, John Edward, 80, 81
Buhle, Paul, 166
Bukharin, Nikolai, 76, 161
Bukovsky, Vladimir, 278, 280
Bujak, Zbigniew, 247
Bureaucratic collectivism, 123-124n, 128. *See also* USSR
Burger King, 28
Burnham, James, 143, 157-158, 162, 168, 169, 179
Business cycles. *See* Economic cycles
Business Week magazine, 23
Bydgoszcz affair, 242
Byrne, Jane, 88

Calhoun, John C., 66
Calverton, V.F., 170, 171
Calvin, John, 209
Cambodia, 132
Campen, J., 48

Capitalism; Cold War and, 9-10; fascism and, 124, 125; feminism and, 113; freedom and, 207, 213, 221-222; labor movement and, 29-30, 44; modernization and, 191, 192; patriarchy and, 111; politics and, 42; post-industrial society and, 188, race and, 63, 78, 80, 83, 84-85; USSR and, 277, 278
CARASA, 112, 116
Carmichael, Stokely, 70, 80
Carrillo, Santiago, 283
Carter, Jimmy, 24-25, 26, 57, 89
Castro, Fidel, 153
Catholic Church, 137, 244-245, 247, 250, 255, 256, 257, 259
Censorship, 258-259
Census Survey of Manufacturers, 50, 51
Central Intelligence Agency, 177
Chalidze, Valeri, 277
Chile, 132
Chronicle of Current Events, 273
CIO, 148, 178. *See also* AFL-CIO
Civil liberties, 141, 142. *See also* Freedom
Civil rights, 99, 175, 276. *See also* Freedom; Race and racism
Clark, Peter H., 71-72
Class. *See* Social class
Cleaver, Eldridge, 70
Cochran, Bert, 156
Cockburn, Alexander, 121, 122
Cohen, Elliot, 169, 170
Cohen, Morris, 170
Cold War, 144-145, 160, 201; DuBois and, 76; intellectuals and, 179; nuclear strategy and, 9, 16; US intellectuals and, 162, 169
Comecon, 261
Comiso base (Italy), 4, 5
Commentary, 155, 156, 165
Commerce Department, 51-52, 53
Committee for Abortion Rights and Against Sterilization Abuse (CARASA), 112, 116
Committee for the Free Trade Unions of the Maritime Coast (Poland), 231
Committee for the Free World, 156, 157

Communism; defined, 124; Fascism and, 119-154
Communist parties, 254-255, 263
Communist Party (China), 127
Communist Party (Czechoslovakia), 256-257, 261-262
Communist Party (Poland), 127; Catholic Church and, 245; Solidarity movement and, 231, 232, 234-236, 238, 240, 242, 250-251, 263-264, 265
Communist Party (US), 72, 135-136, 147-153, 161; race and, 69-71, 73, 77; reformism of, 171-172; religion and, 79; US intellectuals and, 170; World War II and, 70, 174, 175
Communist Party (USSR), 133, 263; dissidence and, 274; Communist party (US) and, 149-150; freedom and, 219; function of, 125, 270, 284; industrialization and, 138, 139; reforms and, 264
Concentration of business, 53
Congress (US), 24, 25, 31
Congress for Cultural Freedom, 186
Construction industry, 49
Consumer credit, 43
Cooney, Terry A., 166
Corey, Lewis, 168
Corporations, 42, 54
Corruption, 186-187
Coser, Lewis, 175
Crisis, 74, 75, 76
Croly, Herbert, 193
Crotly, J., 48
Cruise missile, vi, 4-5, 5-6, 15, 18, 19
Cruse, Harold, 83-84
Cuba, 10, 132, 153, 254
Cults, 190
Cultural feminism, 104, 105
Cultural Revolution (China), 160, 254
Culture; anti-modernism in, 193, 194; Eastern Europe, 259-260; Stalinism, 133
Curran, Joseph, 151-152
Czechoslovakia, 131, 137, 147, 240, 254, 282; Solidarity movement compared, 256; USSR reforms and, 255-264, 265

Daily Worker, 70, 151
Daly, Mary, 104
Daniel, Yuli, 274
Davis, Angela, 65, 77
Davis, Ben, 70
Davis, Elizabeth Gould, 104
De Beauvoir, Simone, 99-100, 102, 105, 106
Debs, Eugene V., 27, 67, 187
Defense spending. See Miliary spending
Deficit spending, 56, 57-58
De Leon, Daniel, 67, 74
Dellums, Ronald V., 77
Democracy, 140-141
Democratic freedoms, 133. See also Freedom
Democratic Party (US); feminist movement and, 115 116; labor movement and, 24, 26, 38, 39; race and, 66, 73
Democratic Socialists of America, 31
Democratic Union (USSR), 277
Demonstrations. See Mass movements
Deterrence concept, 11
Deutscher, Isaac, 142
Dewey, John, 170
Dissent, 155, 169
Dissidence and dissent, 255, 269-287; characteristics of, 273-275; defined, 269; genesis of, 269-273; spectrum of opinion among, 275-282; tasks of, 286-287
Dixiecrat Party (US), 89
Dos Passos, John, 170
Douglass, Frederick, 65, 77
Dragosh, N., 277
Dubcek, Alexander, 254
DuBois, W.E.B., 63, 68, 69, 71, 73, 74-77, 78, 81, 82
Dunn and Bradstreet, 46
Dupee, F.W., 180

Eastern Europe, 142-143; civil liberties in, 141; Poland and, 230, 241, 243-244; USSR and, 131, 254, 255, 260, 262, 264, 265-266
East Germany, 4, 5, 256
Eastman, Max, 156, 169, 171

Ecology movement, v, 198
Economic cycles; labor movement and, 21-22, 40-41, 48; military spending, 54; productivity and, 49-50
Economic determinism, 66-67
Education, 162; blacks and, 81-82; freedom and, 215; USSR, 139, 272
Ehrenreich, Barbara, 110
El Salvador, 122, 145, 156
Employment;business concentrate;53; economic sectors, 22, 27; modernism, 198; productivity and, 46; public sector spending and, 55; union politics and, 33; World War II, 46. *See also* Unemployment
Engels, F., 64-65n, 140; blacks and, 82; feminism and, 105, 111, 113
Environmentalism. *See* Ecology movement
Equal rights, 220
Equal Rights Amendment (ERA), 83, 108, 110, 192
Ethiopia, 132, 173
Ethnicity, 259-260, 270. *See also* Race and racism
Etkind, E., 277
European Nuclear Disarmament appeal, 3, 4

Fadiman, Clifton, 170
Falange, 125
Farrell, James T., 156, 168, 174, 176
Fascism; Communism and, 119-154; defined, 124; Stalinism and, 119; US intellectuals and, 168-169, 173
Fast-food industry, 28
Federal Advisory Commission on Intergovernmental Relations, 56
Federal Reserve Bank, 45, 50
Federal Trade Commission, 52
Feinberg, V., 277
Feminism and feminist movement, v, 97-117; future of, 115-116; radical feminism, 99-106, 107, 110, 113, 116; reform feminism, 107-110, 112; sexuality and, 97-98; socialist feminism, 110-115, 116

Ferguson and Rhodes American Business Careers Institute, 84
Ferrell, John, 71
Fiedler, Leslie, 156
Finland, 260
Firestone, Shulamith, 100, 102
Fiscal policy (US), 54
Foner, Philip S., 70, 72
Foot, Michael, 282n
Forbes magazine, 39
Ford, James W., 69, 77
Fortune, Timothy Thomas, 72, 74, 77
Fortune magazine, 21, 45
Foster, William Z., 149
Fowler, Robert Booth, 177
France, 14
Franco, Francisco, 124, 125
Fraser, Douglas, 25-26
Freedom; negative, 202-207, 210, 213, 214, 216, 217-218, 221; positive, 207-218; socialism and, 218-225; USSR, 274, 284
Frey, John P., 68-69
Fried, Albert, 67
Friedan, Betty, 100, 106, 107, 109
Fuge, Denise, 108

Galbraith, John Kenneth, 32, 197
Garvey, Marcus, 80
Garveyites, 78
Gavras, Costa, 121
Gdansk Agreements, 239, 263
Gender identity, 101
General Motors Corporation, 25, 32, 38, 48
Genocide, 130-131
Germany, 126, 192. *See also* East Germany; West Germany
Gershuni, Vladimir, 274n
Gierek, Edward, 235, 236, 237, 261
Gilbert, James, 156
Ginzburg, Alexander, 278, 280
Give-backs, 32-33
Glemp, Archbishop, 236, 250
Gomulka, Wladyslaw, 263
Gorbanevskaya, N., 278
Gordimer, Nadine, 121
Gordon, David M., 41, 48

Goricheva, T., 278
Gornick, Vivian, 147-148, 166
Graves, Earl, 85-86
Green, Bill, 88
Green, Philip, 157, 209
Greenberg, Clement, 156, 158, 159, 161, 174, 176
Greider, William, 58
Greyhound Corporation, 89
Great Depression, 22, 31, 34-35, 38, 41; Communist Party (US) and, 69-70, 73; lessons of, 44; USSR, 76
Great Purge (USSR). See Purges (USSR)
Great Society programs, 88
Grigorenko, Pyotr, 278
Gulf Oil Corporation, 88
Gwiazdas, 231

Hacker, Louis, 168
Haig, Alexander, 88
Hall, Gus, 282
Hamer, Fannie Lou, 78
Hansen, Alvin, 43
Hardwick, Elizabeth, 157
Harlem Renaissance, 69
Harper's Magazine, 21
Harrington, Michael, 31
Harrison, Hubert, 73
Hartmann, Heidi, 112-113
Haymarket Square riot, 72
Hedonism, 189
Hegel, G.W.F., 209, 279
Helms, Jesse, 120
Helsinki Committee, 274, 276, 278
Herndon, Angelo, 73-74, 79, 147
Herreshoff, David, 67
Hillquit, Morris, 68
"Hire One Youth," 87, 88
Hiroshima, 70
Hitler, Adolf, 126, 127, 130-131, 148, 161, 271, 279
Hobbes, Thomas, 202, 203
Hoffman, Abby, 120
Hollinger, David, 156
Homeownership, 32
Homosexuals, 162. See also Lesbianism
Hook, Sidney, 143, 149n, 155, 156, 159, 167, 168, 170, 171, 172, 173-174, 175,

Hook, Sidney (continued)
176, 177, 179
Hooks, Benjamin, 86
Hoover, Herbert, 35
Hoover Institution, 89-90
Horizon magazine, 74
Howe, Irving, 156, 163, 169, 175
Hudson, Hosea, 79
Human rights movement, 276
Hume, David, 202
Hungary, 4, 131, 132, 142-143, 149, 151, 241, 255, 256, 261, 262
Huntington, Samuel P., 193
Hyde Amendment, 112

IBM, 28, 51
Immigration, 29, 68, 187
Imperialism, 273
Income. See Wages
India, 175
Individual. See Freedom
Indochina war. See Vietnam War
Industrialization, 271
Industrial Workers of the World (IWW), 72
Inflation, 22, 24-25, 51
Initiative Committee, 276
Institute for Labor Education and Research (ILER), 41, 55
Intellectuals, 155-184; Poland, 232; Stalinism and, 129; USSR, 139-140, 276
Internal Revenue Service, 51
In These Times, 140-142, 143
Investment, 33, 38, 42, 51-52, 53
Isolationism, 18-19
Isserman, Maurice, 166
Italy, 125, 132, 173

Jackson, Jesse, 84-85, 86
Jacob, John E., 87
James, C.L.R., 91
Japan; atomic bombing of, 70, 149; black Americans and, 89; competition with, 195; economy of, 22, 192; nuclear disarmament and, 4; rise of, 9; unemployment in, 90; US and, 14
Japanese-Americans, internment of, 70, 148, 175

Jaruzelski, Wojciech, 141, 146, 153, 229, 230, 233, 235, 236, 239, 240, 241, 243, 245, 247, 250, 264
Jim Crow laws, 66, 78, 83
Job creation, 42
Johnson, Lyndon B., 57, 88
Jordan, Vernon, 86-87
Judicial rulings, 23-25, 26-27
Judis, John B., 143n

Kadushin, Charles, 157
Kakutani, Michiko, 160
Kalinin, Mikhail, 76
Kania, 236
Kant, I., 209
Kazin, Alfred, 156, 157, 179
Kekhayan, Jean, 286
Kekhayan, Nina, 286
Kennedy, John F., 57
Kenyon Review, 158
KGB, 273n, 284
Khmer Rouge, 132
Khrushchev, Nikita, 149, 254, 263, 274-275
King, Martin Luther, Jr., 70, 78, 88
Kirkland, Lane, 26
Kirkpatrick, Jeane, 145
Kirov, Sergei, 76
Klare, Karl, 23
Klebanov, 276
Knight, 202
Knights of labor, 71
Kopelev, Lev, 277
KOR, 246, 247, 248, 250
Kramer, Hilton, 157, 159, 164, 165
Kravchenko, B., 278
Kristol, Irving, 143, 146, 153, 155, 156, 167, 177
Kronstadt uprising, 256
Krupnick, Mark, 156
Ku Klux Klan, 88, 97
Kuron, Jacek, 246, 247, 260
Kvachevsky, L., 277

Labor Department (US), 49, 50, 55
Labor law, 25
Labor-Management Group, 25, 26
Labor movement; capitalism and, 29-

Labor movement (continued) 30, 31, 44; Carter and, 26; communist parties and, 255; Communist Party (US) and, 136, 148, 150-152; Congress (US) and, 25; decline in, 21, 22-23, 27; Eastern Europe, 257-258; economic cycles and, 35-36, 41-42, 257-258; economic sectors and, 27-28; future of, 36-40; immigration and, 29; intellectuals and, 165, 174, 178, 179, 180; judicial rulings and, 23-25; membership in, 33-34, 37-38; PATCO and, 26-27; Poland, 229-230, 231, 232, 238, 242, 244, 250-251; politics and, 47; race and, 63-64, 66, 68-69, 71-72, 81, 83; racketeering, 186-187; sexual composition and, 29; Stalinism, 133; successes of, 21-22; technology and, 30-31, 47-48; union politics and, 31-33, 34, 36-37, 47-48; USSR, 140, 276, 283; World War II, 47, 70, 175
Labor Party (UK), 170, 282n
LaFollette, Robert, 150
Lasch, Christopher, 156
Lasky, Melvin, 155
Lassalle, Ferdinand, 64n
League of Nations, 173
Lears, Jackson, 192
Lenin, V.I., 75, 140, 175, 219, 258, 260, 272, 275
Leninism, 178
Lenin Shipyards (Poland), 231, 244
Lert, R., 277
Lesbianism, 97, 107. See also Homosexuals
Levitan-Krasnov, A., 277, 278, 281
Limited nuclear war concept, 11, 14, 15-16
Lipinski, Edward, 248
Lipset, Seymour Martin, 156
Lis, 231
Locke, John, 189
Longshore industry, 186-187
Longstaff, S.A., 156
Lore, Ludwig, 173
Lovestone, Jay, 149
Lubarsky, K., 277
Lukacs, George, 219

Luxemburg, Rosa, 229
Lynch, John R., 80

Macdonald, Dwight, 156, 161, 174, 176, 180
Machinists Union, 36
MacPherson, C.B., 204, 205, 207, 212, 213
Madhubuti, Haki, 81
Mafia, 5, 187, 270-271, 284, 285
Maglangbayan, Shawna, 81
Mailer, Norman, 133
Mail service, 191
Maksimov, V., 278
Malakhovskaya, N., 278
Malcolm X, 70, 78
Malinkovich, V., 277
Mamonova, T., 277, 279
Management prerogatives, 38, 47
Mao Tse Tung, 127, 160
Maoism, 132
Marchais, Georges, 282
Marcuse, Herbert, 212
Maria, 279
Market economy, 204-206, 219, 225
Marquez, Garcia, 143
Marriage and family, 101
Marshall, Thurgood, 73
Marx, Karl, 63, 64n, 75, 104, 140, 160; blacks and, 80, 82; freedom and, 208, 219, 221, 222, 224
Marxism, 202; DuBois and, 74-77; blacks and, 63, 70, 74, 80, 81, 91; feminism and, 102, 103, 110, 112-115; freedom and, 218; Poland and, 249; religion and, 79; Stalinism and, 130; US intellectuals and, 172, 178; USSR and, 229, 271
Mass movements; labor movement and, 39; nuclear disarmament, 4-8
Mazzochi, Tony, 36
McCarthy, Joseph, 120, 185
McCarthy, Mary, 156, 159, 168, 174, 180
McCarthyism, 146, 149n, 165, 174, 179
McDermott, John, 57-58
McDonald's Restaurants, 28
McGovern, George, 177

McKay, Claude, 75
McLellan, David, 64n
Meany, George, 25
Media, 5, 258-259
Medical care, 272
Medvedev, Roy, 277, 282, 283
Medvedev, Zhores, 277
Meiklejohn, Alexander, 225
Menorah Journal, 169, 171, 172
Meritocracy, 186, 188
Metric system, 192-193
Meunier, 286
Milewski, 235
Military spending; corporations and, 54; modernization, 195; redistribution of wealth and, 56; unemployment and, 43; USSR, 139, 276; Vietnam War and, 57
Mill, John Stuart, 202, 206, 207, 216-217
Millet, Kate, 100, 102, 104, 105, 106
Minimum wage, 28. *See also* Wages
Missiles. *See entries under types of missiles*
Mitchell, Juliet, 100, 105
Mitford, Jessica, 120
Modernization, 185-199; anti-modern forces and, 193-196; Stalinism and, 133
Modern Monthly, 170, 171, 172, 173
Monetary policy, 45, 54
Monthly Review, 48
Morial, Dutch, 85
Moroz, V., 278
Morrow, Felix, 171
Moscow Trials. *See* Purges
Multilateral nuclear disarmament, 18
Mussolini, Benito, 132
Muste, A.J., 171
MX missile, vi

NAACP, 63, 68, 69, 73, 74, 78, 80, 85-86
Naison, Mark, 166
Nation, The, 48, 57, 120, 121, 122, 158
National Abortion Rights Action League (NARAL), 116
National Association of Manufacturers, 25

National Committee for the Defense of Political Prisoners, 170
National Endowment for the Humanities, 37
National Independent Political League, 73
National Labor Relations Act, 25
National liberation movements, 77
National Maritime Union, 151-152
National Miner's Union, 69
National Negro Congress, 73
National Network for Reproductive Rights, 112
National Organization for Women (NOW), 103, 107-108, 115-116
National Review, 169
National Right-to-Work Committee, 25
National Women's Suffrage Organization, 108
NATO, 4-5, 6, 8-9, 11, 14, 18
Nazi party, 70, 97, 151, 161
Nazi-Soviet Pact, 148
Negro Business League, 83
Network of Leading Enterprises, 237-238
Neumann, Franz, 134
New Criticism, 158
New Deal, 38, 39, 45, 176-177, 186
New Economic Policy (NEP), 277
New International, 163
New Leader, 163, 176
New Left, 37, 70, 137, 147, 178, 187
New Masses, 170
New Orleans Business League, 85
New Right, 194, 195
New York Age, 72
New York Review of Books, 28
New York Times, 30, 156, 160
New York Times Book Review, 156, 157, 164
Niagra Movement, 73
Nicholas II (tsar of Russia), 279
Nietzsche, F., 279
Nisbet, Robert, 196
Nissan Corporation, 86
Nixon, Richard M, 21, 144, 177
NLRB, 23
Nobile, Philip, 156

Norris-LaGuardia Anti-Injunction Law, 23
Novack, George, 156
NOW. See National Organization for Women
Nozick, Robert, 201
Nuclear disarmament; Europe, 3-20; freeze movement, 4, 18; mass movements, 4-8; negotiations in, 17; nuclear utility concept, 11; political strategy, 11-15; survival and, 8-11; unilateral versus multilateral, 17-18; US and, 4, 6-7
Nuclear weapons, 130, 145

Ofari, Earl, 77
OIC network, 87, 88
Oil, Atomic, and Chemical Workers Union, 36
Olszowski, Stefan, 235
Operation PUSH, 84-85, 86
Opportunities Industrialization Centers, 87, 88
Orlov, Yuri, 278
Orwell, George, 121n
Ovington, Mary White, 68
Owen, Chandler, 73
Owen, Robert, 66

Pavlovsky, Gleb, 274n
Parsons, Albert R., 72
Parsons, Lucy, 72
Partisan Review, 155, 156, 157, 158, 160, 161, 162, 163, 166, 172, 176
PATCO, 26-27
Patriarchy, 100, 101, 111, 113, 114
Peasantry, 270, 283-284
Peoples Republic of China, 10, 126, 127, 132, 160, 254
Perry, William, 86
Pershing II missile, 6, 15, 18, 19
Petty bourgeoisie, 79-82
Phillips, William, 156, 157, 158, 159, 161
Piatakov, 76
Pienkowska, 231
Pinochet, Augusto, 145
Plato, 279

Plekhanov, Georgi, 275
Plyushch, Leonid, 277, 278
Podgorny, Nikolai, 285
Podhoretz, Norman, 121n, 146, 156, 165, 169, 177
Podrabinek, P., 277, 278
Poland, 122, 126, 127, 131, 135, 137-138, 141, 146, 147, 153, 229-252; coup in, 254, 264; Eastern Europe and, 230; martial law in, 245-249; production in, 236-238, 246; USSR and, 229, 254, 281-282; USSR reforms and, 255-267
Polish United Workers Party. *See* Communist Party (Poland)
Politics; bias in information and, 49; blacks and, 78, 79, 81, 82-83, 87; capitalism and, 42; Eastern Europe, 258; feminism, 101, 102, 106, 112, 115-116; freedom and, 213, 214; labor movement, 24, 37, 38-39, 47; modernization, 195; nuclear weapons, 6-11, 12-15; Poland, 233-234, 240; women's movement, 108-109
Popper, Karl, 201
Popular Front, 166, 171-172, 173, 174
Populism, 65
Populist party (US), 83
Post-industrial society, 187-188
Prague Spring. *See* Czechoslovakia
Productivity; bias in rates reporting of, 49, 50; collective bargaining and, 48; economic cycles and, 49-50; employment and, 46; labor force and, 42; modernization and, 195; wages and, 42-43, 44, 48, 54
Profits; bias in reporting, 52; growth in, 52-53; productivity and, 42-43; taxation and, 51; wages and, 50-51
Progressive Era, 99
Protectionism, 31
Psychiatric Commission, 276
Public sector spending, 55
Purges (USSR), 161, 168-169, 172, 270

Race and racism; capitalism and, 63; Communist Party (US) and, 69-71, 148, 175; Fascism and, 128; feminism and, 111; historical impedi-

Race and racism *(continued)*
ments to socialism and, 77-82; intellectuals and, 165; labor movement and, 71; leadership failure among, 82-91; Marx and Marxism and, 64-65n, 74, 91; socialism and, 64-69, 77-82; Socialist Party (US) and, 74; youths and, 89-90
Racketeering, 186-187
Radek, Karl, 76
Radical America, 48
Radical feminism, 99-106, 107, 110, 113, 116
Radicalism, v-vi
Radio Liberty, 287
Rahv, Philip, 156, 157, 158, 159, 161, 163-165, 168, 172-173, 176, 177, 180
Railroads, 191
Railroad strike of 1922, 26-27
Rakowski, Mieczyslaw, 264
Randolph, A. Philip, 70, 73, 74, 80
Raskin, A.H., 21
Reagan, Ronald, v, 144, 156, 189, 282; anti-modernism, 194; blacks and, 81, 82, 86, 87, 88-89; foreign policy, 19; intellectuals and, 178; labor movement and, 26-27, 38; nuclear disarmament, 5, 17; Poland and, 145; standard of living under, 56; tax policy, 59; unemployment and, 90
Recession, 50, 54, 90
Reconstruction, 83
Reed, Adolph, 77
Reform, USSR, 253-267
Reform feminism, 107-110, 112
Reform movements, 107-110
Religion, 190; blacks and, 78-79, 85; USSR, 278, 280. *See also* Catholic Church
Republican party (US); blacks and, 82, 88, 89; labor movement and, 26, 35, 38, 39
Ressentiment, 186
Rich, Adrienne, 104
Road building programs, 43
Robeson, Paul, 78
Robots, 30-31
Rokossovsky, Marshal, 127

Roman Catholic Church. *See* Catholic Church
Roosevelt, Franklin D., 24, 35, 70, 176
Rorty, James, 168
Rosenberg, Harold, 168, 169n
Roskolenko, Harry, 156
Rothschild, Emma, 28
Rousseau, J., 189, 209, 215
Rowbotham, Sheila, 106, 110, 114
Ruas, Charles, 134-135
Rudzutak, 76
Rulewski, Janek, 248
Rumania, 255, 261
Rural Free Delivery, 191
Ruskin, John, 197
Russell, Bertrand, 170, 202
Russell, Charles Edward, 68
Russia. *See* USSR

Sado-masochism, 97, 98
Sakharov, Andrei, 277, 281
Sales, William W., 77
SALT II treaty, 17
SAMOIS, 97
Sandgren, John, 68
San Domingo Revolution, 91
Sanger, Margaret, 66
Scandinavian Women's Peace March, 5
Scarcity, 188
Schapiro, Meyer, 159, 168, 169, 174, 176, 179
Schlafly, Phyllis, 104
Schlueter, Hermann, 68
Schwartz, Delmore, 156, 157, 158, 159, 163
Science, 188
Scottsboro Case, 79, 148
Searches, 273n-274, 276, 280
Second International, 175
Self-determination, 204, 213
Self-mastery, 208-209, 211, 212, 213
Serrin, William, 32
Service Employees' International Union, 36
Seven-Up Corporation, 84, 88
Sexism, USSR, 133
Sex role, 97-98, 100-101, 104, 111

Shachtman, Max, 143, 168
Shechner, Mark, 156, 158
Shelepin, Alexander, 285
Shelest, Petro, 285
Shinhoster, Earl, 86
Shomanov, 277
Shragin, Boris, 277
Shtromas, A., 277
Sicily, 5
Silone, Ignazio, 155
Sinyavsky, Andrei, 274, 277
Siwak, Albin, 235
Slesinger, Tess, 171
Smith, Adam, 207
Smith, Damu Imara, 77
Smith Act, 148, 175
SNCC, 70, 80
Social class; feminism and, 102, 105, 106, 107, 110-115; labor movement and, 32; race and, 63-64, 67, 73, 77, 79-82, 91; Stalinism and, 129, 130, 133; USSR, 139, 273, 284-285
Social Darwinism, 225
Socialist feminism, 110-115, 116
Socialist Labor Party (US), 72
Socialist Party (France), 282n
Socialist Party (Germany), 170
Socialist Party (US), 66, 136; Communist Party (US) and, 170; race and, 67, 68, 72, 73, 74
Socialist Workers Party (US), 175
Socialization, 203, 215
Socrates, 209
Sokirko, A., 277
Solidarity Union (Poland), 137, 143, 144, 145, 146, 153, 229-252; Catholic Church and, 244-245; Communist Party (Poland) and, 234-236, 263-264, 265; compromise and, 239-244; Czechoslovakia compared, 256; economy and, 236-238; membership in, 233-234; outlawing of, 250-251; underground existence of, 245-249
Solow, Herbert, 171
Solzhenitsyn, Alexander, 271, 278, 279, 280, 282
Somoza, Anastasio, 120
Sontag, Susan, 119, 120, 121, 122, 123,

Sontag, Susan *(continued)*
126, 128, 129, 134, 137, 146
Soviet Union. *See* USSR
Sowell, Thomas, 90
Spain, 124-125, 172
Spanish Civil War, 178
Spinoza, 209
SS-20 missile, 17
Stagflation, 32
Stalin, Joseph, 120, 127, 131, 158, 160, 219, 280; death of, 164, 274; purges of, 161
Stalinism, 76, 122-123; fascism and, 119; Trotsky and, 160; US intellectuals and, 163, 178
Standard time. *See* Time
Stanton, Elizabeth Cady, 65-66, 102
Steinfels, Peter, 157
Sterilization, 112
Stevens, Wallace, 163
Stockman, David, 58
Stolberg, 168
Strickland, William, 77
Strikes; General Motors, 38; Great Depression, 44; judicial process and, 23; Poland, 239, 242, 243; post-World War II, 44, 47; right to, 47; Solidarity, 231; World War II, 47; US intellectuals, 178; USSR, 272
Student Nonviolent Coordinating Committee (SNCC), 70, 80
Suffrage; blacks, 66, 67, 102; women, 65-66, 99, 102, 108
Sullivan, Leon, 87, 88
Supermarket employees, 28
Supply side economics, 58-59
Supreme Court (US), 23, 24, 73
Survival, 8-11, 12, 13, 15, 16-17
Suzuki, Zenko, 89

Taft-Hartley Act, 47
Taxation, 195; corporations and, 42; profits and, 51; Reagan Administration, 56, 59
Taylor, Charles, 210, 212
Teamsters Union, 34
Technology, 30-31, 38, 47-48, 193
Thatcher, Margaret, 90, 189

Thomas, Norman, 134, 175
Thompson, James, 88
Thurmond, Strom, 120
Thurow, Lester, 197
Time, 191, 193
Timmerman, Jacobo, 121
Tobin, Dan, 34
Totalitarianism, 122, 131-132; freedom and, 210; intellectuals and, 139-140; USSR, 274, 275
Trade policies, 31
Trade unionism. *See* Labor movement
Trilling, Diana, 156, 157, 170
Trilling, Lionel, 156, 157, 159, 168, 169, 170, 171, 179
Trotsky, Leon, 134, 136, 159-160, 162, 164, 171, 178, 282
Trotskyists, 136, 148, 155, 165, 168
Truman, H.S., 21
Truth, Sojourner, 78
Tucker, Robert, 76
Turchin, Valentine, 277
Turner, Nat, 77
Tuskegee Institute, 83

UFCW, 28, 36
Ukrainian nationalist movement, 278
Unemployment; blacks, 87, 89; government and, 44-45, 46; Great Depression, 44; growth in, 27; inflation and, 24-25; labor movement and, 22; military spending and, 43, 54; technology and, 30-31; USSR, 271-272, 276; worldwide, 90
Unilateral nuclear disarmament, 17, 18-19
Union membership, 22-23. *See also* Labor movement
Union of Radical Political Economics (URPE), 41, 48-49, 51
United Auto Workers Union, 23, 25, 30, 31, 32, 38
United Food and Commercial Workers (UFCW), 28, 36
United Kingdom, 90
United States; cold war and, 9; isolationism and, 18-19; nuclear disarmament and strategy of, 5, 6-7, 12-13,

United States *(continued)*
14-15; USSR and, 8, 16, 145-146;
Western Europe and, 9-10, 16, 19
United States Black Chamber of Commerce, 85
United States Chamber of Commerce, 25, 88
United Steel Workers Union, 31
Urban League, 86-87
USSR, 75; Communist party (US) and, 136; confrontation with, 8, 16; Cuba and, 10; Czechoslovakia and, 240; dissidence in, 269-287; DuBois and, 75-76; Eastern Europe and, 131, 260, 262, 264, 265-266; German attack on, 174; industrialization of, 138-139, 271; Marxism and, 218; military spending, 139; Nazi Germany and, 70, 174; nuclear disarmament, 4, 5, 12, 14, 17-18; Poland and, 127, 137-138, 229, 232; politics in, 125; power in, 126; reform possibility in, 253-267; socialism in, 283-284; Solidarity Union and, 235, 239, 240, 241, 242; US and, 145-146, 161, 162, 163, 164, 172, 176, 178, 179
Vagin, 277
Valladares, Armando, 132
Velikanova, T., 277
Vietnam War, v, 14, 53, 80, 147
Village Voice, 121
Vladimov, G., 278
Voice of America, 287
Voice of the Negro, 73
Voinovich, V., 277
Von Hoffman, Nicholas, 21
Voronov, 285
Voroshilov, 76
Voznesenskaya, Yu., 277, 278
Wages; business cycles and, 48; capitalism and, 30; decreases in, 90; give-backs and, 32; productivity and, 42-43, 44, 48, 50, 54; profits and, 50-51; World War II, 47
Wagner Act, 23
Waldron, J. Milton, 72-73
Walentynowicz, 231
Walesa, Lech, 137, 231, 236, 242, 244, 250, 251, 258

Walling, William English, 69
Wall Street Journal, 58, 90
Wanamaker, John, 191
Warsaw Pact, 261
Washington, Booker T., 65n, 73, 80, 83, 84
Watson, Tom, 65
Webster, Grant, 156
Weisskopf, T., 48
Welfare capitalism, 34
Western Europe, 15-19
West Germany, 90, 195
White, Walter, 69
Williams, Hosea, 88, 89
Willis, Ellen, 97
Wills, Gary, 120
Wilson, Edmund, 156, 159, 168, 170, 171, 174
Winpisinger, Wimpy, 36
Wolfe, Bernard, 156
Women, 83; black socialists, 72; labor movement and, 29, 37; USSR, 272-273. *See also* Women's movement
Women and Russia, 279
Women's movement; racism and, 65-66; USSR, 278-279. *See also* Feminism and feminist movement; Women
Women's Party, 102, 106
Woodward, C. Vann, 65n
Workingmen's Party, 66
World War I, 102, 175
World War II, 161; Communist Party (US) and, 70, 148, 149; employment and, 46; intellectuals and, 169, 172-177; wages and, 47
WPA, 179
Wright, Frances, 66
Wyszynski, Cardinal, 245

Yalta conference, 266
Young, Andrew, 85, 88
Young, Coleman, 88
Young, Whitney, 87
Yugoslavia, 259, 260

Zero option plan, 5, 17
Zinoviev, A., 280, 282
Zinoviev, Grigori, 76

DATE DUE